GAY LIFE

LEISURE, LOVE, AND LIVING FOR THE CONTEMPORARY GAY MALE

EDITED BY ERIC E. ROFES

A DOLPHIN BOOK

DOUBLEDAY & COMPANY, INC.
GARDEN CITY, NEW YORK
1986

To
Tim and Brian

GAY LIFE
was designed by Hudson Studio,
Ossining, New York
and produced by James Charlton Associates,
New York, New York

A Dolphin Book

Library of Congress Cataloging in Publication Data

Gay Life
   "A Dolphin book."
Includes index.
1. Homosexuality, Male—United States. I. Rofes, Eric E., 1954–
HQ76.2.U5G38   1986   306.7'662'0973   86-16541
ISBN 0-385-19386-6

Contents

I. HEALTH & IMAGE

II. HOME

III. LOVE

IV. CULTURE & LEISURE

V. GAY IDENTITY

Introduction

by Eric E. Rofes

QUIETLY, OVER THE LAST FEW YEARS, CHANGES HAVE been taking place. On entering an undiscovered restaurant in an obscure urban neighborhood, one recognizes a table or two of tastefully dressed gentlemen. A weekend visit to a vacation spot—the shore, the mountains, the woods—brings subtle signs of recognition between seemingly unattached single men. In the city or the suburbs, in rural New England or small-town Middle America, dramatic changes have occurred in the ways in which gay men live their lives, develop a sense of community and understand their identities as homosexual men.

Much has been written about the influence AIDS has had on contemporary gay male life. We're not talking specifically about AIDS here. Instead, we are considering changes which have been evolving slowly over the past fifteen years; new and different ways in which a vast population of gay men conceptualize their homosexuality, structure their relationships, pursue their careers and interests. We're talking about men who have survived the repression of the closet, worked through coming-out issues, grappled with contemporary gay male images and emerged intact, relatively satisfied with life and fully at peace with their whole selves.

These are men living in a wide variety of places throughout America in many different lifestyles. Some are single; others are coupled. Others, still, live with friends, perhaps other gay men, perhaps women friends, perhaps heterosexual male roomates. While some of these men are parents, few are living with children on a daily basis. The diverse and creative ways in which today's homosexual men structure their relationships and living arrangements know no bounds.

What these men share is a sense of self, of personal identity, which has comfortably integrated homosexuality into the whole person. While many of us march through the streets, attend political rallies, or wear our gay identities boldly and obviously, most gay men prefer otherwise. They prefer quieter lives, out of the limelight, away from the headlines. They prefer to be who they are without a fuss, without a fury.

At one time sectors of the gay population considered these men "closet cases"—men who concealed their homosexuality, leading lives of denial, secrecy and self-hatred. Perhaps this was once in fact true. Today, however, the situation is different. These men comprise the major portion of the community that turns out for important fundraisers, key social occasions, even gay pride parades. They generally are men who have found a way to successfully integrate their homosexuality into their lives and gone on with the business at hand. They are, if you will, second-generation gay American men.

While most second-generation gay men emerged from the closet during the mid-seventies, amid the Anita Bryant hoopla, many were already confronting powerful personal issues involving their homosexual identities. We use the term "second-generation" in a profoundly American sense, to indicate a period after one has experienced the highly-charged intensity of the "coming out" years. As many second-generation ethnic Americans have found that the substance of their lives are dramatically different from their immigrant parents, so many second-generation gay men discover that their contemporary lives are significantly changed from their lives just a decade ago. The homosexuality, of course, is still there, but instead of serving as a source of anxiety, discomfort and crisis, it has become an accepted and appreciated part of one's self. We know who we are and we're going on with the business of living.

This doesn't mean that the second-generation gay man turns a cold shoulder to activism. We don't. Just as the children of immigrants—who often think of themselves as American through-and-through—still suffer the societal stigma and bigotry their parents endured, gay men who are fully at peace with their homosexuality continue to experience waves of hostility from many sources in society. Whether or not we ourselves lobby public officials or write letters of concern about inaccurate media coverage, we're glad that someone is doing it and we find our own special way to support gay activism. Some of us gladly write large checks to keep our organizations and service centers financially strong. Others find the time to use whatever skills we have for the betterment of our local gay community—serving on boards, catering special events, volunteering at a medical clinic, doing pro-bono legal work, providing flowers for a community fundraiser. Even those of us who simply walk into the voting booth on Election Day with a consciousness of the powerful influence elected officials can have on gay men's lives, are doing our part to help.

Assimilation and ghettoization are issues in the lives of the second generation. Some believe that we're abandoning our interest in narrowly-defined gay community activities and moving on up. We're serving organizations, but rather than gay health clinics or gay newspapers, we're serving our city's planning committee or the local opera company. Actually, it's not our involvement and community participation that's different. What *has* changed is that we're now participating in mainstream institutions in a more openly gay fashion. We're not hiding anymore. While some of us once lead two distinct lives—our "real" life and our gay life—nowadays these lives are merged.

Hence we attend film openings with lovers or groups of men friends. When our women friends join us on social occasions they're there to enjoy the evening with us, not serve as a cover. If we serve on the board of a local theatre company, we feel comfortable suggesting works with particular appeal to gay people— or the plays of openly gay and lesbian playwrights. We dress and walk and speak as we choose, with less self-consciousness and fear that we may "give ourselves away."

Each of us has come to this place via a different path, and we enjoy our lives and our integrated identities in different styles. Some of us feel happiest bringing our lovers along to office social functions. Others prefer to attend by ourselves. Some announce quite openly to coworkers that we're gay. Others prefer to let them interpret our situation as they will. Where we were at one time quite judgmental of gay men who did things differently from us, now we've grown to respect the diverse choices other men have made in living their lives.

And living our lives is what this book is all about. After the crises are over and it's no big shakes to us or to our friends and family that we're gay, we have tremendous decisions to make about our lives. Many of us have the financial resources and the social options available to live quite comfortably.

Books, magazines, movies and television shows bombard us with information pertinent to our lifestyles. We hear news reports or pick up *Esquire* and *GQ* to read about how men manage stress, about appropriate intake of cholesterol in our diets, about next autumn's fashions. But something is lacking. While the mainstream media is rich with viewpoints on men's lives, little is written specifically about homosexual men and the key ways in which our homosexuality impacts on our lives. Sometimes we find ourselves reading two different kinds of publications in order to integrate our identities: the mainstream media and the gay press. We find in the publications of the gay community a great deal of diversity. Some are quite frivolous and others focused solely on our sexual gay identities; others are serious, helpful and well-written. We're aware that the gay press provides us with invaluable information about health issues, politics and leisure activities simply not covered anywhere else.

This book is intended to serve as a source of information and thoughtful analysis for gay men who are seeking to explore various aspects of their lives. While it's a handbook in the sense that it contains specific helpful information to aid gay men in making decisions in their lives, we do not intend this single book to be the final word on these matters. Indeed, the forty-two gay men who contributed to this book are a diverse group of men who share neither a single viewpoint or a specific attitude about their lives as gay men. Nor do we believe this book includes all the analysis and factual information gay men need these days. While the book is extraordinarily comprehensive, many topics have been omitted and some topics which are included in a single essay already have entire books written about them.

However, this volume can serve as a source that you can turn to when seeking advice or specific viewpoints. We intend for it to challenge your thinking, offer you alternatives, and inspire you with optimism. Whether the specific essays are humorous or analytical, we have attempted to convey our attitude about being gay men throughout this book in an upbeat, positive manner. This, we feel, is sorely lacking in literature by and about gay men these days.

Ultimately, there is not a single way to live one's life as a gay man these days. Throughout this book we attempt to respect the choices gay men make and to probe the central issues in our lives: our health and image, home, love, cultural and leisure activities, and our identities as openly gay men. At a time when some would have us go back into the closet, and others would have us focus all our energies on the crises surrounding AIDS, many of us are finding a way to continue living our lives with self-respect, dignity and verve.

Eric E. Rofes
Provincetown, Massachusetts
October 1, 1985

I

HEALTH
&
IMAGE

Serenity

by Paul Reed

ABOUT THE THE TIME WE STOPPED SAYING "TO DIE FOR"
with regard to male beauty, a quiet revolution was under way. At
the outset this health revolution was reluctant, the result of a
tragic situation to which the only sane response was sudden,
drastic change. Now we find ourselves on the verge of a tremendous new era, an exciting time of discovery and perfect peace.

Used to be that we wanted only the *image* of good health—
tan, glowing skin, as if we had done nothing with ourselves but
sit on the beach all season; muscular, well-formed bodies like
those found among cowboys, construction workers and the captain of the high school football team (of course); and, less specifically, an aura of vitality, a certain element of downright sexiness
which some might call sleaziness or raunchiness, but which
was, truly, a spirit of readiness, as if one were willing to try just
anything, the sooner the better.

To achieve this we flocked by the thousands to those palaces
of gay masculinity, our gyms. There we strained ourselves in an
energetic frenzy that not only alleviated our childhood fears of
athletic failure, but that pumped our bodies into a masculine
ideal we called perfection. That frenzy felt like foreplay, so eager
were we, so expectant of the glories yet to be in that time when
every evening contained suspense and hopefulness.

I remember my first few months in the gym, when everything
seemed new and rather exciting to me. Steam rising from the
showers, small white terrycloth towels, the butch-jock sounds of
metal clanking, men grunting, rock 'n roll blasting from sus-
pended speakers—all of it enthralled me and endeared me to
that place where, at long last, beauty could be won.

Magazines of the day celebrated the new gay health consciousness in articles which linked the proliferation of gay bodybuilding with the health craze sweeping the country, though this
was often complete nonsense. For did we not, all of us, know
scores of friends who used drugs to energize their workouts, who

smoked dope, took speed, and shot up anabolic steroids to facilitate that mad, muscular frenzy?

I cared very little for health back then, for I was young, fresh to the city, and filled with excitement at how much there was to do, how many people there were to be with, how much flesh there was. No, I wanted Beauty, and what Nature had failed to supply, Iron would. Heart rates, pulses, protein—none of it mattered (or even occurred to us) in that optimistic push towards being a hunk.

And so, with profound self-discipline I did what had to be done. Day after day, week upon week, I stoically, painfully entered that tabernacle of male perfection and did all those things one does, sweating, dishing, waiting, hoping. It was a constant, mad press of thick bodies, all of us vibrating to Donna Summer and Sylvester, the same loud music which accompanied us later, long after the gym, when at the baths we put it on display and waited to see if the effort would pay off.

Have they turned the music down in gyms? Or have our perceptions of exercise changed so much it seems as though the gyms are now quieter? One often harkens back to the "good old days" before AIDS, but memory often fails. We didn't enjoy good health back then, though we look back as if those were carefree days now lost. Have we forgotten hepatitis? Intestinal parasites? Gonorrhea?

The gyms are quieter now because their members are more sober about exercise and about life. The evolution of gay masculinity has taken us from our original place of bashful non-athleticism to that frenetic decade of muscles and disco, on into an era of transformation—a place I call serenity.

No longer does one hanker for the mere image of health; one is now utterly determined to achieve and keep it. Because of the unpredictable nature of AIDS as well as the undeniable stress of this end of the century, the object now is a deep serenity bred by perfect balance, the peace of mind that manifests itself in a relaxed, fluid body and a rich, hearty soul.

Image is still important, but now we want a new image, the image of perfect health. To this end we have responded with psychology and fashion. We have developed on the one hand what I call the vestal virgin syndrome, which has as its hall-mark the personal (and usually loud) claim that one never went to baths anyway, one hasn't done a thing in years, and one has actually—if you can believe it—reverted to a virginal state!

Congruent with this is an aversion to wearing the kind of clothes—or in any way projecting an image—that might suggest the old feeling of ready sexiness. Much of the conformity which earned us the name "clones" is done. Tight jeans torn and tat-tered at pressure points, t-shirts a size too small, colored jock-straps, bomber jackets, tight red-plaid shirts, motorcycle boots, bandanas—these are now found fluttering in the breeze at side-walk sales, or one stumbles across them while rummaging about in the dark recesses of dresser drawers or in dusty boxes stuck together in forgotten closet corners.

Fashion victims abound, for nothing communicates an image of newness more readily than the "latest" attire. And being a little fat—just the slightest hint of a roll about the waistline—is also a desirable trait. The painful thinness of yesteryear's disco bunnies has yielded to the desire for meatiness, for a man whose appearance bespeaks an appetite for life.

The old practitioners we sometimes still see, though in far fewer numbers: still working out too hard, a lost expression on their faces as they rest between sets, as if unable to snap out of the broken promise; serenity has yet to be learned. But the new gay male, in his loose, relaxed fashions, strolls along the street with an expression of calm, a smile ready when eyes meet (no more the hard frown of heavy cruising), his determination for good health and peace of mind an absolute aura.

To achieve serenity we still flock by the thousands to those palaces of gay masculinity, but we have enriched our health regimens with many new elements. Serenity is induced when we achieve balance amongst these many elements. It is much like the old dictum about everything in moderation.

For strength and physical proportioning we continue to pump iron, swelling muscles into their desired shapes, chiselling thighs, adding bulk here and there, and increasing overall body strength. For endurance, energy, and inner health we add aerobics to our daily plan, keeping heart rates and respiration elevated to strengthen the circulatory system.

For nutrition and freedom from addiction we review our diets, eliminating the things that rob us of energy, things like sugar, caffeine, and simple carbohydrates. We limit drinking, virtually eliminate drugs and completely forbid smoking. We make sure that we take in protein and fiber, lots of fiber.

Rest becomes essential, and it's composed of several things—a good night's sleep, of course, as well as moments of meditation or silence when we create time for ourselves simply to be alone, to quiet all the psychic interference of daily life. It is such quiet moments that create the real appreciation of serenity, because in being still we truly *feel* the calm of a healthy body and we learn that there is a great inner strength in serenity, a strength which combines forgiveness and love. Where tension, fear, worry and judgment once reigned now reside peace, acceptance and love— the kind of love that looks life square in the eye and says okay, we win.

Later, when after all of this we retire to bed and lie thinking in the dark, we remember everything we have done and all the changes we have made. And with a peaceful but plain sense of relief at having left the tensions of the baths and discos behind us for good, we drift off to sleep as we sometimes calculate the odds and always hedge our bets—*we will survive*.

Our priorities have shifted. Surely we have always wanted to look good. Who doesn't? But now we require much more than just the appearance of health. We must have the real thing, a sound mind and a healthy soul in a strong body. That classical goal is now ours, and events have catapulted us forward at a dazzling rate. Where we once aspired to a healthy glow, we now achieve glowing health.

This represents more than a quest for good health, more than a desire to avoid illness, more than a wish for a long life. This shift toward serenity symbolizes a profound transition—we are abandoning materialism and embracing spirituality.

Now this is no minor shift. For too long gay people have been denied spiritual access, if you will. Organized religion has shunned the gay man and lesbian, shutting us out completely and turning us away from the deeper realities those religions represent—tranquility, faith, hope, courage, love and acceptance.

Instead we embraced materialism and physical culture with a vengeance, heaping high value on possessions, beauty, the shape of a face, the feel of muscle. There is nothing wrong with this—materialism has as its ultimate goal to provide comfort, to make this life passage easier and more enjoyable. But as we all know, by instinct perhaps, physical satisfaction can be empty. And here we are again, on that old bandwagon of being on the cutting edge of a new social revolution, demonstrating in our fight against disease and our quest for serenity that real happiness is won by the heart.

Now, there is always a problem when using the term "spiritual." The word has gooey connotations—things like church or temple, or worse yet, all that touchy-feely business we associate with "feeding our souls" or "raising our consciousness." What I mean here has a little to do with all of that, yes, but what I really mean has to do with finding harmony in life—accepting things as they are, being nice to people, not being self-centered but giving, and always looking forward to the future without dwelling on the hurtful past. These require effort, constant and slow, and that effort—and the good feelings it promises—is part of what spirituality is all about.

Of course it runs deeper as well. We all know the feeling of connectedness with nature and humankind, that feeling we humorlessly call "in tune with the universe." It is really a matter of being quiet—keeping still in order to hear one's own thoughts and feelings—and of keeping one's attitude toward life on a positive, loving track, filled with that forgiveness and simple acceptance we learn in silence.

As the saying goes, there are many paths to the top of the mountain, and so we come to this spirituality from many angles. The important point is that we have come to it and that it has colored our values and the quality of life in a significant way. What a relief it is finally to look at each other as just human beings, gentle men with feelings, all of us simply wanting love and comfort and long lives.

W hat, then, has changed? Gay men continue to come out of their closets, migrate to gay urban centers and lead lives in that legendary pursuit of happiness. An edge has been lost, a certain tension is now gone, but it is being replaced by the deeply enriching experience of serenity which blankets our community. We are growing strong in mind, spirit, and body, and at long last we're becoming truly fit. We are on the verge of tremendous success. Serenity is at hand.

Care of One's Physical Appearance From Head to Toe

by Erik McMahan

MOST OF US ARE VERY SELF-CONSCIOUS ABOUT THE WAY we look and how we project ourselves when making that valuable first impression. I know, for I often find myself running to the lavatory after I've finished dining to make sure nothing is lodged between my teeth. When I'm late for a function I still feel under my arms to ensure that there aren't any holes there. I'd just die of embarrassment if there were.

Gay men are often among the few people these days who take pride in their appearance, and through the years I've found that the application of a few sound principles, coupled with a generous helping of common sense, will improve one's appearance. The following tips are applicable to all men, whatever complexion or hair type they might have, and however young or ripe.

First it's essential to stress the importance of vitamins and minerals to one's bodily well-being. Our bodies must have a certain amount of vitamins and minerals in order to function properly and to stay healthy. For most of us our daily food consumption furnishes only a part of these, making it necessary to supplement whatever is not obtained in our food. Vitamins may make the difference between a temporary ailment and a disease that one carries to his grave.

VITAMIN

A	Heals skin lesions, burns, dry or bumpy skin, and acne.
B	Helps many bodily functions, skin problems, nervous system, acne, cold sores, loss of hair, emotional problems, eyes, nails, and headaches.

C   Guards against colds, infections; soothes injuries and
                allergies, etc.
D   Helps bursitis, strengthens nails.
E   Good for circulatory and heart problems; also can be
                used both internally and externally for sores, cuts,
                rashes and blemishes.

MINERALS

Iron   Helpful for anemia and strengthens the blood.
Zinc   Helps prevent acne, body odor, dandruff, facial skin
                care, body skin care, Herpes—Type II, prostate prob-
                lems and severe rashes.

There are several good books on this subject at your local bookstore. Please consult these "encyclopedias" of vitamins and
minerals for more information.

Now, we'll start at the head, with the hair, scalp, face, and
brain, all of which are as important as the rest of us. Breaking this down, I'll show you inexpensive ways of keeping the
zest in these features.

Everyone wants healthy, shiny looking hair that blows
gracefully in the wind and bounces naturally when strolling.
Your hair should catch the light, cast off a healthy shine and be
manageable morning, noon and night. However, you need an
excuse for mussed-up hair during a windstorm.

If your hair lacks luster, is dry, limp, or receding the solution
is easier than you may realize. Some people feel that there isn't
any hope for their hair and have gone to considerable pain and
expense, only to be left with the same problems as before.

Dry hair that hasn't any life to it tends to be just a hassle, and
frizzy. All you need is a small jar of mayonnaise (any brand), a
banana (ripe), a cup of honey, (an egg and a shower cap): *Mix the
mayo with the egg, banana and honey until creamy. Apply this
mixture to your dry hair, put on the shower cap, and let it set for
one hour. Place a towel around your neck and dab your forehead
from time to time.* This mixture will burn your eyes, so be
careful. When the hour is up, simply shampoo and condition as
you regularly do. When dry your hair will be shiny, full, soft and
manageable. You see, mayonnaise penetrates and conditions the
hair follicles and attaches to the scalp. The banana acts as a paste

that fortifies the hair shaft with many valuable minerals. The egg is the protein that hair needs to bring out its natural shine, and the honey locks in the much-needed moisture from the other ingredients.

Be sure to repeat this treatment once a week for a month, and then once every month afterwards. Warning: remember never to answer the door without your shower cap on!

For black men the best treatments for problem hair are non-lye-based relaxers. Be sure to follow the directions on the label. Used in conjunction with the above procedures, you should have no trouble in bringing luster to your hair.

For graying hair, kelp will help. It's a natural source of iodine and will help bring natural color back to your hair. For balding or thinning hair, polysorbate-80, which is found in most dairy products, or which can be purchased from a manufacturer, will help produce new hair follicle growth and thicken your hair.

Scratch and massage your scalp regularly. NEVER BRUSH WET HAIR. Oily hair is not pleasant to have or see. Oil and sweat from your scalp collect dirt, odors and embarrassment. This is easy to remedy, simply by washing your hair every other day with a bar of Ivory soap before shampooing and conditioning as you usually do. Ivory soap cleanses naturally; it's not oil-based, full of perfume or a deodorant. It doesn't dry the skin when proper moisturization is complete. That's all you have to do—nothing more.

Your attitude is most important when caring for your physical appearance or for anything else in your life. If you feel you are fat and ugly and you project this, then you will be. If you do nothing to promote your appearance, then your appearance gives up on waiting for the command to be beautiful, handsome or even foxy. Your body listens to your thoughts, and when you aren't feeling like being radiant, beautiful, and positive it tends to slouche, ache and fart.

Surely there will be times when you just don't have it in you to be positive. Go listen to your favorite album; go for a walk in natural surroundings; or just do something off-the-wall for yourself, to your friends, or your loved ones. You'll be surprised at what the results will be.

Moderation is important when caring for yourself. You can drink, smoke, take drugs, do anything, so long as it doesn't become habit forming. Your body is built to fight off anything that it finds harmful, so long as it doesn't overwhelm your system's ability to battle. Balance out the amount of what you eat and drink with what you smoke, take, and project. Never over-indulge in anything. When taking drugs or smoking marijuana, give your body time to dispose of the poisons before indulging again. If you have a bad experience, listen to your body and never try that substance again. Take care of your body and it will do the same for you for many years.

N ow we'll move on to the face, where a great deal of attention is usually placed.

Wrinkles etch their way into foreheads, usually before they begin forming anywhere else on your face. With proper moisturizing and a gentle massage to relieve tension in this area, the creases are reduced. I find that Vitamin E oil is great for moisturizing.

Your eyes are major expression centers and should be cared for and protected. If your eyes have bags beneath them, look at your diet. You may have too much sodium in your diet. Black circles are usually signs of lack of sleep, or a broken nose. Hopefully you don't have the latter. Also some drugs cause the tissues beneath the eyes to darken and become sallow, which can be remedied by staying away from drugs and taking it easy. Cucumber slices over the eyes help soften the circles and even release tension lines like crow's feet. Liquid Vitamin E pene-trates the skin and helps stimulate regular blood flow, allowing normal flesh tones to reform, thereby fading the circles.

Eyelashes should be moistened with Vitamin E oil from time to time so they won't have a tendency to thin. Stroke the lashes with a drop of Vitamin E oil to enhance a darker and thicker appearance. It works!

For tired and bloodshot eyes, simply splash with warm water and rest with a cool cloth or cucumber slices over your eyes for a half hour. Please, if you get hungry during this treatment, don't eat the cucumber slices! Wear sunglasses in bright sunlight or during windstorms, and always moisturize the skin around your eyes with a non-oily cream. I've found that Nivea works well.

Your nose is usually neglected and never seems to receive the care it needs. Nose hair should never be plucked, but scissored carefully. You may have a need to pick your nose, but I shall not give any tips on this matter.

Oral hygiene is extremely important. Habitual care should form in childhood. I usually brush my teeth three to five times a day, and if I am to be away from home for any amount of time I carry my toothbrush along. I like to have a clean, fresh smile; when I run my tongue across my teeth all I want to feel is a smooth surface. I brush my tongue and gums and rinse with Listerine. Flossing is important to prevent gum disease. If your teeth are stained, don't buy those expensive whiteners; just take a teaspoon of salt, a teaspoon of baking soda and a little bit of water to make a thick paste, and brush gently for several minutes. Soon your teeth will come out of the closet sparkling.

If you have sensitive gums, brush two to three times a day and floss every other day, but never overdo this. Once a week it's good to rinse with warm salt water to prevent oral disease. Whatever else you do with your mouth is up to you.

Your face is usually the center of your appearance and the skin in this region must be provided with a considerable amount of care. The saddest procedure in which most men partake is damaging the skin while shaving. There are certain measures one can take to shave carefully without damaging or toughening the skin. Before you think about your stubble, your skin needs preparation for the abuse it receives during this grooming procedure.

Moisturize your stubble with Nivea face cream twenty to forty minutes before shaving. If you're going to bathe before you shave, apply Nivea and bathe without washing your face.

Apply shaving lotion or cream directly over the Nivea. Wet the razor with warm water and rinse after two gentle strokes. You'll already notice the difference in skin texture after you shave.

Once shaving is completed you're ready for your facial. There are two facials I recommend: one is Apricot Facial Scrub; the other is a homemade solution that gives a wonderful awakening to your skin. Mix 1/2 cup of honey, 1/3 cup of corn meal and a tablespoon of salt, and apply to your face, massaging gently for one minute and making sure it doesn't get into your eyes. This same mixture may be used for calloused hands and feet.

The Apricot Facial Scrub (instructions are on the tube) is a quick and easy method of removing the dead skin cells that clog pores and produce many skin problems, such as acne and blackheads. When preparing for facials, steam or apply hot compresses to your face to open the pores. I usually boil a large pot of water and steam the pores open by placing a towel around my head and the pot of water; breathing the steam is beneficial if you boil the water with two tablespoons of salt and a capful of vinegar or Vicks Vapo-Rub. This helps congestion, clogged nasal passages and lungs, and it's great for colds.

After the pores have been opened, the skin will become red and tender. This is a good sign that you're still alive after inhaling the steam. Apply the facial. While scrubbing your face remember to scrub the areas affected most by problems, and pay particular attention around the nose and especially the sides near the nostrils. This region usually causes major skin problems throughout life.

Rinse off the facial with warm but not hot water and pat dry. It is important to remember that after each facial you should pat your face dry—never rub. The scrub is an abrasive and you have received all the rubbing you'll ever need to bring blood to the surface of the skin.

Moisturize the face lightly with Nivea face cream. Stand back and look in the mirror at your new radiant face that glows with health. Feel the softness with the back of your hand and begin feeling good about yourself.

From your neck to your waist use only a mild soap, such as Ivory, while showering or bathing, and remember to moisturize afterwards. Your skin is always losing moisture and is continually shedding dead skin cells. To help lock in and add moisture, you must apply it in the form of creams, whether you have oily, normal or in-between skin. Learn to work with your body and it will always work for you.

Armpits need a good washing and a chance to air before applying deodorant. Otherwise you'll trap moisture between the deodorant and skin. When you perspire the moisture mixes with it and harmful bacteria may develop, causing odor. If you have no luck with deodorants, don't use them. Lightly powdering baking soda under your arms absorbs odors and soaks up wetness. To some, baking soda may be irritating. If it does become irritating, apply white vinegar with a cotton ball or a wash cloth instead. Vinegar doesn't prevent wetness, but stops perspiration odor.

Trimming underarm hair is fine if you feel the need to do so. It's your body, and you should feel at ease with any grooming procedure that may complement or make you feel more comfortable.

As we proceed towards the abdomen, the navel is our next quest. Washing this area gently will prevent odors and bacteria from forming. Sweat collects in this region, and foreign objects such as lint or dirt may adhere. When this occurs just wash with Ivory soap and dry thoroughly with a soft towel. Do not apply a moisturizer or deodorant, for they may be irritants.

When sunning, try not to use oil-based suntan lotions. When you apply lotions remember that your pores open in the heat and in goes the lotion. The pores may become clogged, so remember to bathe after tanning.

If you tend to burn more frequently than tan, use good common sense and apply apple cider vinegar to affected areas every twenty minutes for three hours. Replace the moisture burned away with 400 IUs of Vitamin E capsules, and you'll relieve the pain. You may look like a lobster but you won't feel the pain of being boiled.

Never use baby oil when tanning. Baby oil attracts the sun and causes a magnification of the ultraviolet rays, thereby causing the burn to deepen and become more painful. Baby oil should really be used on the infant and not the adult.

Exercising and dieting are too complex to be mentioned briefly; however, they are very important and should be a part of your daily routine. Consult your physician when considering any form of strenuous exercises, and remember the basic rule of dieting is: *if you eat less and exercise more, you should lose whatever you want.* If you eat a great deal and do a little, then be prepared to resemble the Goodyear Blimp.

On to the nails—not the kind that you hit with a hammer but those used for scratching, clawing, showing off and tapping.

Your nails say a lot about you; they may indicate nervousness, style, class and charm. Your nails accentuate the person you are. If you bite your nails you probably have a great deal of time on your hands. If your nails are long and sharp you may be the type who uses them in quarrels ("tooth and nail"). If they're properly taken care of, then you're a down-to-earth person who enjoys just being yourself.

People spend far too much money on their nails. For everyone there are simple at-home methods that can replace costly hand jobs. Moisturizing the nails can be accomplished with two Vitamin E capsules and a tablespoon of Crisco. Simply puncture the capsules and mix with the shortening. Make sure that the two ingredients are blended well. Apply the mixture to your nails and place your hands into plastic gloves (or wrap each finger in cellophane) for twenty minutes. Remove the wraps and wipe the excess over your hands while gently pushing the cream well into the cuticle area. Use this same home-made cream to freshen hands and nails whenever they feel dry or rough. Soak nails in Vitamin D and warmed milk (for calcium).

Common sense is essential in caring for your nails. If you want your nails to look clean and healthy, then you must take care of them when they need it. If your nails become cracked, moisturize the nail, let dry, then use an emory board and file the nail until you overpower the crack. Brush on an enamel to seal any remaining splits. Try to avoid filing with metal files, as they may lead to more splits and snags. The emory board is best when used gently.

Lightly tapping your nails does strengthen them. Blood is brought to the cuticle and stimulates new growth. Be careful not to do it on rough surfaces.

On, now, to the area between the legs. Most people feel that this area doesn't need much attention; oh, but it does! Sweat causes pubic odor and the skin to become tender during activity. If you have an excessive amount of hair, it's quite alright to trim the hair carefully. Brushing the hair gently allows air to reach the skin so that odors may escape. Try to brush your pubic hair at least once a day. Washing this area is essential. Never scrub—simply wash with a bar of Ivory soap and dry with a soft towel.

Consult a physician immediately at the first sign of abrasions or lesions that just seem to appear, and avoid touching the affected region. If you are not circumcised, be sure to wash your penis daily. The foreskin in the area can easily collect dirt and may cause infection. When washing the penis, be careful that soap does not enter the tip, except after sexual contact. This may cause a burning sensation that may persist for an hour. Washing the pubic and anal areas must be done gently and without rubbing. The skin in these areas is usually sensitive and can easily become irritated during intercourse and may burn, itch, swell, and become extremely sensitive. If these symptoms persist, consult your physician and be more gentle the next time you're intimate.

Not every itch or inflamed tissue means you have hemorrhoids—there may be more to the matter than meets the eye. There are many forms of disease that affect the genital region. Parasitic infections are common and you may have symptoms for months before your body becomes tired of warding them off and succumbs. Cleaning these areas thoroughly after sexual contact should help to reduce the risk of disease. If your symptoms persist, consult your physician and be prepared for some possibly painful treatment.

We move on to the legs. Not much is needed here, other than a good moisturizing, like the rest of you! If your legs tend to become tired or begin to ache after some form of activity, your body is telling you to sit down and take it easy for awhile. Listen to your body.

You probably neglect your feet more than any other part of your body, and so they need more care than you realize. People never seem to provide enough attention to this area and yet complain when their feet become tired and sore. First of all, your feet are furthest from your heart and may tend to lose circulation. They frequently become cold, and the skin may become tough. All of these can be prevented with proper care and simple treatments.

It's good to massage your feet every evening, taking time to apply pressure to sore spots. Use lotion while massaging to moisturize the skin and relieve tightness in the tissues. To soften dry heels and corns, soak your feet twice a week. After a long day in shoes, go barefoot for awhile. Let your feet breathe. Otherwise they may become afflicted with several forms of fungi, including athlete's foot.

Many people neglect the area between the toes where, on occasion, more than dirt tends to collect. Washing the webs is important so that corns do not develop from the friction of two dirty toes rubbing together. Manicuring toenails is equally important as caring for your fingernails. I suggest clipping the toenails—it's better than filing. Remember to moisturize and push cuticles back gently.

There we have it. From head to toe, a few at-home treatments that help put proper grooming in its place. One should remember the four keys of maintaining a radiant glow: 1-common sense; 2-moderation; 3-attitude; and 4-general care of oneself, including faith in vitamins. You don't have to spend a whole lot of money on expensive lotions and beauty salons to look radiant and alive; and although some of the tips in this article may sound unusual, these recipes really do work.

Good luck, and good grooming!

Bodybuilding—Gateway to a Better Life

by Roy F. Wood

WHY IN THE WORLD WOULD ANYONE SPEND THREE, FOUR, five or even six days a week lifting weights in a smelly old gym? Surely anyone who attempts such a thing must have lead in his head!

If you compound the situation by having the bodybuilder work out at home, away from scenes of gorgeous hunks strutting about in their near-naked sweatiness, then obviously you are dealing with the worst sort of masochist. Right?

Not really!

Bodybuilding does have a great many rewards which are, for the most part, open to anyone. Only when physical illness prevents an individual from being able to exercise regularly is the sport unable to benefit a participant. Bodybuilding is an arena where progress is made as rapidly or as slowly as the lifter wishes to work at it.

For a gay man as for anyone else the reasons for lifting may be many. Certainly the results can be gratifying if one trains consistently and adheres to a strict schedule.

Along with the rest of the nation, gay men's interest in good health and general overall self-improvement is a recent phenomenon. But this new interest appears to be serious—bodybuilding is here to stay. Witness the large number of general purpose gyms as well as numerous "gay" gyms which continue to thrive and expand.

For a gay man, however, bodybuilding should be more imperative than for a heterosexual man. Gay society, whether one likes it or not, is based very much on looks. A person's physique, not his personality, often attracts the initial response. When men first seek out other men they don't generally inquire, "Does he have a brilliant mind?" The presentation of one's flesh gets first notice. That presentation depends on a body which is in good shape, coupled with other features that are not repulsive.

Most people can do little with the faces they are given; they can do a great deal with their bodies. Certain physical characteristics can't be altered. A person's flesh can be changed. Weight can be lost or gained. Chests can be expanded. Pecs can be rounded and firmed. Biceps can be made to bulge—in the right places. And stomachs certainly can be solidified into rock-hard layers of muscles. Stomachs do not expand, bulge and drape over one's belt by accident. Nor is it usually an act of nature when these features are kept in their optimum condition for a man—defined, solid, firm.

Certainly other sports such as biking, swimming, running and many team sports will assist a man towards a better body. But these activities generally aid only a few bodyparts. Most also presuppose participants to be in good, healthy form.

Bodybuilding, however, is exactly what the word implies: building one's body. Which is very different from weightlifting, where the emphasis is on the amount of pounds one can lift.

With a proper program a man can mould his flesh into any form he desires. He can become a sculptor creating his own David. If his legs displease him, he works harder on these. Hard work and dedication can change any single part of the body into an outstanding attribute. There are no limitations. The only limitation is in the mind of the lifter.

Which is not to say that a forty-year-old man who has never lifted anything but a beercan is going to become Mister Universe in five years. He won't (although the current holder of the Mister Universe title is over fifty!). All the same, someone starting a bodybuilding program can make definite, visible improvements in his physique. The amount of improvement depends primarily on the amount of work one puts into lifting. Common sense dictates that the earlier one begins the more improvement will be possible. The forty-year-old who is just beginning should proceed with caution. As one ages one generally accumulates a number of habits which are at best unhealthy. These include poor nutrition, lack of exercise and simply allowing one's body to run down. The man who becomes dissatisfied with this general malaise and resolves to do something about it is to be commended. At the same time the older the man is, the more attention he should pay to his general health before starting a bodybuilding program. A medical check-up would not be remiss. These considerations taken into account, however, the maxim still holds: *if you begin to lift weights, no matter how carefully or how slowly, and work diligently, visible improvements will* occur.

For a beginner, there are generally two options: training in a gym or at home. Your selection will depend on a number of variables.

If you live in an area which doesn't have a gym, or which doesn't have any that are adequate for the serious bodybuilder, lifting at home is probably the best option. Stay away from those places which have separate days for men and women. Under such a system the most you would be able to lift would be three days a week, which is a great limitation for anyone who is serious about bodybuilding. If you are in an area, however, which offers suitable facilities, a gym may make a lot of sense for the beginner. You'll have the chance to see other guys in later stages of development, which ought to encourage you. The professional who operates the gym will be able to show you basic lifting routines. It's important to begin correctly. Once you've got the basics and know which parts of your body you want to work hardest, you should be set. Don't be intimidated by men larger than you . . . everyone started somewhere! A gym routine for the first year or so can be advantageous for most beginners.

Lifting at home, however, also has advantages which you generally won't find discussed in most books and magazines on bodybuilding. Anyone who reads the bodybuilding bible *Muscle and Fitness* (assuming you can find anything to read amongst all the ads for Weider products) will soon realize that working out at home is unheard of to these folks.

At home you have the flexibility of lifting at the most convenient time for you, without having to contend with a crowded gym. You can push yourself according to your limits. The faster you can do each set while maintaining proper form, the better.

About the only disadvantage of working out at home, unless you have a lifting partner, is the need to use somewhat lighter weights on some routines (notably benchpresses) than you might handle if you have someone around to spot for you. In gyms, however, you can waste a lot of time waiting to use equipment.

Don't be in such a hurry to finish your routines that you don't enjoy yourself along the way. Lifting shouldn't be a chore. It shouldn't be something to be endured in order to improve your physique enough to please yourself and pick up the tricks you want, or to attract the lover you hope will one day turn up.

Lifting is a struggle . . . a struggle against yourself. Conquering the barbells can be exhilarating. You can assist yourself by maintaining a careful training record: which routines you do, how much weight you use, how many reps you perform. At the end of even three months you'll be surprised at the advances you've made . . . at the end of six months or a year the changes will be startling.

Bodybuilding is above all a sport of perseverance. It's not something which has a "season" that arrives, lasts a few weeks and then passes.

It helps to have mirrors in your lifting area so you can watch yourself. You can't watch yourself do each exercise; some routines don't lend themselves to visual effects, not if you're exhibiting proper form. But on sets like benchpresses, preacher curls, concentration curls, eyeing yourself in a mirror can be exciting. As you strain to lift your allotted number of pounds the required number of times, you can see your flesh responding. Pushing the barbell up slowly . . . raising it to the limit of your arms, then back down . . . your chest heaving as your lungs gulp in air and expand (always watch your breathing!), growing stronger, more powerful with each upward thrust. Or watching your bicep grow and bulge with every attempt at curling the iron bar. The sheer joy of such exertion should instill any man with a feeling of power, with an exaltation that he is in control of his own life and his own destiny, not simply a pawn in the hands of others. For gay men this can be as beneficial as the improvement in their physiques.

Bodybuilding is first, last and always an individual effort. It's an effort motivated by a strong desire to better oneself, a desire to be the very best you can be. Certainly there are elements of arrogance and "machismo" involved, but most men who work and lift and strain in order to achieve a physique which both they and others can admire are driven by an overwhelming desire to improve themselves. Bodybuilding starts with a lot of mental guts. The individual is challenged daily, having to overcome his own weaknesses, his own personal inclinations to skip a workout "just this once." But those who meet the challenge, those who continue working towards their goal, can achieve it. Their mirrors will show them the results. Pride in themselves as human beings will replace feelings of inadequacy. For gay men the pride may be more intense, which is why bodybuilding remains an arena where gay men can excel beyond their own expectations. Twenty years ago the notion of a gay man achieving success through bodybuilding would have caused snickers everywhere—even among the gay populace. In those days muscles and homosexuals didn't go together. They do now.

Facing Up to Compulsive Lifestyles

by Ronald E. Hellman, M.D.

EACH OF US IS ENDOWED WITH THE ABILITY TO CHOOSE from an infinity of potential pursuits in our daily lives. Our choices are formed in the context of their necessity for survival, their personal and social usefulness, and their pleasurable qualities. We derive a positive sense from those activities that help to sustain our lives, realize our goals, and make living enjoyable and worthwhile. Some of us, however, feel consistently compelled towards certain activities that work against our real aspirations in life. We focus on an arena of behavior that provides no lasting sense of self-affirmation. These compulsive activities may substitute for a lack of personal love, meaningful relationships, and social approval. They can be so pervasive as to dictate our style of living.

Many factors may predispose the gay man to compulsive and addictive problems, including one's age, ethnic and religious background, heredity and temperament, as well as familial and social influences. Society's prejudices certainly increase the potential for such activity. Gay men commonly grow up in families, around friends and within a social environment that disregards their real emotional needs. We are denied avenues of emotional expression, and a painful struggle ensues in adapting to the tensions that one's homosexuality creates in others. Stifled feelings build within, until their intensity demands some form of discharge.

For the individual enmeshed in a compulsive or addictive lifestyle, one activity usually predominates as a way to alleviate uncomfortable feelings. Anger, loneliness, or feelings of inadequacy are so persistent, annoying or overwhelming, the individual feels compelled to act to reduce the anxiety associated with these feelings. Compulsive activity becomes a way to self-medicate against such anxiety.

Compulsive activity provides immediate gratification, temporary structure, and safety from a pained and disorganized existence. But this behavior doesn't resolve the deeply conflicted feelings that gave rise to the anxiety, and the activity is repeated. The compulsion can distract from painful memories altogether, and the individual may be largely unconscious of why he feels compelled to act.

The individual feels driven by an irresistible force, and quickly learns which drug or activity reduces anxiety most efficiently. With practice the activity is competently initiated, and carried out almost automatically—the person is habituated to a compulsive activity. The brief satisfaction and control experienced during the compulsive act substitutes for fulfillment in other areas of life. There is a loss of interest in other areas of living, and the compulsion itself is established as a lifestyle.

The individual may suffer from one or many compulsions depending on circumstances and availability. The activities become part of a practiced and planned repertoire that serves to relieve emotional pain that is poorly understood, and lost to insight and control. As one multi-addicted, compulsive gay man recalls:

> I had such a terrible sense of myself, I would just spend all my time in the bars. I could forget about myself and open up on alcohol. I small-talked my way into bed with one or two tricks a day. I put AIDS out of my mind—I just didn't think about it. With an "up" to get through work, and a "down" for sleep, I had my act down cold.[1]

The compulsive activity becomes a signature for the person in his style of functioning. It "possesses" the person. His need for the activity grows to be well outside any useful or pleasurable function of that activity. This man continues:

> I stopped enjoying sex. I just needed it because the rest of my life was so empty. It filled time. It was a pleasureless pleasure.

The compulsive activity is potent in its temporary tranquilizing effect, and the individual feels helpless to resist it. Failure to

resist the impulse and its subsequent repetition further intensifies feelings of personal inadequacy, heightening anxiety which
reinforces the compulsive act. As the individual becomes more
preoccupied with his compulsive behavior, lover relationships,
friendships, work, and family ties may be increasingly affected.

The term "compulsive lifestyle" is not a diagnostic entity. It is
a descriptive term that has its usefulness, but confusion
about it has bred some debate. As a diagnostic term the American Psychiatric Association officially uses the word "compulsive" to describe three distinct disorders: obsessive-
compulsive disorder, the familiar example being the compulsive
handwasher; compulsive personality disorder, characterized by
formality, rigidity, perfectionism, and rumination over trivial
details excessive enough to impair one's ability to function; and
compulsive conduct disorders, characterized by an inability to
resist the impulse to gamble, steal, set fires, assault, and on.[2]
Freudians classically view compulsions as irrational, repetitive
acts, in which the person feels driven to "undo" guilt relating to
some past or future circumstance. Others see compulsions simply as repetitive, uncontrolled behaviors that reduce anxiety.
Still broader conceptualizations use the term in a positive sense,
as when one feels "compelled" to do the right thing, or when one
is "addicted" to running or meditation.[3] A distinct personality
that leads to a compulsive lifestyle has not been found. Still
much remains to be learned about the complex interaction of
factors that lead to a compulsive style of living.

Because the term conveys such a heterogeneity of meaning,
concern has been raised over its potential misuse. For gay
men confronted with the difficult task of altering their sexual
activity in the face of AIDS, some have feared that the term
"sexual compulsivity" will be misapplied in a pejorative and
socially controlling way. They fear the indiscriminate use of this
label among gays themselves will fuel homophobic embers within fundamentalist and other sexually repressive groups that
have always viewed gay men as nothing but compulsively sexual
beings. As one gay man put it:

> If you're heterosexual and have a compulsive problem, society calls it a neurosis. If you're gay and compulsive, they think it's part of your character.

Homosexuality itself can seem like a compulsion to the person with deeply internalized negative feelings about his sexual orientation. A middle-aged, heterosexually married father describes how he experiences this:

> It interferes with my family life. I don't want it to be there, but I have this compulsion to have sex with men. I stop at a bookstore for sex on my way to or from work. That takes care of it, and no one has to know.

This man has a poorly integrated homosexual orientation. It is not his homosexuality per se that is compulsive, as he would believe, but the psychological context in which his behavior occurs. He is in conflict over an accepted social role and an unacceptable sexual orientation. His homosexuality is so unacceptable to him that he experiences it as coming from outside himself—it "compels" him. In actuality his inner conflict generates great anxiety, and he has found that the most efficient way to reduce this tension is through isolated homosexual acts. Although this temporarily reduces the intensity of his sexual attraction, and his anxiety, it does not resolve his conflict and the behavior is repeated.

For gay men with a more integrated sense of their homosexuality, numerous factors may explain a tendency toward sexual activity as a compulsive outlet. Many therapists experienced with the problems of gay people have noted a striking difference in the emphasis on sexuality between gay men and lesbians. This is not surprising to many who see sexual conquest as acceptable for men, while bonding and nurturing are expected and encouraged among women. The difference in emphasis is exemplified by the institution of the baths, which is virtually an exclusively male phenomenon. Biological differences between men and women may contribute to this sexual dichotomy as well. Others, however, emphasize that as gay men discover their homosexuality they are also confronted with the widespread belief that this is synonymous with being "less than a man."

For some, therefore, compulsive sexuality reduces anxiety because it is a constant assurance of one's masculinity. For others, defined by society in sexual terms, and simultaneously negated for being sexual, compulsive sexual activity reduces anxiety because it affirms one's identity as a sexual being. For still others, alienated from family and friends during important years of development, compulsive sex provides immediate intimacy, reducing anxiety associated with strong feelings of isolation.

It should be emphasized that sexual compulsivity has little to do with the frequency or anonymity of sexual activity, or with the number of sexual partners. An example:

A 31-year-old gay man has frequent, anonymous sex with other men that he meets in a park near his home, or in bars in other cities. He works as an airline steward. He enjoys living alone, traveling, and not having the responsibilities of a lover relationship. He finds that these encounters satisfy his need for sex, and his sexual style fits nicely into the overall pattern of his life.

It is not an activity per se, nor its frequency that deems it a compulsion, but its repetitive use as a way of reducing anxiety generated by other problems in the individual's life.

By this definition, relationships, themselves, can hallmark a compulsive lifestyle. Here is an illustration:

A middle-aged gay man has always felt an overwhelming need to be in a relationship. Without a lover he becomes so anxious that he panics. When this happens his ability to judge and reflect on new relationships becomes impaired. Nothing matters but to have someone. Compatibility and an interest in resolving differences is barely considered, and inevitably the relationship fails. The cycle begins again.

For this man relationships medicate against feeling abandoned. He admits that he "knows better," but his immediate sense of relief in not being alone overwhelms his critical abilities, and he "compulsively" falls into each relationship.

A compulsive or addictive lifestyle may go unrecognized when the repeated behavior is socially acceptable, only to be viewed as maladaptive when social values change, as when the health risks of sexual activity increase or the Surgeon General warns that smoking is dangerous. Certain activities may be so admired and seem to be so beneficial as to completely elude their compulsive underpinnings for some gay men:

> I began weight-lifting when I was 20. I felt effeminate, and not very aggressive physically. Androgyny was the last thing I was comfortable with. Bodybuilding took care of all that, but after a while I realized I couldn't stop and I wanted to. All my recognition—my whole sense of self—came from my physical appearance, and I didn't have anything else.

For this man weight-lifting initially enhanced his physical appearance and improved his sense of well-being. It grew into a compulsive activity as it substituted for other needed areas of fulfillment. In time it came to function primarily as a way to reduce anxiety associated with strong feelings of non-physical inadequacy as a person.

Compulsive behaviors are sustained through a complex interaction of social, psychological, and biological factors. The pleasurable effect of a drug or activity reinforces the tendency to use it. A subculture of peers involved in the activity fills a social void. Alcohol and other addicting drugs alter brain chemistry, so that more drug is needed to produce the same tranquilizing or euphoric effect. Lack of a drug after significant use can induce uncomfortable, even life-threatening physical withdrawal symptoms. And some individuals inherit biological factors that increase their sensitivity to a drug, placing them at higher risk for addiction, once exposed to it. But no matter which factors increase susceptibility to a compulsive lifestyle, the individual must ultimately take responsibility for his behavior in order to change.

One of the most difficult problems that is pervasive within the gay community is the compulsive use of alcohol. Studies estimate that 10 percent of gay men are alcoholic, while an additional 20 percent believe they use alcohol excessively.[4,5]

Drinking is acceptable and a seeming necessity in bars, at parties and other social gatherings. For many gay men, the bar and alcohol are synonymous with refuge from an imperfectly benevolent and homophobic world. Growing up in a society less than accepting of same-sex intimacy conditions many gay men with an avoidance response that must be overcome each time intimacy is attempted. Alcohol reduces anxiety, disinhibits, and produces a mild euphoria that facilitates overcoming this response. For the compulsive drinker alcohol is repeatedly used to reduce tension. Progression to alcoholism occurs as control over drinking is lost, and physical or emotional health becomes further impaired. In the later phase of alcohol dependence the drug becomes necessary to prevent physical withdrawal symptoms, such as tremor, inability to sleep, fever, and hallucinations.

While many factors motivate an individual to use a drug, including curiosity, pressure from friends, recreational pleasure or the desire to enhance or attenuate a bodily function such as sleep, the primary motivation for the compulsive drug user is the constant need to restore a sense of well-being. A compulsive lifestyle builds around the conviction that the drug is the only reasonable way to do this.

Compulsive drug use is undoubtedly a problem for a significant number of gay men, although research data on the extent of this problem is presently unavailable. The choice of drug repetitively used depends on its ability to offer escape from a particular uncomfortable feeling. Those who feel anxious may use Valium and other similar anxiety-relieving drugs. Amphetamine-type stimulants relieve sadness, while cocaine is often used to overcome boredom, emptiness and a lack of energy. Heroin users find the drug attenuates anger, aggressive impulses and depressive feelings. Even compulsive use of an addictive drug like heroin has less to do with its addictiveness than other longer-standing, personal factors. This was borne out in a study of Vietnam veterans who used heroin during the war.[6] While half of the soldiers exposed to it became addicted, 90 percent used no drug on their return to the United States. The key predictor of continued drug use was abuse of the drug before going overseas.

Although not typically thought of as a drug, food also works for many as a medication. Many more women than men seek help for compulsive eating, but there is some evidence that gay men are over-represented among those with such problems, especially when sexual dysfunction is present. A study from the Eating Disorders Unit of Harvard's affiliated Massachusetts General Hospital found that 26 percent of men who sought help for eating problems were homosexual, more than double the 10 percent estimate of gay men in the general population.[7] Almost all led isolated lives and were sexually inactive, although some gay men did not fit this pattern. In explaining the basis of food as a compulsive outlet, analysts have emphasized the symbolic need to fill oneself when emotionally empty. Others believe that eating disorders may be a particular problem for gay men because there is excess pressure in gay culture to be thin and attractive.

For the man who is bright, industrious, disciplined and competitive, work can be an efficient, compulsive outlet. For the workaholic a career can be an all-encompassing way of staving off confrontation with other insecurities and inadequacies:

> A 56-year-old gay executive grew up feeling deeply rejected by his father, who could never accept his homosexuality. His father never expressed approval of anything that he did. Other areas of life became meaningless to this executive, as he unconsciously strove for that approval from his superiors at work. With determination he was elected chairman of his medium-sized corporation. But there was no longer anyone above him that could fulfill that need, and he slumped into a depression.

Ironically, the work situation itself often contributes to a compulsive working style in gay men. This is so because it is often necessary to conceal one's homosexuality to varying degrees at work, and to lead a double life with varying degrees of deception and avoidance. Even when coworkers are tolerant or accepting, a company may worry about its image and customer attitudes. Insecurity intensifies when one is passed over for promotion. Self-doubt raises anxiety, compelling the individual to work harder.

The compulsive gambler, like the workaholic, tends to be bright and intolerant of boredom. In areas of the country where it is available and accessible, gambling can be a potent release from anxiety. The compulsive gambler's sense of self is tied to the game. A win brings an immediate feeling of gratification that is lacking in other areas of life. A loss brings on intolerable anxiety that pushes him back to the game. The compulsive gambler is intelligent, knowledgeable of the game and good at it. A very large win is not uncommon and induces an extreme euphoria that is sought after, but rarely found again. Judgment becomes impaired as bets increase and losses mount. Bad checks, illegal loans, and loss of job and lover can lead to imprisonment or even suicide unless help is sought.

Often there is a lover, close friend or relative of the person with a compulsive lifestyle who unwittingly reinforces and perpetuates the problem. This caring person may benevolently go along with the alcoholic's alibis or bail out the compulsive gambler. But what this does is give the compulsive person another chance at his compulsion, because someone else has now assumed responsibility for the consequences of his actions.

The transition from a compulsive lifestyle to one of freedom and choice can be difficult. When change is desired and attempted, a period of intense psychological withdrawal often occurs (physical withdrawal can occur with alcohol and other drugs, as well). The individual is frequently preoccupied with thoughts of the compulsive activity, as time that had been devoted to the compulsion is now free. Many report having dreams in which they engage in the compulsive activity. These can be upsetting and anxiety-producing. Unpleasant feelings that triggered compulsive activity may return and persist. Often the decision to change itself works as an immediate euphoriant, and the determination to change wanes as the realities of a long-term commitment emerge. Motivation to abstain from the activity is tested often and may erode. Feelings become overwhelming once again, objectives are confused, critical judgment is lost, and relapse can occur. It soon becomes clear that abstention from the compulsive activity is not enough, as abstention doesn't resolve the problems and conflicts that originally fueled the compulsive behavior.

Once a commitment is made, therapeutic change can take place in a variety of professional and non-professional settings. An understanding lover, an interested friend, or a sympathetic religious practitioner can be of help. Other personal interests can be developed and pursued on one's own. Supportive fellowships are also available, including Alcoholics', Sexual Compulsives', Narcotics', and Overeaters' Anonymous, all of which now have groups for gay people that facilitate sharing of common values and experience, mutual support and strengthening of one's gay identity. Similiar groups such as Al-anon and Nar-anon help those close to the person with a chemical dependency pattern. It is important to be sure that any therapist, group, or fellowship is sympathetic to and knowledgeable of the gay experience, as change and growth can be inhibited in surroundings that fail to acknowledge and support one's gay identity.

For many people careful professional assessment and help may be necessary when other approaches do not produce the desired change. A therapist should be sensitive to the individual needs of each client: compulsive problems demand a practical and person-affirming approach. The binge eater that purges may require medical attention to correct imbalances in body chemistry caused by vomiting or the use of laxatives. The gambler may need practical help in scheduling debt repayment. Those physically dependent on drugs should be under medical supervision, as withdrawal is potentially life-threatening. Individual and group therapy can promote insight into the problems that generate compulsive behavior. Therapy can help the individual develop personal goals, reduce stress, and resist the urge to return to the compulsive activity.

Change begins by taking the time to look at oneself. Real solutions come with sustained, often painful effort. But when the man who suffers with a compulsive lifestyle takes the responsibility to become his real self, a process begins that leads to true emotional and spiritual growth.

Notes

[1]All clinical examples are extrapolated from cases in the author's private practice.

[2]*Diagnostic and Statistical Manual of Mental Disorders* (Third Edition): American Psychiatric Association, 1980.

[3]Glasser, William, *Positive Addiction*, New York: Harper & Row, 1976.

[4]Lohrenz, Leander, J., et al., "Alcohol problems in several midwestern homosexual communities," *J. of Studies on Alcohol*, 39:11, Nov. 1978, pp. 1959–1963.

[5]Saghir, M. T., et al., "Homosexuality III. Psychiatric disorders and disability in the male homosexual," *Am. J. Psychiatry*, 126:8, Feb. 1970, pp. 1079–1086.

[6]"The Polyaddictions," in the *Journal of Clinical Psychiatry*, 45:12, p. 44.

[7]Herzog, D. B., et al., "Sexual conflict and eating disorders in 27 males," *Am. J. Psychiatry*, 141:8, Aug. 1984, pp. 898–992.

Other References

Carnes, Patrick, *The Sexual Addiction*, Minnesota: Comp-Care Publications, 1983.

Peele, Stanton, *Love and Addiction*, New York: New American Library, 1976.

Shapiro, David, *Neurotic Styles*, New York: Basic Books, 1965.

The Way Back, Washington, D.C.: Gay Council on Drinking Behavior, Whitman-Walker Clinic, 1981.

Love & Pain

by Philip Pannell

HERE ARE FAR TOO MANY VIOLENT EPISODES AMONG those who are involved in relationships. Yet this belligerence is rarely discussed openly. Just like battered wives, those who are abused at the hands of their lovers often suffer in silence.

Being beaten by your lover is a humiliating and embarrassing experience. After all, who wants to admit that one's lover is constantly kicking one's ass? I, like many, had never realized how often abuse occurs among us. But my eyes were immediately and dramatically opened to this problem when I became a victim of abuse by my lover.

I had fallen deeply, impulsively, and unrealistically in love when I had rid myself of some of my possessions and moved in with my lover. Although overtly he seemed like a person of superlative character, before two months had elapsed he had beaten me.

If this violence had been defensive on his part it would have been understandable. Everyone has the right to defend himself. But this was a beating, not a fight, since I did not defend myself. Of course afterwards he was contrite and apologetic, and I forgave him. Nevertheless, I recalled hearing that if violence happens once in a relationship most likely it would recur. And it did, again and again.

It became nearly impossible for us to have the slightest verbal disagreement without him behaving bellicosely. His pugnacity escalated to the point where one night I had to be taken by ambulance to the hospital with a case of badly injured ribs. When I arrived at the emergency room, I insisted I had fallen down a flight of steps. The members of the medical staff were incredulous. After my release my lover told me how terrible he had felt while he was sitting in the waiting room. He said it would never happen again. And again I forgave him.

But it did happen again. Five times. The final incident was almost like Armageddon. His violence culminated in an attempt to stab me. Needless to say our relationship had reached its lowest point, and I moved out shortly thereafter. Even though the relationship had plunged me into financial chaos and left me a mental wreck, I felt relieved and liberated. I had ceased being the fool; my nightmare was over.

After our bitter breakup, I was in a quandary as to how to handle what had happened to me. At first I felt it best not to discuss my relationship. But during conversations with others about the violence in my relationship, they confided that they had had similar experiences, but were embarrassed to talk about them. I had in-depth discussions with several men who told me they had been beaten by their lovers because of situations arising from petty jealousy or financial problems. Some of them stated that their lovers had been drinking when the violence took place. But the most harrowing experience was related to me by a young man I will call Charles.

Charles and his lover had been together for several years. Throughout their relationships there had been innumerable battles, with Charles often on the losing side, since he was the smaller of the two. But one evening about three years ago they had their last fight. In the midst of a particularly vicious beating, Charles shot and killed his lover. At the end of a sensational trial, where he testified about the years of abuse, Charles was acquitted on the grounds of self-defense.

Not having had any easy solutions when I was a victim, I asked the men I talked to what in retrospect they would have done at the start of the violence. Several possible approaches were offered:

Defend yourself. Some of the victims felt that had they fought back initially, the violence may not have recurred. However, more problems could be caused by this approach, since the person who initiates the violence may be physically superior. This may result in the victim being even more seriously injured than if no attempt at self-defense had been made. Also some persons may "get off" on fighting. There is something to the adage *Violence begets violence.*

Try to get away. This will work temporarily, since you minimize the chance of being injured. However, it does not solve the underlying and persistent problem.

Seek professional counseling. This approach may prove helpful, but it also may take a long time. Besides, the ideal situation is for *both* parties to seek help. Unfortunately, many persons who engage in violence fail to see the rationality of this approach and consequently eschew professional help.

Press charges. This will most likely be successful only if the persons *are not* living together. For those who *are* living together this may only heighten the enmity and could result in a tragic ending.

Move out. This would seem to be the best solution, since the persons would no longer be living together. But some individuals' financial affairs may be so intertwined that such a move may be extremely difficult, if not impossible. One person that I spoke with related that his lover was supporting him, so that when he moved he had to drop out of college and return to his parents' home in another city.

These approaches in no way constitute an exhaustive agenda for dealing with this problem, since this type of abuse is an extremely complicated situation with few easy solutions. However, I offer some suggestions that may help in dealing with the problem:

After the first beating or fight, make sure you let someone know what has happened. You will need support mechanisms and possibly some place to go. Remember, it is a poor rat that has only one hole.

Don't engage in overrationalization. Do not write off the violence as a result of your lover's problems, such as drinking, job pressures, or financial problems. And don't attempt to rationalize a love/hate relationship; it is not worth it.

Be open about what has happened to you. Talking it out may help. Don't feel that you are airing your dirty linen or putting your business in the street. You are the victim, and intelligent, sensitive people will be sympathetic to your plight. Also you may be doing others in the community a favor by exposing a violence-prone individual.

Don't let anyone belittle or minimize your situation. Once, when I relayed what had happened to me to an individual who holds my erstwhile lover in high regard, he asked, "Well, didn't you ask for it?" When I replied that I hadn't, he responded with amusement, "Well, didn't you enjoy it?" Don't pay any attention to insouciant, insipid, and insensitive ignoramuses like that. Your problem is real.

What we need is a greater sense of respect and love among ourselves. It is irrational for a person to hurt what he or she supposedly loves. We gays face enough societal discrimination, oppression, and abuse without inflicting harm on ourselves. If you are not a faith healer, you should avoid the laying on of hands.

On Hating Ourselves

by Darrell Yates Rist

"**A**N INCURABLE DISEASE," HE SAYS. JOHN HATES HO-
mosexuality.

Today's occasion is Chicago's gay pride parade. The usual
pastiche of seriocomedic, the sliding scale of homosexual politics from angry lobbyists to fetishists to revelers whose op-
portune intent is nothing more or less complex than ribaldry.
Here are politicians, then gay clergy and their congregations,
shrinks, teachers, parents who are gay, parents of gay children.
There are a group of bankers, a sewing club, a softball team, a
marching band, a chorus, a fraternity of "slaves" and "masters."
Ardent patrons of the bars and baths ride floats.

Drag, leather, and near-nudity have offended John, as well as
flagrant sex (holding hands and kissing on the street). He says
acridly, "They seem to think it's sick to be discreet."

John's utterance is tensely aspirate. He dares my eyes with
his, moist and nervous, as though an anxious stare alone belied a
counterpremise. "Gays shove everything they do in people's
faces," he spits *sotto voce*. "Why should anyone put up with
this? Let me tell you something, if I had *kids*"—he backhands the
air towards a man, a woman, and two small boys (the four of
them delighted by a drag queen's dole of cock-shaped candies)—
"I'd do everything I could to stop it."

At this I heat. "When *I* was a kid, I'd have been a hell of a lot
happier," I object, almost hissing, "if I'd seen just one thing like
this and learned I wasn't the only one like me alive."

"*Happier?*" John snaps, angling abruptly away to leave the
scene. "This makes people *happier?* That's the trouble with *gay
rights*"—he bites the words—"all this openness. This . . . *display*. If things were less available, some of us"—his voice
stings—"would really never have thought about it. Never tried it

out. And never gotten hooked. There are a few of the human urges that *ought* to be suppressed."

With John, as with few others, I have been forgiving. He compels my pity, he seems to cling to me. Despite my obsessive interest in gay politics and my adamant opinions on homosexuality, hostile to his. Despite my unembarrassed public mien (at least I'd like to think that, unless I fear inviting bodily attack, I'll take my lover's arm or hand, hug or kiss him, that I'll speak freely—say, in restaurants—not censoring my remarks in deference to the squeamish sensibilities of straight people, or gay people, nearby). In spite of myriad attributes which mark me as an unrepenting homosexual, John seeks me out. In fact, although abashed by any behavior which passes for a sign of homosexuality, John nonetheless almost exclusively selects his friends among gay men; and though repelled by his own insistent homosexual impulse, he pursues—not fleet, anonymous encounters—but romance and has had (a few brief times) a lover. I reason he is not all bad.

Sometimes I've lost patience, once (it's now been several years) when John invited my lover and me to join him at the symphony. A senior partner at the law firm where he practiced had given him two seats, center orchestra. He reserved the second for a date and suggested I buy tickets for the balcony. "If we sit together," he explained, "well . . . I think it'll cause too much attention." Bemused, I didn't answer. "My boss's friends sit in that section," he precipitated, apprehensive, I conjectured, of my silence. "I don't want to raise suspicions. You know, I can't let that happen." My silence teased him. He teased back, as though compelled to tempt intolerance with truth. "You're not exactly *butch*," he condescended. "And you know as well as I do you don't try. If you acted straight . . ."

"What the hell is *that* supposed to mean?" I raged, then assailed him with emasculating vignettes of his looks, his gait, his mannerisms, speech, his taste in food, in clothes, in decorating, art—whatever facile accusation I could conjure to disparage his virility. "I really don't want to hang around with someone," I continued, "I can't trust. And I can't trust a homosexual who wants gay men as friends just as long as they pretend they're something they are *not*. I have to wonder, John," I shouted, "if they started rounding up the queers, like they did in Germany in the Thirties, or baiting us, like in the Fifties here, would you help your friends—or cooperate to save yourself and turn us in?"

Some days later, fuming, I recounted this episode to Larry, a friend who'd known me well for years. "Politically," I said, "you have to come to the point of swearing off on gay men like John. They're there, they always will be, hating themselves the more as time goes on. But we don't have to harbor them. They use the rest of us for some perverted kind of comfort. But believe me, in the end, they'll do us in. Befriending them, it seems to me, would rather be like Jews condoning members of their synagogue who sympathize with Nazis."

Larry stared at me a moment, impertinently tipping his head to the side. "You forget you're talking to your sister," he indulged me campily. "I've known you since the first time you came out. I helped you meet the boys. Suddenly you started falling in and out of love—and loved it, all your newfound freedom. Then I saw you get afraid, just as suddenly, of everything. Who you were, what you did, who you hung around with, what your future would be like if you 'stayed' queer.   You couldn't stomach being gay. So you found a woman, told everyone you were in love, and dropped your gay friends one by one. You even went so far as to explain to us you didn't think homosexuality was a particularly healthy adjustment to life. And you were guilty of making a few cracks about 'people who choose to live their lives as queens.' Now none of us thought that very civil. But most of us were rather kind. Quite a few of us even went so far as to come to the wedding, though we thought you'd lost your mind. And I was crazy enough to be an usher. That's not a little bit of loyalty to a friend who's losing it—and in a nasty-tempered way, at that.

"What I want to say is this. We were deeply offended, hurt, by what you said and what you did. But your closest friends stuck by you—waiting—somewhat charitably, I might add—until you found your senses. And when that marriage fell apart, I think I can say we were there to nurse you back to normal. So all this talk about rejecting other homosexuals for acting out their own self-loathing, however twisted you may think they are, dear, ought to give you pause. Few performances, after all, could be more grand than yours. You have very little room to be self-righteous."

I n the late 1960s, when I first came out, nothing scared me more than drag queens. In Chicago, where I lived in those days, they proliferated—some bedraggled number of them, it seemed, habitating every bar except the Gold Coast, an asylum for the leather/Levi set. I liked to dance and went to Broadway Sam's. There "Ethel" was a drunken fixture at the bar. Her penciled eyebrows arched her little, glassy eyes. A nylon page-boy, oily black, squared her pudgy, drooping face, which sat on several chins. Her short, fat fingers always clutched a cigarette and a fresh Manhattan. Ethel ruled her kingdom soporifically, only sometimes managing to moo, "Come and talk to mother."

In the back of the bar, on a tiny square of floor for choreography, we boys did "routines" and sang along (Marilyn McCoo, Burt Bacharach, the Supremes). There were a few impassive types, standing stolid in the shadows, motionlessly eyeing the clientele with manly scrutiny. But most of us were light and squealing, trivializing one another with feminine pronouns and names and high, self-conscious camp. Most of us—perforce, I'd say—were "nellie." When the public iconography of homosexuality is contained almost exclusively within a stereotype, the stereotype encroaches on the homosexual's expression. Before Stonewall energetically began to set us free, the cultural mythology summarily defined the male homosexual as effeminate, and the definition pressured gay men to conform. Being nellie was the sign that one was gay, the member's badge. A sissy found community among gay friends.

I'd been called a sissy all my life. Now I teetered on the balance. I despised the epithet. I hated being that. I loved that I belonged. Acceptance was rewarded for embracing what I loathed. I seized on Ethel as an emblem: she was, I feared, a pure epitome of homosexuality. The pathetic gene that somehow languished at the heart of homosexual desire, the end of every homosexual who left his sordid tendencies unchecked. I fled, intimidating femininity with marriage—the proof of cultivated manhood, the prize for exercising masculinity's prerogative.

M en are made to sire. (That is, anatomically and biologically: I'm not arguing divine or moral purpose.) Women are constructed to conceive, support the embryo and fetus, and give birth, to milk until the infant's weaned. Hormones capacitating reproduction also make cosmetic—we can call them that—distinctions: for example, women have generally less body hair. The ebb and flow of hormones may as well affect the cycle of emotions. During her menstrual period a woman's feelings are expected to be tenuous. This phenomenon, of course, has all the force of maxim which conveniently ignores a like "disability" in men. Male biology is now believed to stimulate hormonic ups and downs, manipulate the masculine psychology with monthly whimsy that is, categorically, considered feminine.

The differences in male and female bodies, should I have to say it, are sexual. Rooted at conception in the enigmatic dialogue of chromosomes, their ultimate expression is the propagation of the species. Aside from this, they're insignificant. But they're *socially* elaborated, like the simple mysteries of religion: nature, we have seemed to think, was not enough. Between the sexes we've constructed walls of artifice—fictions of distinction in the spiritual, emotional, and intellectual capacities of men and women and, consequently, differences in social roles, mannerisms, and dress. As if—and feminism has only impotently assailed this—women are by nature better equipped than men for nurturing. As if, say, grace and poise and emotional spontaneity, as if vulnerability and weakness were exclusively a female province. As if earrings, make-up, dresses and high heels complement vaginas as naturally as blooms adorn the pistils of flowering plants. Masculinity and femininity are art, not nature; disparities of, not sex, gender, the substance and the symbols of a caste system which enforces men's control and women's compliance. Tyranny exists as long as genitals determine social roles: as in any cultural opposition, the idea is to be on top; one side predominates. Heterosexual relationships, as they're commonly practiced, exemplify this dominance and submission. Marriage is the purest model: it's every man's proprietary right to keep a cunt beneath his cock. The order of the ages is maintained.

This is the sexual power structure which the Women's Movement has resented, analyzed, railed against, and failed to change. It's entrenched because it seems so natural. One guesses since Neanderthals its tenets have been passed—father to son, mother to daughter—as though genetically, like beauty or deformity, intelligence or idiocy. Both sides—the women's and the men's— are committed to it: if men will not give up the privileges of rulership, women are as resistant to forswear the privileges of being lorded, the compelling, paltry fantasy that, if they're good enough, they'll be wholly taken care of. Both sides enjoy their territorial prerogatives. Wars are fought to preserve historical advantages like these.

It's no wonder, then, male homosexuals are so despised. They offer no comforting promise to women. They pledge no unified purpose with heterosexual men. They're fakes, traitors to the birthright of their genitals, specious patriots. Because they don't own women, they weaken the structure of power: White slave masters in an ante-bellum South who liberate their Negroes and implicitly incite new vision and unrest. Heterosexual men enrage at the horrifying specter of a world they don't control. Heterosexual women tremble at the menace, responsibility, of being "unprotected," free. The homosexual threat obsesses them. In their governments and social institutions, in their arts and entertainment, they defensively exaggerate, celebrate, adulate the benefits of being straight. They set themselves to decimate the enemy: there is no peaceful coexistence. They fabricate philosophies, theologies, psychologies to assault the homosexual and buttress them with legislation and so teach against him, preach against him, try to cure him, lock him up. They ridicule him, beat him, kill him if they can. Children learn antipathy for homosexuals at home: It's as right as love. If a boy finds out he isn't drawn to girls but rather falls in love with other boys, he's learned to hate himself. He knows he is a fag. Other disrespected groups of people—Blacks, Jews, women—though they suffer stigma and injustice, learn at least a feeble sense of self-worth and belonging from their families. At worst they have a meager social place. Fags have none.

I t's tempting to blame my friend John's reaction to gay pride parades wholly on self-hatred. But that would be simplistic and unfair. John disliked parades, no matter whose they were. He thought most of them obnoxious. But his observations of some other parades we saw together weren't so venomously laced. One March 17, while shopping in Chicago's "Loop," John and I got stranded at the St. Patrick's Day Parade. We watched a little mob of sottish revellers stumbling by, blowing a cacophony of home-made horns and bellowing. "This is why my grandparents left Ireland," John laughed, partly disgusted and partly amused, and rolled his eyes.

"Maybe if they can't behave, they shouldn't have a parade," I goaded him. "That's what you seem to think about the gay parade."

"Don't be absurd," he barked. "That's not the same at all."

What would render homosexuals acceptable to John, what would render John acceptable to himself, has always been elusive.

John's discomfort with his homosexuality is so extreme and instigates so many wrenching inconsistencies, he seems a caricature. So much more, then, is his life illustrative of countless, if more subtle, homosexual lives. Homosexual children, reared to hate themselves, don't easily grow up believing in their dignity, nor in the dignity of people like them. They don't grow up assuming they will find respect or love, or that they are deserving of the emotional fulfillments—certainly not the social privileges—most heterosexuals expect as if these were their patrimony. We homosexuals are psychologically battered as children. As adults we're all too often prone to torture ourselves.

Ron and Tom, two friends of mine, go through something which I call their yearly penitential rite, a kind of Lenten flagellation for—I've sometimes said—their having been in love so long (something like ten years). Each fall Ron's mother makes a pilgrimage to Chicago from the East. On the way she spends a week in Pittsburgh with his sister and her boyfriend, who've lived together several years but out of principle won't marry. Ron and Tom are frantic for that week: they rearrange the house in preparation for their guest. They turn their study into a bedroom for Tom, setting up a full-sized bed which they normally stow in the basement. (These machinations take up all the extra room: Ron's mother's relegated to the sofa in the living room.) Then they transfer clothes, putting all of Tom's things in the closet in what *was* the study and what will again be when Ron's mother's gone. (The illusion is that everything is "his and his," not "ours.") They take down pictures of the two of them and stash away the memorabilia, which might arouse suspicion that they're more than just good friends.

For years I asked Ron why they put themselves through such contortions. "Doesn't your mother know you're gay?"

"I don't know," he'd say. "It's never been discussed. But changing around the bedroom is the least we can do not to rub our sex lives in my mother's face."

I asked him once if his sister showed his mother this same scrupulous respect.

"What?" he answered, looking at me blankly.

"Do your sister and her boyfriend set up separate bedrooms when your mother is in town?"

"Why should they?" he spat back. "My mother certainly would like for them to marry. But any way they work it out, it is a straight relationship. This is not."

Each Christmas Ron and Tom do what I call their Advent penance, cruel but less grueling. The family, including Tom, gathers at Ron's mother's house. His mother, all her qualms about it notwithstanding, beds her daughter with her boyfriend. She puts Ron and Tom in different rooms, following the example which they set during her visits to them.

What Ron and Tom turn in upon themselves, some of us turn out, assaulting other homosexuals with disparagement. This sort of thing may seem innocuous when it only takes the form, let's say, of dishing some gay men for being fey. "Too gay," my friend Ryan says, dismissing guys from his consideration as potential tricks. Like John, he thinks gays should "act straight," but then no one can ever be man enough once Ryan knows for sure the man is homosexual.

There's a nastier side to this belittling. On a vacation in Key West I was walking with a new acquaintance who'd been badly fag-bashed only days before. His face was full of stitches, one eye covered with a patch. We ran into some of his friends.

"That's twice in about a month," one said.

"What did you do to make the straight boys mad this time?" asked another. "Were you camping it up? Or holding hands with a trick?"

Protestations of sympathy only *followed* their interrogation. Like blaming the woman for her rape.

Things get more pernicious still when this is the kind of thinking we apply to tragedies like Acquired Immune Deficiency Syndrome (AIDS). One gay friend of mine suggested that the hideous disease would do the "gay community some good if we can learn to quell our promiscuity. "I think," he said, "we brought this thing upon ourselves."

"And what about the straight people who get it?" I asked. "What are they supposed to learn?"

He huffed, as if disgusted at the question. "But it's not their fault. They weren't the ones who spread it with their irresponsibility."

Americans, both straight and gay, have a penchant for apocalypse. Catastrophes have all the force of prophecies: there are equal moral lessons to be learned by the victims of earthquakes, airline crashes, random murders, herpes and chlamydia. We inmates of Judeo-Christian culture serve a vengeful god. Such interpretations have much greater force for gay people, however, when they're able to attribute their misfortunes to their homosexuality. After all, if calamity befalls us—like being beaten on the street or getting AIDS—we've been asking for it, even less for what we've done than who we are. The seeds of retribution lie within our sexual character. We have a taste for guilt because we're weaned on it.

Self-loathing—internalized homophobia, as it's been dubbed—informs many scenes of gay life, is central to some acts (as in the case of my friend John), but certainly, at least since Stonewall, doesn't sum the drama. Anyone who knows gay life by more than torrid stereotypes doesn't need to be reminded of the depth of homosexual friendships or the stable, rich relationships we call our "marriages." From our closets and the anonymity of bars and parks and public restrooms, from a few, feckless homophile associations—almost our whole world before Stonewall—we've built a powerful community which heterosexuals have learned they have to reckon with and, if only grudgingly, respect for its social and political accomplishments. Nearly ex nihilo, but for our defiance, we organized ourselves to cultivate our interests—witness the multitude of clubs, choruses and athletic teams—in an ambience where we would not be stultified by bigotry. We created businesses which understood our needs and, doing that, enhanced our power in the market-place. Ignored or disparaged by the general media, we built our own to tell us about ourselves. We've grouped to lobby for our civil rights.

Still the shame we feel about our homosexuality enfeebles us, reaching hatefully beyond our private angst and the wretched judgments we impose upon ourselves and other homosexuals, poisoning the public institutions we've set up as safeguards. As though faintly underlying our perfunctory self-preservation, we entertain a death wish. We deprecate whatever's gay more glibly and severely than we do what we identify as straight. Gay pub-lications, which we often anxiously dismiss as "rags" no matter what the merits they've attained, are a case in point. By mid-decade in the AIDS crisis one gay newspaper, *New York Native*, was followed with esteem by major media for stories on the medicine and politics of the disease. Editors and reports at the news wire services and the *New York Times* pursued it as a credible, if controversial, source. Its coverage incited programs on formidable network news shows like *Nightline*. It earned its writers interviews on the *Cable Network News*, the *Today Show*, and the BBC. Its features were picked up by European slicks like *Paris Match*. At the same time, though, it didn't fare so well among its own constituents: its readership was a fraction of one percent of the million and a half or so homosexuals in New York City (the other local gay paper, *The Connection*, did no better). For most New York City homosexuals a gay perspective, even one respected outside the gay community, seemed not to warrant reading. A reminiscence of the scripture: a prophet is not with-out honor except in his own country.

More implicating still was many gay men's response to any disagreements with the paper's editorial positions. At one point *New York Native* published an attack on a prominent heterosex-ual physician who was staunchly thought of as an ally of the gay community in the politics of AIDS. She'd misspoken herself, seeming to suggest that gay men must somehow bear responsibil-ity for spreading AIDS to straight people. The paper's broad-side—despite her long, unqualified support of gay concerns—was truculent and unforgiving. What's worse, it was poorly documented, badly reasoned: it deserved an angry outcry from the paper's readers, which it got. But criticism of this shoddy journalism was often fueled, it seemed, by something sinister. Many of my friends insisted that the paper was "embarrassing," full (one friend said) of "typical homosexual immaturity," and refused to buy it. These, I wondered at, were people who, yes, complained about the attitude towards homosexuals in the *New York Post*—whose reports and editorials persistently vilified gays—and the *New York Times*—which had nearly ignored AIDS until it became more than a homosexual concern—but never got so angry as to boycott them. We often judge straights' foibles as the minor flaws within some greater good. We often judge our own as if they were the sum of who we are, something which evokes unmitigated condemnation.

More telling yet, perhaps, of our opinion of ourselves is our response to groups whose single purpose is to advocate gay rights. In little more than ten years after it was founded, the National Gay Task Force, the nation's premier gay political organization until the 1980s, had succeeded in such efforts as securing statements from major corporations like AT&T disavowing anti-gay discrimination in employment. It had won landmark legal decisions, like the Supreme Court's declaring unconstitutional an Oklahoma law prohibiting homosexuals from teaching in public schools. Its successes were protections of the civil liberties of more than 15 million gays: the names it listed on its members' roster numbered something like 8,000.

Homosexuals cannot plead ignorance of the dangers to their civil rights: preachers, politicians, the press and, according to the polls, the majority of the American population, revile them. People fight relentlessly to guard whatever they most value. Most homosexuals see scanty worth within themselves.

Bill, who's gay, had been a member of the gym for months before he talked to any of the openly gay men. When I got to know him well, I asked him why he'd kept his distance for so long.

"Were you giving attitude or are you shy?" I asked facetiously.

"No." He laughed hollowly. "One day I saw the guys I work out with being friendly with you."

"What difference would *that* make?" I puzzled. "Were you waiting for an introduction?"

"Just waiting to see how my workout partners felt. They're all straight, you know. I didn't really know what things were like around here. So I thought I'd take my cues from them."

If Bill achieved some greater freedom than he'd had before he sensed permission to associate with me, he did it at the cost of acquiescing to his heterosexual friends' control. It was they, straight men again, deciding what's allowed. Still I felt I should admire the progress Bill had made, however slight, in this society in which gay people's liberty, even the conception of it, is imperfect. And I wondered whether Bill and I, for all my touted liberation, really were much different. I'm reminded that I couldn't stomach drag queens till I went to Provincetown one fall to do a story on the straight transvestites and their wives who'd gathered for their annual convention.

"Strictly speaking," the guest psychiatrist explained, "cross-dressing is a heterosexual phenomenon. The vast majority of transvestites are heterosexual men."

I was comforted, relieved—a vague, guilty burden had unrolled. "If straight men do drag," I perversely calculated, "then there can't be anything so horribly bad about it. It's got to be all right." And rather suddenly, Ethel, who many years ago had haunted me at Broadway Sam's, and everything she represented, started seeming more benign. I estimated drag queens needn't be pariahs in the gay community, dirty family secrets which we were obliged to cover up.

I enthused, confessing to a drag queen at the Provincetown affair who said that "she" was gay, and didn't mingle much among the others. She had a dimmer view than mine of my discovery. "Listen, sweetheart," she said, holding out her newly polished nails to dry, "I'm not in this dress and heels because some *straight* man thinks drag's O.K. And I'm not here because I'm welcome. The way they see it, what they do is fine because they've got their girlfriends and their wives along. And *nothing* I do's right because I'm queer." She paused to blow her nails.

"All this brand new insight you got, baby . . . something's wrong with that. Let this girl tell you something." As she crossed her legs, she saw a run. "Oh shit," she cried, searching for a bottle of clear polish in her purse. She daubed a little on the lesion in her hose. "That'll stop the little bitch," she muttered, turning back to me. She fixed me with an angry stare. "I'm a queen, I act like one, and I enjoy it. I don't need anyone to tell me I'm allowed. And till you stop waiting for straight men to pat you on the head, you ain't learned a goddamn thing. Way down underneath it all, underneath all that gay pride, most of you boys are still just terrified of being gay. And acting like the straights won't work, doll. 'Cause to them you're just a fag. They'll hate you anyway."

Our friendships, romances, our businesses and clubs, our politics—the strength of the community we've built. All of it perhaps is tenuous, as insubstantial as our fears. We never will be free, I guess, until we're really not afraid of being fags.

Safe Sex: Guidelines That Could Save Your Life

by Michael Helquist

IN OHIO, BARTENDERS DO IT; IN MINNEAPOLIS IT'S CAPTAIN Condom. In Houston they do it with bears, rabbits, frogs and turtles; in Los Angeles it's a movie actress playing a mother. In San Francisco it's advertised with large bold letters, while in Atlanta it's done under the shadow of Georgia's pornography laws. In Washington, D.C., they tried to do it on the city buses. (But the Centers for Disease Control hardly do it at all.)

All of the above warn, cajole and encourage gay men to avoid either exposure to the AIDS virus or transmission of it. These AIDS-risk-reduction campaigns also include recommendations of such common-sense health practices as good nutrition, adequate sleep, exercise, and reduction of drug and alcohol use. But the main focus of the campaigns is to promote no-risk or low-risk sexual activities. Within the last two years an entire industry of safe sex and healthy sex programs has sprouted around the country.

Gay men have always categorized their sex acts—from the basic top and bottom positions to other options signaled by hanky colors, uniforms, even miniature teddy bears. In the midst of the AIDS epidemic new categories have appeared. This time, however, they don't expand the sexual repertoire as much as they limit the transmission of a deadly disease.

It has taken several years for some of the controversies and assumptions about what is safe, possibly safe and definitely not safe, to settle down. Research and common sense now permit gay men to chart their way from former high-risk behaviors to safe and healthier practices.

The description sounds absolute, but proponents of safe sex will admit to a little confusion about what really is completely safe. For example, the San Francisco AIDS Foundation placed bold-lettered, full-page ads in gay newspapers listing safe activities as "massage, hugging, mutual masturbation, social (dry) kissing, and body-to-body rubbing." But a few physicians have suggested there may even be risk with variations of the standard "circle jerk." They warn that open cuts on hands, feet and other areas of the body may be exposed to a partner's semen during the heat of passion. And "jack-off only" clubs in New York City forbid kissing or any oral contact with a partner's body, for example, sucking on tits.

Most researchers, however, would agree that the above is a list of safe activities, as they believe that AIDS is transmitted by a virus—variously named HTLV-III, LAV and ARV—via bodily fluids. Since none of these activities involves the exchange of fluids such as semen, blood, urine or saliva, each merits its label as safe.

AIDS educators fully realize the importance of sex to an individual's overall mental and physical health. Most of these educators are also familiar with the role of sex in the gay liberation movement. They attempt to broaden the definition of sexual activities to include touching, fantasy and playing with erogenous zones in new ways. Gay men, especially those who have yet to adopt the new sex guidelines, face a formidable challenge in changing well-established and much-enjoyed sexual patterns. But the alternative is likely exposure to a deadly disease.

Many gay men who believe they've already been exposed to the AIDS virus think that there's no reason for them to modify their sexual behavior. AIDS educators, however, strongly disagree.

Robert Bolan, MD, chairman of the board of the San Francisco AIDS foundation, put it this way: "Any infectious agent must get into the body in sufficient numbers to overcome the body's defenses. This is called a virus 'load.' We don't know how much of an AIDS virus load is needed for disease to result. We don't know if this load can be acquired at one time, or if many exposures may be necessary." Bolan summed up: "By continuing unsafe sex practices, you virtually assure that you will be repeatedly exposed. It's a dangerous risk."

I f gay men recognize AIDS as a sexually transmissible disease to be avoided at all costs, what good are the guidelines that include a whole set of "maybes"? Every day gay men make decisions to reduce risks with no guarantee that physical harm will be averted. Risk-reduction is just that: a means to lessen possible exposure to dangerous events.

At first risk-reduction was based only on the behavioral or environmental factors that people with AIDS said they had in common. Those epidemiological data have now been supplemented by discovery of HTLV-III/LAV/ARV, the virus most researchers believe causes the immune disorder. Such viruses, like the one linked to hepatitis B, can be spread from one person to another through the sharing of most "body fluids." That indelicate phrase serves as a "buzz word" for AIDS educators.

To date the AIDS virus has been isolated in semen, blood, saliva, urine, and tears. Physicians explain that the virus needs to enter the body, not just come in contact with the skin. So possibly safe activities are those that allow more sexual options while blocking the passage of potentially infected fluids from one partner to the other. Possibly safe, however, means possible infection with a deadly virus.

Anal Intercourse with Condom. The basic bottom position with new kinks: condoms. Take your choice: latex or natural membrane. Almost from the start AIDS epidemiologists—the scientists who study the spread of the disease—determined that the receptive partner in anal intercourse (the partner getting fucked) appeared to be at the greatest risk of later developing AIDS. This was based solely on statistics gleaned from hundreds of questionnaires completed by gay men with AIDS. When researchers compared the responses of preferred and most frequently performed sex practices, getting fucked always appeared near the top of the list.

Do condoms block the AIDS virus? Even two years after isolating and duplicating the virus, federal researchers have failed to test whether condoms can block it. The experiment is neither lengthy nor especially difficult, and yet the only study to test the AIDS virus with condoms was undertaken by researchers from the University of California San Francisco. In that study, Drs. Marcus Conant and Jay Levy tested five different commercial brands of condoms, both those made of latex and natural membranes. Each was found to block the AIDS virus in laboratory experiments.

The condoms were filled with a fluid containing a high concentration of the AIDS virus. Conant said the concentration was 5000 times greater than what has been found in semen. No virus particles penetrated the condom membranes even after three weeks. When the researchers subjected the virus-filled condoms to pressure, there was still no leakage.

Conant said he believes that condoms, especially when used with a spermicidal jelly, are safe for anal sex "100% of the time."

James D'Eramo, Ph.D. of New York's Gay Men's Health Crisis expressed a few reservations about condoms during the 1985 International Conference on AIDS in Atlanta. "Condom use greatly reduces the risk of sexually transmitted diseases," agreed D'Eramo, "but it shouldn't be viewed as the sole answer. Sometimes condoms break, and you have to be careful in how you handle them." AIDS educators are careful to specify the proper use of condoms. The San Francisco AIDS Foundation advises the following steps:

(1) Place the condom on the erect penis by starting at the tip and rolling back until the entire penis is covered.

(2) Hold the nipple end with finger tips to prevent filling with air.

(3) Do not make sexual contact without the condom in place.

(4) Do not use petroleum-based products, grease, or any other oil-based products with latex condoms.

(5) While withdrawing after ejaculation, hold the rim (open end) of the condom with fingers to prevent spillage.

Oral and Anal Sex: Stopping Before Climax. This is the *interruptus* method. If sex partners are vigilant and their timing is good, both measures could ensure that semen would not be swallowed or shot into the rectum. Health educators advise that this method requires knowledge of your partner's seriousness about the "interruptus" as well as his ability to control his orgasm. This isn't easy to do with new or anonymous sex partners.

The other problem lies with one of the body's minor fluids, that of the preseminal type—in the vernacular, "pre-cum." Does the AIDS virus or any other virus reside in pre-cum? Again, there has been no research. AIDS educators believe the risk is reduced—certainly less than that with semen—but nevertheless that it is present.

Several gay men now report that they have begun to use condoms during oral sex as well. This new practice would greatly reduce risk. Those who are interested should consider using non-lubricated varieties to avoid tasting a chemical solution.

Watersports. Is it safe for skin to be in contact with urine? As long as there are no cuts or abrasions and as long as there is only external body contact, there is reduced risk when someone pisses on his partner.

Deep Kissing (Wet). The prospect of the AIDS virus in saliva continues to stir up controversy and panic among the general population. The fear is related to casual contagion. But what about direct saliva exchange during passionate, deep kissing? In October, 1984, Dr. Robert Gallo, the prominent AIDS researcher at the National Cancer Institute, revealed that his laboratory had isolated the AIDS virus in the saliva of eight men who had AIDS Related Complex or who had had sexual contact with people with AIDS. Other studies have been unable to isolate the virus in saliva. Even with these differing results, the presence of the virus in a fluid is not considered a guarantee of transmissibility.

Dr. Edward Brandt, former assistant secretary for Health, responded to the saliva question soon after Gallo's research was released. "Epidemiological patterns of transmission consistent over the past three years lead us to believe that AIDS is transmitted only through blood, blood products and semen. After more than three years and more than 6,000 cases in the United States we have not seen a case where saliva seems to be the plausible route of transmission."

Many viral diseases are spread as a result of "infected" saliva. The common cold, flu, cold sores, cytomegalovirus and mononucleosis are a few. But not all diseases can infect individuals easily. For example, although the hepatitis B virus is present in saliva, there is little evidence that the virus can be spread by kissing.

AIDS researcher Dr. Jerome Groopman offered this analysis. "Saliva is very unlikely to be an important means of transmission for this disease . . . but it is a potential vector."

As a potential means of transmission, saliva exchange, and therefore deep, "wet" kissing, falls in the possibly safe category.

No poll has determined it, but many sexual activities that gay men would have once listed as their most favored are now clustered together as high-risk and unsafe. Fucking, sucking, rimming, fisting, sharing sex toys, exposure of the mouth or open sores to urine—scientists regard all of these as high-risk activities. Why? Because they involve a sharing of possibly AIDS-infectious fluids.

While the high-risk nature of fucking and sucking is readily apparent, controversies still revolve around fisting and rimming.

Fisting. Enthusiasts of fisting ("handballing") object to what they feel is a prejudicial response to the practice. Porno movie star and safe-sex educator Richard Locke asserts that fisting involves neither an exchange of fluids nor the introduction of microorganisms into the rectum. Locke predicates this discussion on the presumption that fisting partners are careful, knowledgeable and clean (with a preliminary thorough body scrub, especially the hands, nails and arms). To avoid the dangers of fisting—rectal trauma, tears of rectal wall—practitioners must also be fully aware of the anatomy of the rectum.

Most health officials are unyielding in their advice to avoid the risks of fisting. And though many practitioners of fisting are now using disposable surgical gloves to further prevent any possible transmission of infectious agents, health officials continue to cite the dangers of tearing rectal tissue and providing an entrance to infectious agents as reasons not to practice fisting.

Both sides seem entrenched in their stances. The real limits on resolving the issue rest with the lack of research into sexually-transmitted diseases.

Rimming. A bright and energetic Finnish scientist presented unexpected data at the Atlanta AIDS Conference. Dr. Kikka Valle, a gynecologist from Helsinki, is a primary AIDS researcher in her country. A study Valle conducted among patients with AIDS revealed rimming as the activity that correlated the highest with development of AIDS symptoms. The second highest was getting rimmed.

In an interview following her presentation, Valle added that the rectal wall is often inflamed, a condition that summons white blood cells to the area. The Finnish researcher suggested that during the act of rimming such an inflammation might facilitate the spread of the AIDS virus (possibly present in saliva) to the rectal cells.

Independent of Valle's data, American health officials had already listed oral/anal activities as dangerous because of the ease with which disease can be transmitted, especially other sexually-transmitted diseases. Since AIDS can "flare up" as the body's immune system weakens, proper AIDS risk-reduction includes the avoidance of other diseases damaging to the body's defenses, as well as exposure to the AIDS virus itself.

Sex Toys. Sex toys are often exposed to body fluids and fecal matter as well as to the microorganisms in them. Although high temperatures and a 10-to-1 solution of water and bleach have been found to kill HTLV-III in laboratory tests, health officials advise that sex partners use only their own toys.

Gay health workers will attest to the somewhat surreal quality of AIDS scientific gatherings. Gay men have become accustomed to nongay society's curiosity and fascination with what gay men do in bed together. But now, four years into the AIDS epidemic, the most conservatively attired scientist glibly discusses research data about fisting, rimming and watersports. And they no longer bother to explain what the words mean; all the other nongay scientists there already know.

Although the word is out on the varieties of gay sexual activities, the development of risk-reduction guidelines has not been imposed from on high. Gay physicians and organizations have been on the front line of efforts to determine what safe and healthy sex means today. Gay men can be assured that the guidelines as outlined above reflect a genuine concern about a deadly, sexually-transmitted disease rather than a moralistic attempt to limit gay sexuality. As Dr. James Curran, director of the

AIDS Activity Office for the Centers for Disease Control (CDC), recently acknowledged, "The challenge to remain uninfected for gay men is an extremely difficult prospect. How would heterosexuals deal with this?"

Along with all the recommended sexual changes, physicians also advise gay men to protect their overall health through good nutrition, sufficient rest and exercise. They also advise avoidance of undue stress and reduction or abstinence from alcohol and recreational drugs, including poppers.

Curran has called the sexual behavior change recommended for gay men "the most dramatic sexual revolution since the 1960s." Studies done in Madison, Wisconsin, and Chicago confirm that gay men are changing their sexual behavior and have greatly reduced the number of their sex partners.

Curran emphasized the importance of the reduced numbers during the Atlanta conference. "A gay man in San Francisco with 12 partners in 1980 would have been exposed to AIDS by three of them. In 1984 sexual contact with three men may have resulted in exposure from two of them," Curran estimated. He based his figures on a study that showed 64% of gay men in San Francisco with evidence of exposure to HTLV-III. A more recent study using a more representative sample of men in that city revealed a 37% exposure rate. While the second finding alters Curran's projections, reduction of sex partners has taken on a different meaning today than it did when AIDS first appeared.

The Chicago study, conducted by Dr. David Ostrow, found that from 1982 to 1983 gay men reduced certain practices, compared to a similar study done in 1978. Rimming was down 88%; getting fucked, 77%; and fucking, 62%.

There are other indications that gay men have changed their sexual habits. The rates of rectal and pharyngeal (throat) gonorrhea in Manhattan decreased a remarkable 59% from 1980 to 1983; the Denver health department reported similar statistics. In 1983 San Francisco claimed the second-highest number of gonorrhea cases in the nation—by mid-1984 the city had dropped to thirteenth. During the five-year period between early 1980 and 1985, San Francisco recorded an 86% plummet in numbers of gonorrhea cases. Safe sex campaigns appear to be working, and gay men are definitely changing their habits. No gay man should worry that he is alone in his efforts to adopt behaviors that enhance health.

The various safe sex campaigns that have been established across the country attempt not only to educate about specific practices, but also to encourage and support the changes that gay men are adopting. An ongoing study of sexual changes by gay men in San Francisco has noted that men in the sample reported a lack of confidence in changing behavior. Researchers Leon McKusick, MS, William Horstman, Ph.D., and Thomas Coates, Ph.D., advise that "public information must consistently reinforce the notion that it is within the individual's power to change behavior to avoid contracting AIDS." They also recognized the power of peer support to facilitate change.

The study by McKusick and colleagues found that among their selected sample of gay men the practice of monogamy did not increase appreciably. On-the-street talk, however, does suggest that many more men are indeed coupling up, a situation that for most will mean far fewer sexual partners. Researcher Coates said that in examining the data from this study an important trend has become apparent.

"Gay men have not substituted one sexual activity for another, but rather have declined in overall level of sexual activity." Coates added that the decline probably results not only from safe sex campaigns but also from awareness of the rising number of AIDS cases and from seeing people die of the disease.

It is not too uncommon to hear men testify to a certain peace of mind from becoming celibate. There has been little research into this option, however, and few AIDS educators—or anyone else—expect it to catch on in a big way.

And what of romance? Although the greeting card distributors, florists and confectioners might wish it were so, gay men do not indicate a sudden eagerness to adopt straight courtship patterns. Nevertheless, a quick glance at The ADVOCATE's classifieds will reveal several personal ads from men looking for relationships, not just a quick night of sex. The radical changes required in today's sexual relationships do tend to make it easier for interested men to pursue romance without being caste as oddities.

But beyond all the professional ad campaigns, bartender outreach programs, and behavioral research data, what are individual gay men thinking and, more importantly, doing when it comes to safe sex?

In a popular cruising and sex-in-the-bushes park in San Francisco, one cute gay man explained his afternoon trek to the hilltop open space. "I need a break from my work, and the weather is great today. But you know what surprises me is how much I've taken to jacking off with men. I never used to do it much, and now it's my favorite sexual act."

Writer Paul Reed relates that "getting bold about safe sex" is a necessary step in adopting the new guidelines. "This means refusing to feel less than hot about saying: 'Let's fuck, but safely.' Chances are the other guy will be relieved to find somebody else who's as worried as he is," Reed wrote in the Bay Area Reporter. "And the nasty little mistake of slipping into unsafe sex in order to preserve one's hotness will be avoided."

Negotiating safe sex requires new social skills. At one time gay men could initiate a sexual encounter with a nod or a touch, but now many must get accustomed to talking about sex, health and what activity is acceptable. Even this verbal negotiation may be a necessary but passing phase. Men in cities most aware of the AIDS epidemic find that safe sex is so widely practiced that it can be taken for granted. There's little reason to negotiate the norm.

The primary AIDS organizations in the two cities hit hardest by the epidemic—New York and San Francisco—tend not to pull any punches when it comes to risk reduction. One of the New York Gay Men's Health Crisis newspaper ads posed the challenge to gay men this way: "Sex and Danger vs. Sex and Fun. Gay men confront a stark choice: safer sex or flirtation with death. . . . We're not trying to scare you. We just want to get across the simple message that this epidemic is worse than ever and you may be in real danger."

"THERE IS NO LONGER AN EXCUSE FOR SPREADING AIDS," read the big, bold, black letters in the West Coast gay and lesbian press. The San Francisco AIDS Foundation decided to take their message and put it on the line. A few paragraphs capture particularly well the necessity for safe sex:

"Whose life is it, anyway? It's yours. Your partner's. And the community's. . . .

AIDS is not just a physical problem. There are political, social and economic effects as well. There is already evidence that social freedoms may be restricted because of AIDS. AIDS can be used as an excuse for anti-gay action and legislation.

Making decisions about sexual practices is difficult. Sticking to those decisions is even more difficult. But this isn't a moral issue; it's a matter of life and death."

Fighting Our Sexism

by Brian McNaught

MOST WOMEN I KNOW ARE SEXIST. MOST HOMOSEXUALS I know are heterosexist. Most Jews I know are anti-Semitic. It is the rare soul who has deprogrammed herself or himself today.

When you meet a woman who doesn't consider herself a person without a penis; who rejects a preconceived role; who celebrates the gifts of her womanhood and who sees equal rights not merely as a justice issue but as an opportunity for society to become enriched, spend some time talking with her. Consider what such a woman has overcome.

Can we men imagine growing up in a world in which every supreme authority is female? What if God, Jesus, Santa Claus and the breadwinner in our family was a woman? What if every U.S. President, every judge, every visible police officer, every priest and rabbi, every major author and corporation president was a woman? What would that do to our sense of importance? Our sense of pride? Our sense of equality?

What if men's penises were thought of as elephantiasis of the clitoris? What if male body hair was socially offensive and we were forced to daily shave our underarms, legs and chest? What if we had to resort to electrolysis or bleach to remove that which grew naturally? What if male puberty was considered a "curse," wet dreams disgusting and semen a frightening sight which should be disposed of with a sanitary napkin? What if our culture demanded that men insert devices into our penises to prevent pregnancies? What if developing massive pectorals at age 14 was viewed by society as essential if we wished to get a date?

Speaking of dates, what if we weren't allowed out at night unless a girl asked us out? What if women stood every time we went to the "powder room," opened every door, pulled back every chair and paid every check? Would we not feel weak and dependent as opposed to "special"?

What if we only had two sexual role models in life, the whore or the saint? What if girls who peeked into our locker rooms when we were naked were considered "red-blooded" and when we did the same to them we were labeled "sluts"?

What if a limited family income only allowed our sister to go to college because boys don't need an education to be happy— they merely need to meet a successful woman? Besides, our only career options would be teaching and secretarial work.

What if we finally did get a job in the women's world and discovered that to compete we had to not only be equal to women but better? And what if we found that on payday, women were paid nearly twice as much for the exact same job? What if a successful male was always described as being cute or handsome rather than sharp, intelligent and industrious?

Would we not be angry? Would we not become assertive— even "aggressive"? Would we not begin demanding that womankind share power with us? Would we not demand that language be changed to reflect the presence of men in the world, and history books be changed to reflect the achievements of men in history and customs be changed to reflect the self-sufficiency of men? Some of us would but many of us would not.

Given those circumstances, many of us men would be afraid to challenge thousands of years of culture. Many of us would fear that if we boldly proclaimed our disgust with the status quo, women might not date us, like us or stay friends with us. We would fear the reaction of our families and male friends. Worst of all, many if not most men would have a hard time believing that we were equal to women. While we talked about pride, we would feel in our gut that there is really something basically inadequate about being a man. We would ask women to help us understand ourselves just as we had in the past when we plopped ourselves down on the couches in the offices of women psychiatrists, the examining tables of women doctors and the pews of women spiritual leaders. We would be sexist because we would believe that if we had our druthers, we would really rather be women. To paraphrase the line in *Animal Farm*, "All people are equal but women are more equal than men."

As a man living in a male world, I acknowledge my sexism. I work hard at eliminating it, but it shows its ugly face more often than I would like to admit. I have attempted to understand what it is like being a woman but it is difficult to feel fully the rage most women do or should feel. My best bridge in spanning the emotional gap between myself and women is my reflections on what it is like growing up homosexual in a heterosexual world. As a homosexual who is outraged by my heterosexist tendencies, I feel more comfortable suggesting the awful truth that many women today are sexist.

Heterosexism and sexism are prejudices based upon the assumption that one sexual orientation or one gender is more equal, more preferred, more "normal" than another. Most of our battles against heterosexism, sexism, racism, anti-semitism, etc., have been based upon arguments of injustice. But even when arguments are cogent and we are successful in eliminating inequalities, we don't succeed in eliminating prejudice; we don't root out of ourselves and others the sexism, for instance, which is at the core of the injustice. What has helped me attack my own heterosexism is the process of examining not only why my sexual orientation is "just as good" as that of heterosexuals but, more important, what makes me special. I am less likely to be heterosexist when I begin celebrating the unique beauty of my being gay and the unique contributions I am making to society and nature because of my homosexuality.

My sexism and that of my women friends is best attacked when I examine, with the tutoring of women, the unique beauty of the female, the unique glory of the female perspective, the unique contribution to society and nature of the female mystique. I don't owe it to women to eliminate my sexism by discovering the unique perspectives and gifts of women; I owe it to myself.

Like most men today, I have been deprived of half of reality. It's as if one of my eyes and one of my ears have been eliminated; as if I have only been allowed to eat pre-designated foods and read pre-selected books; to smell only half of the flowers; to encounter only half of the truths. Men have deprived me of my entire inheritance as a human being by burying half of life's treasure under mounds of ignorant, self-serving bias. I am less whole because of this deception. I am less healthy, less liberated, less in tune with nature because of this deception.

If we doubt there is a special new beauty to be discovered, it is our sexism, our years of indoctrination which gives birth to and nurtures those doubts. To challenge those doubts and to set about the task of discovering the whole melody of creation is an exciting, compelling adventure. It is for that reason that I suggest if you meet a woman who celebrates her womanhood, do yourself a favor and listen to her song.

II

HOME

A Guide to Urban Living

By Edmund C. Sutton

NEW YORKERS SMILE AS BENEVOLENTLY AS GRANDPAR-
ents at stories of trial and travail by new city arrivals. Smugly
they reminisce and recount their own experiences becoming
familiar with the city's frenetic pace and how they once labored
to absorb even the most basic city survival information. Street
etiquette, dining protocol and dressing oneself with style are
hard facts of contemporary urban living, and acquiring these
skills may prove to be highly demanding of innocent nerves and
sorely try one's patience.

Despite the difficulties encountered in orienting oneself to life
in the city, for many the attractions are deliciously obvious. The
shimmering urban landscape just a cab ride away and the de-
lirious possibility of notoriety at a moment's notice are sugar-
coated dreams bound to be soberly crushed after just a few days
in the city. If, shortly after arrival, you find yourself accepting
abuse as if it were somehow wildly exciting, consider yourself
already fully integrated. For those to whom absorbing the city's
beat becomes an exercise in futility, however, we offer some
sensible information on the basic components of contemporary
urban life.

FINANCES

Few things can keep one from enjoying the pleasures of metropolitan life; the largest stumbling block seems to be an absence of
abundant cash. You'll easily understand this block when you
succumb to city-induced depression caused by a lack of funds.
In the city it quickly becomes evident when finances are limited;
you'll notice too little space, a shortage of heat, few essential
services and an impressive amount of filth and noise. Something
must be done.

Perhaps the most expedient method of replenishing your cash

supply is the 24-hour teller. These computer-controlled cash registers dot the city landscape and are usually within a block or ten of your unpaid dinner checks.

Since the human contact you'll be accorded by most city banks is approximately as long as the coital syndrome of hummingbirds, you'll do well to shop for a bank based solely on the amount of automated self-service machines provided. This is more a matter of logistics than anything else, so try to choose a bank that has a lot of automatic tellers. Keep a map in a convenient place which lists their locations—you'll need it at the most hectic times. When shopping for a bank, look for teller units that are enclosed, off the street, and require your banking card to gain access—the reasons are obvious. Unsavory individuals have been known to haunt them, striking down unsuspecting bankees as cash issues from the slot and "Have A Nice Day" appears on the screen.

Though credit cards require respectful handling, it's a good idea to possess at least one major card. Even if that card is rarely used it provides a substantiating credential of identity when writing checks, renting automobiles and making reservations for theater and airline tickets by telephone.

If you don't already have a credit card, or possibly lack credit entirely, you may be neglecting the credit history you've already earned. Your landlord, for instance, with whom you are unabashedly on good terms, receives a regular amount from you, and knows something of your character. Likewise the phone company, utilities, school loans and almost anything you've repaid or pay regularly, is considered part of a credit history and can be included in applications for credit. If you've had a bank account in any one place for a prolonged period, say your whole life, this is the best place to apply for a credit card. Bankers will be more accommodating if they've known you since you were "knee high."

Some credit cards will permit you greater access to cash or its facsimile, traveler's checks. The American Express card holder, for example (this is a charge—not credit—card, requiring payment in full with the monthly statement), have traveler's-check dispensers in convenient (apparently only to them) places in major cities and their corresponding airports.

LANGUAGE

Early on in my city tenure I felt as if I spoke another language from those I encountered daily on the streets of Manhattan. I was unable to communicate basic coffee chemistry to the Greek who bellowed my order at the corner deli, and more than once I was embarrassed when I didn't know how to hail a cab that wasn't off duty. This is understandable when you realize that outside cities, one rarely signals a taxi; it's usually arranged by phone.

I discovered the proper urban method of hailing cabs, courtesy of an understanding acquaintance, and this clue seemed to unlock an almost zen-like wealth of understanding. It wasn't so much that I had an uncanny ability to signal unavailable cabs, but the method in which I did this was perhaps not as assertive as it could have been.

For the record, New York City medallion cabs have identifying lights planted in their roofs. Should all lights be dark, this is a busy cab. If the medallion number is lit, you're in luck. Otherwise, when the lights to each side of the medallion number are lit also, this means the driver is off-duty. Off-duty cab drivers will stop for you if they think you're going their way, usually to an outer borough, and in this case you may be able to negotiate an off-the-meter fare. Do so before the cab moves.

All this street nuance is only one step in the achievement of the "integration effect" you're hungry for, and it boils down to the ethics that are the pressure-cooker intensity of city life. The level of street competition, vying for sidewalk space, jockeying for cabs or dinner reservations, breed a "sink or swim" sensibility. Hence, folks can seem just a bit callous to your good old-fashioned gentlemanly deference in the face of a majority of harried "coffee achievers."

This is by no means license to be any ruder or inconsiderate than the next person, but if you're politely assertive, move with intention and aplomb, the city will open up to you.

REAL ESTATE

To give you an idea of the difficult housing market in some cities, during the summer of 1985 New York City's vacancy rate was .05%. This rate refers to the number of available apartments and indicates that at that particular time roughly one-half of an apartment was available to approximately one hundred people. These people not only are already living here, but have had an eye on that specific apartment since the turn of the century. If you live out of town and have your heart set on a move into Manhattan, it might be wise to meet with a consoling friend and consider alternatives. Should you decide to proceed and begin a quest for an apartment, I'm happy to provide insights into the current, socially acceptable methods of stalking a rental in any sizeable urban center.

The best thing you can do is your homework. Check out the territory before plundering it. Reliable sources of information about housing in any city are contained in local newspapers. Many local entertainment weeklies list rental classifieds and are usually a good place to turn in these desperate times. Publications like these will have listings for sublets, roommates or specializing agencies. When reading advertisements for apartments, be aware of fixture fees. The ad may indicate an immense space with expansive panoramic views for $200 a month, but you'll find out that a move-in fee for fixtures is going to cost you—a fee ranging from exorbitant to a randomly selected five-digit figure.

The fixture fee, or key money, is something entirely unique to areas where the primary form of housing is an apartment. The fee suggests that the tenant, existing or former, has invested labor, materials, and especially funds that can't be recouped from the landlord for structural changes on property he or she doesn't own. Most rental contracts will contain a clause permitting you to make alterations on the structure with the owner's permission. This clause also stipulates that if the alteration is affixed to the structure it becomes permanent and therefore, on departure, property of the landlord. This applies to tenant-installed windows, skylights, or refinishing a kitchen or bathroom. Fixture fees are generally illegal in New York City, but people still charge and get them because the market will bear it and housing is scarce. If the lease is long, the rent low, and the fee manageable, you might convince yourself that it's worth the investment, or else promptly develop more creative methods of quickening the hunt.

An annoying amount of apartment listings reads like executive want ads: "Perfect for company relocator," or "executive suite," which translates as sparsely furnished studio rooms in slightly tacky hotel style. These are meant for a seller's market, and since $1400 a month rent is meager compared to a couple of weeks in a hotel, they go fast.

A renovated apartment is an extremely broad term used to suggest rents that require two incomes, and implies anything from no bathtub in the kitchen to new windows or as much as a complete interior overhaul. These are usually older buildings or smaller ones, unless you're shopping lofts, which are commercial spaces made livable from scratch.

Local colleges and universities offer bulletin board listings of nearby housing. Though you may not be a student, these can be good resources for wholesome shelter. But remember that those offering these listings expect quiet, sincere academics to reply, so respond accordingly. Also many of these listings are for shares, sublets, or a room in a family home, and should be considered only as temporary.

Many savvy apartment hunters use agencies as a last resort. The New York Times is where most Manhattan property agencies advertise apartment listings, and it's rare to find in that paper an independent listing at a bargain rate. An ad in the Times may seem very romantic, but your image of a clean and spacious hearth may be cruelly shattered by a visit. All agency listings must indicate as much, and the words "fee" or "agent" let you know the party handling this transaction is not the principal. Real estate agents stand to gain 15% of your first year's rent.

Terms like "nook" are often used when "pit" would be more appropriate, and "full bath" when "complete stall" is more accurate. "Pioneer" usually means you'll require attack dogs and federal disaster assistance, while "developing" generally implies tofutti stands and take-out Chinese only moments away.

Do not overdress for your appointments with agents. Instead, dress simply and well. Be demanding and virtuous in your dealings with agents and decline all party invitations until your housewarming. You should be aware that many agents may know the same people that you do, so be tight-lipped. No scurrilous rumors are to be perpetrated in the presence of real estate agents.

One of your most valuable resources is your address book. Though everyone needs a better apartment, if you poll and query all your friends at least one of them will yield a lead. An additional advantage is that friends know something about your habits, the living conditions you're willing to tolerate and, in suggesting roommates, can act as a screening intermediary.

Before you visit an apartment with an agent, have them show you pictures if possible. No one has enough time to run from one prospective apartment to another, and since using an agent is to save you footwork, let *him* do some. If an agent promises you repairs or anything else, *get it in writing* from the landlord. The agent (unless his firm is also the managing agent) has no authority to promise anything the landlord ultimately will be responsible for. Try to meet the landlord before giving anyone money. It rarely happens, but the multiple rental swindle is a sickening tale. Find out who pays for building services—water, gas, electricity, heat and trash removal.

Discover if the building is rent-controlled or rent-stabilized. City housing laws exist to protect you from rent overcharges in these two designations; and they are enforced, albeit lethargically.

If there is no doorman, is the building secure? Do intercoms, door buzzers and door bells operate? Be sure to check water pressure in bathrooms by turning on showers and flushing toilets. Knowing how often the building is fumigated or sprayed for insects can also clue you in to how much attention the landlord pays to the smooth maintenance of the building.

Once you've found a place, write down the phone number of the Central Building Complaint office, since most landlords need an occasional nudge from city agencies to keep your home livable. You'll also want your landlord's and building superintendent's numbers handy in case of emergency. Be sure to have a phone number for your building's supplier of heating oil, since should an emergency arise it's your right to have oil delivered at a moment's notice and billed to the landlord.

Not all landlord-tenant relationships are abusive, so relax, because ironically the beauty of an inner-city abode is to make more readily available the city's activities and conveniences. Hence you'll discover you really don't spend as much time at home as you did before you became metropolitan.

LAUNDRY

Laundry is a bigger drag in the city than anywhere else in the world. Laundromats are always ridiculously overheated and invariably unglamorous. My strongest recommendation is to find a reliable laundry to *do it for you*. If, however, you think it therapeutic and humbling to do your own laundry, pack your walkman and bring along your diary.

I recently heard that someone in Texas has opened cafe/bars in the laundromats—it's a wonder we've put up with boring launderettes this long.

FURNISHINGS AND HOUSEHOLD APPLIANCES

Always be on the lookout for things you'll need to furnish your apartment. A futon seems to be a very popular substitute for boxspring and mattress, particularly for those with backs strong enough to withstand this form of oriental abuse.

Since most city apartments are from small to minuscule, keep your eyes peeled for furniture that stores, folds, rolls or in general will go away when not in use.

If you haven't considered your apartment's security, it's imperative to do so. Door locks should be a deadbolt, cylinder variety, and vulnerable windows should be gated with fire department-approved units. Gates should contain protective stationary tracks to prevent their being pried open. They can be bought second-hand in hardware stores.

In the age of cryogenic cuisine a toaster oven is a bridal gift with enough cooking potential to keep you in at least food for one.

If you've installed your apartment with a mammoth sound system, be very considerate. Keep speakers away from walls and rest them on foam bases to absorb the bass "punch." Conversely, if you have a neighbor who tends to play the beat box a bit loud, a friendly offer of foam bases and a bottle of wine is more effective than banging on the walls or yelling your request.

Most tenement dwellers rely heavily on steam heat and no air-conditioning. You must give priority to your comfort, so it may be wise to invest in adequate air-conditioning and heating units to supplement what little comfort your landlord will provide.

Another anomaly to city apartment tenants is the habit of tipping the superintendent. This works in your favor when you need something fixed, and palming a token of appreciation of the labor involved is good form. Don't make a big show of it, but when the repair's major or involved it's appropriate. When you need something minor done your past generosity won't be forgotten.

CLOTHING

There's not a soul alive who isn't prepared to defend whateve. statement is made by his or her choice of clothing, and you'll soon learn that though you may have dressed in a similar style for the majority of your life, you now have innumerable options. It's important to know that one may combine several distinct styles of costume and dress to create a single, integrated persona.

While it certainly remains safe to stockpile standard issue Brooks Brothers' garb, it's equally important—and perhaps even more useful—to collect the key elements of an eclectic wardrobe or: party clothes. Striding up almost any big city street, it doesn't take long to realize that every sort of clothing has its purpose. If you're of the social chameleon ilk and wish to look "correct" in any situation, there are as many choices as are people, perhaps a few more.

The current passion for combining almost anything has been dubbed "street chic" by "fashion" arbiters, who've discovered and defend the use of eccentric combinations and patterns as the answer to the sober post-apocalyptic look with which the Japanese recently swept us.

All of this is to indicate that those individuals to whom success is paramount take their clothing very seriously but don't overintellectualize it. Interpreting your apparel should come from an innocent playfulness and an inherent self-confidence which allows you to wear red suspenders with a sober suit if the mood strikes. This depends entirely on your personal daring, the amount of confidence you're willing to muster, and whether you actually look right in the clothes. After all, some men were born to wear skirts while others must bear responsibility for upholding the tradition of the double-breasted suit. Far be it from this writer to determine which is right for you; only you and your haberdasher can come to that decision.

But in New York, known for its extremely style-conscious population, an initial examination of one's wardrobe may well fail the sartorial test. At least it did for me, looking as I was for parties full of glitter and lamé in any configuration. Don't fear, however, New York isn't really all that daring; in fact, I'm one of the few in my social circle who doesn't continue to wear button-down shirts.

At times it seems almost anything is acceptable, and while it's unlikely that you'll encounter many who are overly zealous in regard to current style, you may discover an entire city of people who can spice up an otherwise pedestrian ensemble with a simple twist at a moment's notice. The whole point of dressing is in working the accessories. Trouser braces worn front to back, bright socks, a single carat in a single earlobe, or unmatched shoes are the whole point of turning the sartorial screw and taking none of it seriously. Making fun of the whole idea of fashion is what works best.

Of course it's always important to consider the milieu in which you and your clothing and accessories will mingle. Due consideration needs to be given to the general audience of a given function, whether or not business is likely to be conducted, and if you want a starring role, cameo appearance or simply to be lost in the crowd. Clothing will make it happen.

On walking through town—as you're bound to do on occasion—you may be impressed by the particular fashions which are indigenous to an area. For example, some denizens of the East Village sport closely-cropped, occasionally multi-colored hair, combat boots, leather of an undesigned sort and impenetrably dark glasses. A flavoring of Eastern European peasant is also obvious in the East Village, while a look on the Upper West Side may mean the latest denim fashions, bouncy haircuts and "big" tops from shops on Columbus Avenue.

Dare. Don't be afraid to experiment. If it requires a grand and sweeping gesture to pull it off, do it. The point is, there are really no rules—haven't been for at least a decade—and the fashion misdemeanors that remain are falling away at a rate that renders them meaningless. If you like a smily face in the center of your leather jacket, so be it. A strand of pearls, bravo.

DINING

After cocktails, a city dweller's most prized pastime is dining. This can easily become, ahem, a consuming passion, since there are innumerable options and every cuisine to sample in New York.

In Lower Manhattan, Little Italy and Chinatown border one another. In Little Italy you can easily sample mussels marinara, pasta primavera and an almond soda, then traipse over to a cafe for double espresso and baba au rhum. The Italians are particularly fond of food festivals and celebrating anything that can be fried and put into a paper bag or on a hero roll. New York Italian restaurants aren't that different from those outside the city. Most are either of the sawdust-on-the-floor variety or garishly tuck-and-roll. Walls are tiled with effusively autographed celebrity photographs, and all have menu specialties that of course, no one makes *quite like them*. In this particular case, as has been my experience, asking the advice of the waiters on menu choices can be inspiring and delicious.

The Italians are also well-known for their wine-making and imbibing abilities, and many *trattorias* offer comprehensive wine lists traceable to every culinary province. Many of these wines are not only good bargains, but can be as delicious as the entree itself.

Chinatown, on the other hand, just south of Little Italy, has the distinctive reputation of containing more neon lights per square foot than any other area in Manhattan. Menus vary greatly; some cater to milder Western palates and still others have entirely separate menus for Oriental and Western diners.

Chinese restaurants are rarely of an opulent strain. The preferred decor leans toward formica surfaces, ceiling fans and a generally clamorous ambience. Disregard these distractions and pay attention to what the Chinese patrons are ordering. Take a few minutes to see what intriguing sizzling noises and provocative smells issue from the kitchen. If you're adventurous stray from the beaten menu path and you'll rarely be disappointed. Query your waiter on the dishes you see and solicit suggestions.

It required an entire year to discover the correct way to ask for coffee from Greek coffee shops. Of course one may naively request his coffee black/with cream and/or sugar. Not so in Manhattan, where you order coffee a) regular or b) black. My own problem was discovering what regular coffee contained. For some coffee shops regular is both sugar and milk, while others only milk. All of this investigative coffee drinking was put abruptly on hold when summer arrived and I was forced to drink regular coffee, iced. Soon after, someone else from my office fetched coffee, and I can now authoritatively inform you I still don't know what regular coffee is.

Delis are sandwich shops which litter the city, having accepted the dubious responsibility of feeding you a meal between bread. Delis are also responsible for a variety of food slang and jargon, and have been known to confuse many by requiring the customer to distinguish between a cream cheese sandwich and a "bagel wid a schmear." I feel obligated to inform you that the difference exists in the price tag: a sandwich costs substantially more than a schmear.

Americans have come up with something that slurs all ethnic parameters and combines them into one highly-overpriced, overrated offering—the trendy restaurant. Trendy restaurants can be identified by the inclusion of "baby" anything—particularly vegetables and animal organs—proclamations of exotic woods flavoring your food, a surly and ignorant staff, ambitious American wine lists or even wine bars, and are considered by some to be the quintessential mondo-consumer delight. All right, you've caught me, I'm a poor snob. But honestly I can't eat someplace that doesn't have at least a trace of wadded gum under my table. I also advise avoiding any place that serves blue or unnaturally-colored blender drinks as their specialty; unless, of course, you're poolside.

City dwellers converge on restaurants like moths to a flame. Since most haven't the enormous kitchens of their parents' suburban homes, they're forced to conduct their entertaining in large, noisy restaurants. And though we're clearly the benefactors of a democracy, one isn't required to subject oneself or one's guests to the unctious preferential treatment often accorded patrons in restaurants of current popularity. Therefore it pays to scout your area, the better to become acquainted with your "neighborhood" restaurants and soon establish yourself as a "regular."

It won't be long before you'll feel you're on the insider's track of city living, and though you'll occasionally bristle at the brusqueness of urban abuse, you'll soon be taking it in stride and hurling it back with the same bravado. Challenges aside, you'll walk as briskly as anyone else, navigate traffic as if you owned the place, and without fail (except for inebriated miscalculation) hail the available cab, and make your exit only after the correct tip.

The Gay Ghetto

by Greg Jackson

I HAVEN'T CONTRIBUTED TO THE CENTENNIAL CAMPAIGN TO save the Statue of Liberty. Instead I'm collecting funds to erect a statue in my own Boston neighborhood, the South End. The statue will be called the Queen of Liberty and although I'm no Emma Lazarus the inscription on the base will read:

> Bring me your tired old queens, your poor drags, Your horny masses yearning to be free, The disco bunnies of this teeming land, Send me these tempest-toss'd homos And I will lift my skirts and take them in.

The South End, you see, is Boston's premier gay ghetto, the promised land for thousands of refugees from homophobic hamlets all across New England. There are more homosexuals per square block in the South End than in any other area of the Northeast, except New York's Upper East Side and Greenwich Village.

At certain times, on a Sunday afternoon, for example, when the streets of the neighborhood are thick with men on their way to a tea dance, it's easy to believe that everyone is gay. But of course there are straights in the South End and we try to keep an open mind about them. After all, heterosexuals are just like us except for what they do in bed. Besides, we feel they add a little diversity to our little ghetto.

To call the South End a ghetto is both accurate and misleading. In the most objective sense of the word, a ghetto is simply a part of a city where members of a minority live because of social, economic or even legal pressure. And in this sense of the word the South End is certainly a ghetto. Perhaps a third of the residents are gay, and we've moved here because we feel safer, freer and more comfortable than we would in any other part of the city.

But ghetto is not exactly the term to describe an area where the average house now sells for around $400,000. The term ghetto brings to most people's minds a host of complex images, most all of them negative. In the popular sense ghetto conjures up a blighted, impoverished, violent and hopeless area of a city. And although the South End once fit this description, that is no longer the case.

Twenty-five years ago no gay man would have been caught dead in the South End. And being caught dead would have been a distinct possibility because the area had hit rock bottom. But today any gay man would be proud to give an address on one of the South End's shady squares or tree-lined avenues.

In the 1850s and 60s the South End was Boston's most fashionable address for Victorian yuppies, even though the term hadn't yet been coined. Now it's the address for post-high-tech guppies. A few gay men still insist on Beacon Hill or Back Bay, but if the New Right ever comes looking for us they know where we'll be—squeezed into fifty-odd blocks of lavish townhouses and luxury condos. Herd up all the gay men in the South End, send us off to the quarantine camps and you wouldn't be able to find a hairdresser or interior decorator in all of Boston.

The great influx began in the early 1960s. At that time a gay man could buy a five-story Victorian townhouse for a few thousand dollars and spend years restoring it. In those days the neighborhood was a real ghetto—in the generic sense. But the generic ghetto became the gay ghetto—almost overnight. After the first few gay men came the deluge. As if heeding the call of a gay Pied Piper, men flooded into the South End by the thousands.

Where winos once stumbled across garbage-strewn squares, clutching bottles of Wild Irish Rose, guppies now rush back to their condos with bottles of Chablis. Bag ladies used to push their worldly possessions through the streets in shopping carts. That was before the local historical society declared shopping carts incompatible with the historic character of the neighborhood and banished the bag ladies forever. Once soul music blared out of open windows. Now if you listen carefully you can just make out strains of Beethoven coming from behind the facade of a restored brownstone. Spanish used to be the second language of the neighborhood; now it's "queens' vernacular." A few years ago hookers strutted down the street in halter tops and platform shoes; now queens in Calvin Kleins walk their poodles on diamond-studded leashes.

But the greatest change is the value of real estate. House prices are inflating so quickly that I make more money by going to bed in my ready-for-condo-conversion townhouse than I do by getting up and going to work. In the South End real-estate market everything is seen through rose-colored glasses. What was once servants' quarters down an alleyway is now advertised as "an adorable dollhouse on an interesting mews." An abandoned bowfront becomes "a neglected queen." And any inner city wreck has "lots of potential."

Real-estate developers have discovered the neighborhood and are falling all over one another to buy up the few houses that haven't been renovated. When I used to see a long, sleek car moving slowly down the street I thought "pimp"—now I think "developer."

Once I had to watch out for junkies and winos when I walked the dog. Now I keep an eye out for fast-talking developers who are much more persistent. Retreating into the house will not discourage them. They ring the doorbell, leave offers to purchase on the answering machine and occasionally climb up the fire escape to peer longingly into rental units which could be converted into condos.

Unfortunately, the real-estate boom has squeezed out many of the South End's old-time residents. The neighborhood is quickly becoming unaffordable to all but the most affluent. As a result what attracted many of us to the South End in the first place— the enclaves of black, Hispanic, Chinese, Middle Eastern and Irish residents—are being transformed into a homogenized neighborhood of guppies and yuppies. The South End will remain integrated due largely to the number of public-housing units in the neighborhood, but the days of the racial and ethnic patchwork are gone. It's unfortunate that gay men have played such a heavy role in forcing people out of their homes so we can make our own ghetto. But the truth is, life in the "new South End" (as the realtors love to say) is very pleasant for gays.

I often think life in the South End in the 80s must be a little like life was for blacks in Harlem fifty years ago, a place where an oppressed minority can breathe more freely. By most accounts

Harlem was a nice place for blacks to be in the 20s and 30s. Whatever its drawbacks, Harlem was certainly preferable to the Jim Crow South. And for many gay men the ghetto is certainly preferable to the rest of homophobic America.

Life in the ghetto is an altogether reassuring experience. It's possible to be openly gay in the South End, a boast precious few other places in the country can make. Some straight neighbors undoubtedly share the homophobic epidemic, but they're either too polite or intimidated by our numbers to make their opinions known.

The pleasures of the ghetto can be small ones, too, like gazing out the window at gay men passing by or, when weather permits, coming home to find a group of neighbors congregated on the stoop, drinking beer, sizing up the passersby and generally camping it up. At such times I know it's my neighborhood and that I belong.

In the ghetto we don't have to be invisible. Outside the ghetto we simply don't exist; but in the ghetto nothing could be more natural than being gay. The clerk in the corner store is gay; the restaurants are gay-owned; so are the gyms, even the garages. Now there's the true test of the gay ghetto—any small town can produce a gay hairdresser, but it takes a real ghetto to provide tattooed lesbian car mechanics. We're so numerous in fact that I've learned gay men are, unfortunately, just like everyone else except for what we do in bed. In my idealistic youth I believed that all gay men were brothers, but after eight years in the ghetto I know the only thing I have in common with most of my neighbors is sexual preference.

Life in the ghetto is so comfortable that there is a real threat we'll forget our life here is the exception rather than the rule. After a while it's hard to remember that we're a privileged few living in a few dozen neighborhoods of America's largest cities, and that we're all refugees from less tolerant parts of the country. Such forgetfulness can be dangerous. I'm often alarmed to see how many of my gay neighbors vote their pocketbooks rather than their heads at election time. The appeal is luring, I'll admit; a healthy economy means a more comfortable ghetto. But my neighbors have apparently not drawn any lessons from the fate of the Jewish ghettos in Eastern Europe during World War II. It's true that the Jewish ghettoes were not self-defined and that Jews were forced to live in them. We aren't forced to live in the gay ghetto, but we are certainly pressured to do so—unless we're willing to hide who we are. And, in the end, it has the same effect—they've got us where they want us.

But who knows? Perhaps the jack-booted storm troopers will never arrive. Until they do I'll continue to collect funds to erect the Queen of Liberty—who will shine her beacon of welcome for those of us the rest of the country excludes. Someday we may feel free to live anywhere we choose. In the meantime, thank God for ghettos.

DO YOU LIVE IN A GAY GHETTO?

Your neighborhood is gay if:

1. There's at least one card shop on each block.
2. The restaurants have hi-tech decor and high-priced menus.
3. During traditional business hours the streets are thronged with men of working age who are obviously not working.
4. Drivers of cars stopped at red lights can be observed checking their profiles in the rear view mirror.
5. Older men drive youthful sports cars such as MGs, Porsches and Mercedes 280 roadsters.
6. Young men drive the latest Japanese GT coupes.
7. Women drive beat-up Japanese cars which appear to be held together by bumper stickers.
8. There's at least one clothing store that deals exclusively in beachwear, even though the nearest beach is a hundred miles away.
9. Bookstores have large collections of art magazines.
10. Corner groceries have stockpiles of Perrier and yogurt.

Creating a Home in the Country

by Dick Harrison

I'VE ALWAYS HAD A LOVE OF THE COUNTRY, EVEN AS A BOY growing up in the suburbs of Buffalo. I looked forward to those weeks at summer camp, miles away from the traffic, concrete, and noise of the city. After graduation from a small-town college in upstate New York, I decided to move to the city—"to take advantage of what it had to offer." I headed for Boston and there I found out what the city *really* had to offer. I began coming out.

After five years in Boston I decided city life wasn't for me. Rather than remain there, hoping to meet that special man who wanted a country life, I realized I had better chances of finding a country man in the country. I'd spent three summers in Maine and recalled how much I enjoyed it there. Exploring maps, I decided to make a move to the central or southern part of that state—anyplace south of Bangor.

I ended up in a small community at the northern border of the state—over 200 miles *north* of Bangor. Van Buren is an Acadian town—French is spoken on the street. The culture shock I experienced, moving from an urban, sophisticated, liberal, anglophone city to a rural, isolated, conservative, farming and lumbering francophone community of 4000 people was overwhelming. This was further compounded by my being a gay man living just outside the closet door. I was a school teacher, the only art teacher in the four-town consolidated district, and I didn't want to lose a job which had taken so long to find. I retreated into the closet, but made sure the door was louvered.

On first arriving in Van Buren I was struck by the lack of anonymity. Though small town people seem friendlier and more caring towards others in their community, for one attempting to remain aloof these aren't always desirable characteristics. Urban gay men can lose themselves in the crowd; people don't care. In a small town, however, you're known. After less than a week in Van Buren, while sitting at the counter of a local greasy spoon, the man serving me approached. He didn't ask if I were new in town, how long I'd been there or what I did for a living. "What do you teach?" was his initial question. He already knew! Exposed!! The whole town must know about me, and it's only been a week!!!

I decided to move, not far, but far enough. The house I rented was in town where my comings and goings were seen by all. I found an old, secluded farmhouse three miles away. No neighbors. I learned about heating exclusively with wood. Just wood— no oil or electric back-up system. I wanted rural living and I got it! I bought myself a four-wheel drive vehicle with a plow to keep the snow out of the driveway during the long winters. I was adapting.

My social life, however, was dull. My local gay bar was in Augusta, Maine (five hours south), or Quebec City (three and one half hours west). I decided to place an advertisement in the personal column of *Mainely Gay*, the statewide gay periodical at the time. I received two responses from men who lived within an hour's drive of Van Buren. Another thing I had adapted to was travel. The towns in Aroostook County, Maine's northernmost and largest, are few and far between. Traveling forty miles one way for an evening's visit with gay friends is not unusual. It surprises city folk, but I point out that I travel that distance in 45 minutes, the same time it takes them to get across town by subway.

I met three men from that advertisement. One of them, Roger, was a native—Acadian and bilingual. The other two, Walt and Jack, had been together almost ten years, including seven in the northernmost part of Aroostook County along the Saint John River. From those meetings a rural gay support system began. There were gay men throughout the region, but they were isolated from one another. The network started with the rental of a post office box and a notice placed in the County edition of the *Bangor Daily News*. It's grown to the point where I can now travel to any community in northern Maine and some in New Brunswick, Canada, and visit friends. For me the friendships

and gay male bonding in this rural area are much more meaningful than what the city had to offer. When we're so few and far
between, each of us is truly special.

I found my country man up here, too. Phil is originally a city
boy, but his family's roots are in northern Maine. We met less
than a year after my arrival, at Walt and Jack's tenth anniversary
party. Phil and I lived about seventy-five miles apart. Because he
worked every other weekend, we saw each other for a total of six
weeks that first year. After that I left teaching, and we lived
together in three different Aroostook County towns over the next
three years. We decided we wanted to settle in the county and
purchased a big old five-bedroom farmhouse with ten acres of
land.

Rural life suits me just fine and I'm lucky to have found a job
doing art-related work. Our life is very comfortable, even though
we're "known" more than I'd prefer to be. Because people are
very independent around here, they pretty much mind their own
business. Despite the few homophobic teenage boys who drive
by once in a while, honk and yell "Fags," people are very nice.

Since reading stories by other rural gay men in publications
such as *RFD*, I've realized *how* rural and *how* isolated I am.
Many men write of their lives in very small towns—perhaps 50
or 100 miles from cities of 40–50,000 people. I live in a town of
700 and the two closest cities have populations of 9,500. That's
it. Any city of substantial size with even a moderately active gay
community (read: bar or disco) is hours away. This isolation
makes this place very special to me. That's probably the primary
reason our small but growing gay community tends to be so open
and welcoming to strangers.

Despite this isolation ("There's a new face—I've got to meet
him!"), we're not immune to AIDS up here. Two of my very
closest and dearest friends have died of AIDS. One of them was
Jack. In at least one respect my life here is similar to my gay
brothers in the urban centers.

I love my partner, my home, the large family I have here, and
the life I'm making for myself. As long as I can spend some time
each year in the city, I don't need to move back. I find it easier to
live in the country and visit the city, rather than living in the city
and visiting the country.

If you're thinking of moving to the country consider these questions:

Is there a job there? If Aroostook is any indication, rural areas tend to be economically depressed. Check out the communities in the region. If there's a small town of appreciable size (15,000) there's probably work to be found, maybe not in your field, but there's a job if you're willing to do it. Check your public library for the community's phonebook and see what the yellow pages has listed. It will give you some idea of the opportunities. Write to the local chamber of commerce, too. If you can be self-employed, that might be the best route to follow.

Is your personality such that "lack of anonymity" is not a factor?

Self-reliance is important. Country people tend to do for themselves, whether it's handywork around the house or making one's own entertainment. If your spare time is now spent at films, performances, window shopping and the like, you won't find much of that in the country. Oh, that's not to say there's no "culture"; it's like the towns—few and far between. Often you must create your own leisure time activities.

Are you moving to the country alone or with others? It will be easier with a friend or a partner, but it's not impossible to do on your own.

What's important to you? Is what you currently feel to be essential to your "lifestyle" *really* that high on your list of needs? Is it worth it to give up some of what you enjoy now for the pleasures offered by rural living?

Finally, is there any gay support in the area? If you're moving from a place with gay bars, bowling leagues, religious groups, hiking clubs and the like, you won't find all those resources in the boonies. Chances are there's *something*. Check the *Gayellow Pages*.

Since Stonewall, the gay communities in major urban centers have grown in strength and numbers. It's an easy and comfortable life there. A natural extension of "the good gay life" is to create a comfortable *rural* gay life. Gay men who have fled small town America for the glitter and support of the city should consider returning to the country. There are countless gay men who have never left the small towns as well as those of us city folk who've chosen to join them. We've brought some of the glitter and chintz of the city with us, and country living adds an extra special dimension to our lives. Our growing numbers show that gay men *can* and *do* live everywhere.

Living the Gay Life in a Resort Community

by Rondo Mieczkowski

IF PROVINCETOWN IS ANYTHING IT'S BEAUTIFUL. SITUATED at the tip of Cape Cod, Provincetown is surrounded by constantly shifting sand dunes and beaches. Everyday the tides rise and fall, changing the picture-postcard vistas. The light is reflected off the sand and surrounding ocean and bay, bathing the town in an otherworldly glow. Provincetown looks magical, and this magic has for many years attracted tourists, various artists, and gay people. On a year-round basis all of us live together in a town that's three miles long and only two blocks wide.

Often gay men believe we can only live in a large urban setting, where we can share the joys and comforts of organized gay communities. Some of us, however, long to leave the big city and find a smaller place where the pace of daily life isn't so hectic, yet the prospect of the middle of Nebraska isn't appealing either. We assume the pressures there would force us right back into the closet.

There is an alternative. Openly gay men are living productive lives in small towns across the country and many of them are resorts.

Provincetown is one of them. Others include Ogunquit, Maine; New Hope, Pennsylvania; Key West; Saugatuck, on the eastern shore of Lake Michigan; the Russian River and Laguna Beach, in California, and Lahaina on the island of Maui. These are places where a gay person can live life with a degree of freedom most of us can't imagine in Smalltown, U.S.A.

What is it like living in a resort community? Why do gay men choose to live in these places? I'm currently in my fifth year of living in Provincetown. One of the things I like best is its small-town atmosphere. If you want to talk to a friend the easiest way is to sit out on the benches in front of Town Hall (affectionately referred to as "The Meatrack"). While you're sitting there you can chew the fat with your neighbor on the bench—gay or straight, resident or tourist. This is the place where you'll hear the latest news along with a healthy dose of gossip.

Living in a small town helps me examine my life and take responsibility for my actions. When I lived in larger urban areas it was too easy to lose myself in those concrete canyons or avoid someone or something unpleasant. But in Provincetown, with one main street and most people getting around on foot or bicycle, it's not so easy. Relationships are ongoing and you have to make decisions about them. It's impossible to hide from your life—past, present or future. But beware! The residents know what you're doing, sometimes even before you do! Tongues will wag—the inevitable feature of smalltown life. While the peak population on a summer weekend may be 40,000, in the heart of the winter we're a small town of 3500.

Gay people are everywhere in Provincetown. We're integrated into every aspect of society. We serve you food, write you speeding tickets, sell you nail polish, babysit your children, remodel your home, harvest shellfish, serve on boards of directors, regulate zoning policies, sweep streets, write for local newspapers. And some of us still have the energy to go out dancing in the local gay bars. There is no geographical "gay ghetto" in town. We live in apartments, flats, cottages, houses, condos, rooms, boats, dune shacks, on the water, in the woods, in the middle of the action and as far away from it as we can get. Alone, with lovers, with ex-lovers, or with too many roommates, we find a place to live wherever we can afford.

One advantage of the lack of ghettoization is that gay men are exposed to many other kinds of people. I've made more friends with gay women than anyplace else I've lived. The Portuguese community, involved in the local fishing industry, makes Provincetown special, adding spice among the somewhat dour New Englanders; many of the Portuguese ladies in town function as surrogate mothers to the gay men, watching out for us and sharing in our fun and heartbreak.

The artists of Provincetown also make it a special place. It seems every other person who lives here paints, writes, sculpts, dances or is involved with local theater productions. You can stop by a friend's house for a cup of coffee and see his latest masterpiece. And artists serve to inspire the local gay community. When you're around people who are creating what they want, what they have to, it inspires you to be the person you want to be.

The natural beauty of Provincetown helps keep me going when I need encouragement, especially when I work as a waiter each year from April till October. Since this is a resort town, many of us are forced to make a year's wages in six months. During the summer season a sixty-five-hour work week is not unusual and an eighty-hour work week is by no means unheard of. But half a year of demanding work means another half year of little or no work, and that's the point—to have a chunk of time to call one's own. Whether one has a novel to write, crafts to make, artwork to labor over, or just wants to spend time with friends, the "off-season" gives you time—and plenty of it.

In Provincetown there is a supportive atmosphere. If you want to try something, go for it! People will support you. There are many avenues of expression open to you, and no one will look at you funny because you're gay and not hiding it.

Are you interested in politics and community action? There are few things more exciting than small town politics, and the annual Provincetown Town Meeting, which can last up to two weeks at five nights a week, is the best show in town. One can stand up in front of fellow townspeople and speak out on any issue. One can make a big difference in the life of the town as an individual, serving on town committees and boards. One can create policy, and not have to be a big-shot politician to do it.

Do you like to dabble in the arts? Classes are offered year-round, taught by some of the best regional and national artists, gay and straight, who live here. The local Provincetown Art Association & Museum sponsors open shows during the winter open to anyone wishing to exhibit their artwork. Last winter I showed a "primitive" painting of mine (a tree and sun and three stick figures), next to work by other artists whose paintings hang in major museums.

One can have a radio show on WOMR-FM, our community radio station which includes gay programming in their format, or appear in a theater production by any of the numerous theater groups in town. Have you always wanted to run a shop or guesthouse? The members of the Provincetown Business Guild, which promotes gay tourism in Provincetown, will lend you support and camaraderie.

There's no need to remain in the closet in Provincetown. The energy that was previously used to build walls of self-protection can be used to create whatever kind of life you want.

But make no mistake about it. There is homophobia in Provincetown—harassment, physical violence, discrimination. But there is also support and concerted action against homophobia—from gay people and straight people, concerned citizens who want to keep Provincetown a "live and let live" town.

There are other dangers of living in a gay resort year-round. When living amidst such freedom, some go overboard. That's one reason Alcoholics Anonymous has meetings every day, sometimes twice a day in town. Part of this comes from the crazy partypartyparty atmosphere in the summer contrasted with the loneliness that some feel in the winter. You see the same faces and boarded-up shops day after day. The winter can be lonely, especially in January and February, if you don't have someone warm to snuggle next to. But you can get out and mingle with friends and meet people if you don't isolate yourself. Winter is special in Provincetown for potluck parties and reading groups.

During the winter there are readings, aerobics, a gym, classes, art openings and community movies. The public library is open five days a week. Many organizations in town need volunteers and welcome gay men.

In Provincetown you always know that you're amidst nature. I've picked cranberries in the dunes within earshot of highway traffic, then gone down to the harbor to gather mussels for dinner. I've sloshed through a quaking bog in search of carnivorous plants and orchids found nowhere else in New England. Every winter seals migrate from the north and play on rafts in Provincetown harbor. A few years ago a killer whale called our harbor home for a few weeks. One can collect herbs in the forests and harvest rose hips from plants rumored to have been imported from China a century ago. And in the ten-minute walk downtown from my home I've seen the ocean change from a hard silver to a gorgeous palette of blues, purples and greens. Every day in Provincetown I see something more, something special that takes my breath away. And a part of me connects. Clicks. And I feel very lucky to be who I am, where I am.

Living Alone and Loving It

by John E. Jones, Jr.

SO WHAT IF YOU AREN'T EVEN LOOKING FOR MR. RIGHT? Dinner for one is most enjoyable to you and you never feel like a fifth wheel or a third—but platonic—member in a fourposter.

Being single in a society of couples shouldn't be considered an obstacle, but a stepping stone; maybe even a blessing rather than a curse.

Living alone and loving it says that you enjoy yourself. There are advantages to living alone that often surpass those of being half of a couple.

For instance:

You can squeeze the toothpaste in the middle or start at the end of the tube and no one will bitch. You can even do both to the same tube.

Dinner—if there is one—is enjoyed at the time of day when you're hungry and not at his appointed time.

There's no one to fight with over which television program to watch—or even if the television is to be turned on at all.

You can be Felix Unger one night and Oscar Madison the next day. It all depends on whether you want to pick up or step over.

There's no one to say, "Not tonight, dear, I have a headache."

You can order a small pizza with only pepperoni and plenty of onions if you want.

You can go to the theater on Saturday matinees. You'll probably get a better seat if you only want one ticket.

You can smoke as much as you want or not have ashtrays in the house at all.

You can arrive at and leave parties when you damn well feel like it—if you damn well feel like going in the first place.

To starch or not to starch is never a problem.

You can have someone stay for breakfast whenever you choose.

An unplanned trip to Cleveland, Atlanta or New York can happen at your whim. It's hard to have corresponding whims.

Flowers in a home, apartment or on the dinner table are acceptable even if there's only one person in the house. You can send yourself flowers.

Living alone doesn't mean you have no one with whom to share the sad times and the best of times. You can still have someone who's more than a friend and less than a lover to hold you when you hurt and are in pain and tell you that he likes you—likes you a lot. It was once said to me, "There are worse things in life than not having a lover." Think of the destructive relationships you know.

There's only one set of parents to visit on a holiday. Kind of a relief, isn't it?

You'll always have a spare bedroom when folks come in town for a conference and need a cheap place to stay. Living alone allows for new and interesting experiences.

You'll have plenty of time to read and stay in bed as long as you want or get up as early as you like on Saturday mornings.

Living alone doesn't mean you can't or shouldn't have a Christmas tree if you want one. And you don't have to put it up on Thanksgiving day if you want to celebrate the Twelve Days of Christmas. Best of all, there'll be no one to object if you want to "Bah, humbug" the whole thing.

Nowhere is it said that he who lives alone cannot have a lover. There are perfectly logical and rational reasons for lovers to maintain separate residences. The reasons may be professional and they may be personal.

Don't feel sorry for the person who lives alone and loves it. Remember, one-half of a couple may be totally miserable.

The person who lives alone and loves it has made a choice. He knows what he wants and he's got it.

Dinner for one can be an enjoyable adventure. Don't be afraid of it. Don't be ashamed of it.

Live alone and love it.

Living With a Lover
or
How to Stay Together Without Killing Each Other

by Bryan Monte

CONGRATULATIONS! YOU'VE MET SOMEONE WHOM YOU find compatible as a lover and you're interested in moving in together. Great! You should be glad to know that you're about to become one of the more than two million households in the U.S. run by two people who aren't related by blood. You should also congratulate yourselves on having overcome a great deal of negative social conditioning designed to discourage same-sex households. *Amor omnia vincit!* Although a gay household is not a new creation—ask anyone at New York's SAGE project, which provides support and encouragement for some couples who've been together more than forty years—information on how to run a gay household is rare. What follows are some suggestions on how to enrich your new domestic life and stay together by overcoming the more common emotional, financial and legal hurdles that gay couples encounter.

FINDING A PLACE, OR WHAT TO DO ABOUT THE LANDLORD

The best way to find an apartment congenial for you and your lover is to look for one *together*. This is beneficial for two reasons. It will allow you and your lover to compare notes simultaneously, and it will forestall any future problems that may come up with your landlord if he or she has to acknowledge from the first day that two men over twenty-five want to share an apartment. If the landlord appears to be straight and isn't the least bit suspicious why two thirty-year-old professionals want to share a one-bedroom apartment—then you're home free. If you'll be sharing a two-bedroom apartment, your landlord will probably assume you're straight unless you decide to declare otherwise.

SHARING THE FINANCIAL RESPONSIBILITY

In obtaining a lease for an apartment, insist that both your names are on the lease, so that from the start you contractually share the financial responsibility of living together. A lease with both names on it also protects both roommates from being evicted or locked out of the apartment without due process. Splitting the utilities is also a good idea. For example, one person should have the telephone in his name while the other has the gas and electric. Some couples also fill out separate inventories of their individual belongings, such as furniture, TV sets, books, etc., which they then have notarized. This prevents your lover's relatives or creditors from seizing your property due to his death or sudden departure from town.

MEETING THE NEIGHBORS

Before you decide to move into a new apartment, try to get a sense of who your new neighbors will be. Do you notice any other gay couples? Do your prospective neighbors keep to themselves or stop to talk to each other in the hall? Are your prospective neighbors noisy or quiet? Visiting an apartment at dinnertime will give you a good idea how loud your prospective neighbors are and how they interact with each other. Ask your landlord who your new neighbors will be and how long they've lived in the building. If the building is in good condition, the tenants tend to stay for years at a time. Your landlord will probably also know the occupations of his tenants, so you may know in advance if you have professional interests in common with your neighbors.

How you choose to introduce yourselves to your new neighbors is up to you. You may wish to greet them in the hall as you run into them. You may prefer to knock on their doors and introduce yourselves or throw a housewarming party and invite them. Do whatever you feel comfortable doing whether it is to introduce yourselves separately or as a couple.

GIVING EACH OTHER "SPACE"

Keep in mind that no matter how deep your love and respect for one another, there will be times when due to the pressures of modern living you'll temporarily view each other as *the enemy*, and therefore need to retire to neutral corners. Men are very territorial animals and need their own space to stay mentally healthy.

Two-bedroom apartments will solve a multitude of emotional and logistical problems. If both lovers happen to be busy professionals who sometimes bring work home, both of you will need your own desk in a quiet room. Two bedrooms are also convenient if you tend to have out-of-town guests who drop in frequently. If you are only able to afford a one-bedroom, try to designate a portion of a common room for the exclusive use of one roommate. You can cordon off this area with a room divider or arrange the furniture away from this area. One roommate may want to claim the kitchen table as his workspace if, for example, the bedroom is at the other end of the apartment. This situation, however, requires a tremendous amount of cooperation, caring and scheduling.

REGULATING THE HEAT AND THE AIR CONDITIONER

Unless your apartment is equipped with separate thermostatic controls for each room, you'll have to come to an agreement with your lover as to how to heat and cool your home. This can cause great problems for a couple if one lover likes to dress like an extra from *Buster Goes to Laguna* while the other wears multiple sweaters as a sexual fetish. Usually moderation in heating and cooling an apartment (which means keeping the thermostat somewhere between 65° and 72°) will keep both lovers happy. Once again, two bedrooms may be a godsend for a couple if one roommate can't sleep without the air-conditioner on while the other "simply freezes." Lovers should sit down and discuss their heating and cooling needs without being miserly or extravagant—and they should always keep in mind their lover's comfort.

COOKING AND CLEANING SCHEDULES

A dirty bathtub or a sink full of dishes as probably caused the breakup of more relationships than most people would care to admit. That's why it's important that *from the first day of living together* lovers set up a cooperative and an equitable cooking and cleaning schedule. You can choose either to cook your meals separately or together. Cooking separately allows very busy professionals the freedom of cooking what they want, when they want it. If one lover tends to work late fairly often it doesn't make sense to always cook dinner for him. If you do cook separately, then you're responsible for washing your own dishes.

Cooking cooperatively requires a great deal of planning and patience which can be rewarded by the joy of sharing a meal in your lover's company. The first week you move in together it's good to sit down and talk about what you can or can't cook or what you will or won't eat. You may even prefer washing the dishes every night to cooking, period! Get a large calendar for the kitchen on which you can plan in advance who's cooking on a particular night, and maybe even what you'll eat. You can decide whether you want to alternate cooking with washing the dishes, or switch both chores every other night. Some lovers may choose to cook or wash dishes for an entire week. Whatever schedule you decide upon, it's important to keep it simple so that both of you can remember it without having to consult the *I Ching.*

If two lovers have significant dietary differences—i.e., one is a vegetarian and the other a carnivore—this doesn't mean you can't share meals together. The meat eater may decide to eat an entirely vegetarian meal every now and then or share some of the vegetables or fruits that his lover prepares every night. The vegetarian may also cook certain types of seafood as a main course. The important thing, once again, is to discuss in advance what you will or won't eat and then respect each other's choices by sticking to the meals you plan.

Housecleaning schedules can be constructed and alternated by dividing the apartment into different areas. Cleaning the bathroom can be combined with vacuuming and dusting the living and dining room, while cleaning the kitchen can be combined with emptying the garbage for a week. Lovers are responsible for cleaning their own rooms. The longer you live together the more you'll discover who likes to do what, but for the time being it's good to stick to the schedule.

SHARING THE PHONE AND THE TV

If one or both lovers were living alone prior to moving in together, they may have some difficulty sharing the two most heavily-used appliances in the home—the phone and the TV. If you're in the habit of talking on the phone for two hours every evening, this may upset or alienate the lover who uses the phone infrequently or is worried about missing an important call. He may feel shut out psychologically if he always arrives home from work to find you on the phone or if your dinner conversation is interrupted by phone calls.

If one or both lovers feel in conflict concerning phone use, you should sit down and discuss plans for sharing the phone equitably. Maybe you should consider ordering call waiting. If one lover is upset by phone calls during dinner, then friends should call afterwards. If one roommate makes an unusually large number of business or personal calls at home, maybe he should consider having a second line installed.

If your lover watches TV infrequently while you become a zombie in front of the tube, he may feel shut out psychologically by your inattention. Furthermore, if you own only one TV set you'll have to plan in advance which programs to watch or get a VCR. The lover who watches a great deal of television should do so out of earshot to allow the other to work or relax as he pleases. Once again, one lover may prefer that TV not be on during dinner. TV should be used for entertainment, not as a weapon to block out or isolate one's lover.

ENTERTAINING GUESTS—BRINGING TRICKS HOME

With two men sharing an apartment there are bound to be some conflicts in social calendars and sexual desires. If you're moving into an apartment as a new couple it's good to discuss in advance whether you'll be having an open or closed relationship. In a closed relationship both lovers are monogamous—they only have sex with each other. In an open relationship one or both lovers may have sex with a casual or a regular partner outside of the couple. Usually if a couple decides that they want an open relationship, they also decide whether or not they're going to tell each other when they've had sex with someone else. Telling one another has its advantages, especially during the AIDS crisis. It allows your lover to decide whether he wants to risk indirect exposure to your sexual partners. On the other hand, not telling a lover about a casual or a limited love affair may also avoid a great deal of unwarranted jealousy or emotional tension. Neither an open nor closed relationship is always best for two lovers. Talking this issue out ahead of time, though, and deciding upon the nature of your relationship, may keep you together longer.

Remember, if you are sharing an apartment your roommate may feel obligated to entertain if you bring home friends unless you tell him otherwise. If you're planning to entertain in advance, talk this over with your roommate to make sure it doesn't conflict with his schedule. Keep in mind important appointments your lover may have the next day, such as a presentation at work or an examination at school. By scheduling visits in advance, you and your lover will have the time to prepare and "put on a happy face."

Bringing guests home for sex is usually not advisable, even in a very open relationship. No matter how passionately two lovers pledge undying fidelity to one another, the unexpected presence of a third attractive body usually provides enough tinder to set off an emotional firestorm that makes the burning of Troy look like a quiet marshmallow roast. Even in the most open relationships it's best to do tricking outside of the house. A lover's philosophical decision not to become jealous may be out of sync with his feelings. One way that couples may trick without jealousy is if they do it together. Keep in mind, however, that this may cause problems once your lover sees how well you connect with that blonde Adonis from the gym. If you feel the need to trick regularly, however, you should reexamine your commitment to one another to make sure it's still mutually valid.

VISITS FROM PARENTS

A friend once said that parents are just like children to new couples—they're always testing their limits! The same people who seem perfectly normal before they arrive somehow manage to become transformed into twin turbos of terror, wreaking havoc with every comment and raised eyebrow. Parents may wrongly surmise you've invited them over for their approval, that they have the right to criticize or ridicule your apartment, its furnishings, how you're dressed and even your lover—in his presence! For these reasons it's good to discuss ground rules with your parents before they come over for a first visit—including what they can or can't discuss. It's also a good rule not to invite parents over for a visit until you've been together at least six months and have developed a sense of stability and autonomy. Many relationships have been wrecked by a parental visit.

A first visit should be short, probably no more than an hour or two. Your lover may or may not elect to be present, which is his right since they aren't his parents. Two against two, however, has always been better odds than two against one, so if there's any way you can talk your lover into it, do so. Offer to take out the garbage for a month! You and your lover should also decide upon a non-verbal signal, such as tugging on your left earlobe or pointing to your nose, so that if your parents become too obnoxious you'll be able to whisk them out the door together before they can say: "There's no place like home!"

A COUPLE'S BEHAVIOR

Couples should maintain a semblance of calm decorum when out in the public eye. Arguing in public about intimate details is to be discouraged for two reasons: one, visible gay couples are rare role models and should strive to present the best possible impression. Two, due to societal prejudices that argue to be gay is sick or bad (which become institutionalized in the form of no health benefits for gay spouses or anniversary presents from relatives), it's important not to provide them with extra ammunition. *Staying together as a gay couple is very difficult and it's crucial that you be gentle, kind and forgiving to one another.*

If couples find themselves arguing a lot, it's not advisable to break up immediately or separate. What a couple might do is go to a counselor to see if they can work out their problems. Living together is not automatically heaven. Everyone argues. It's a way of working out aggression and frustration, and occasionally removing roadblocks in a relationship.

Living With an Avowed Heterosexual

by Mark A. Perigard

I MET JOSH IN THE FIRST CLASS OF MY FRESHMAN YEAR AT Boston University. We became fast and good friends, though I was still deep in the closet. I realized I would have to come out to Josh when, at our first joint celebration of Chanukah and Christmas, he gave me a gift-wrapped condom and advised me to "go for it." When I finally told him I was gay, months later, he paused thoughtfully and simply asked, "How do you feel about blind dates? There's this guy I know, and I think you two would be great together."

His unflinching support cemented our friendship, and we took an apartment in our junior year of college. Now quasi-professional people ("aspiring yuppies" we tell each other), we've been together for years. A devotee of beauty pageants and women's mud-wrestling, Josh is hopelessly heterosexual and makes no apologies for his orientation. Based on my experiences, I offer some pointers to gay men on surviving and thriving with an Avowed Heterosexual roommate.

ASK YOURSELF A FEW QUESTIONS

The decision to move in with an Avowed Heterosexual shouldn't be an onerous one. Is he someone with whom you can be completely open? Will he be comfortable around your gay friends? Will you be comfortable around his straight friends? Will you mind waking up and sharing the bathroom with his girlfriend? Will he have a problem eating breakfast with your boyfriend? Are the two of you compatible as housemates? Is he a neat freak who panics at the sight of a mote of dust? Are you a slob who couldn't pick up a dirty jockstrap if your life depended on it?

Find a housemate you're compatible with as a friend, and not as a potential lover. Avoid moving in with someone you're romantically interested in. (Be honest, there are one or two straight men who are physically attractive.) You'll only be letting yourself in for endless frustration. Psychiatrists tell us that Avowed Heterosexuals are notoriously difficult to seduce away from their chosen lifestyle. It seems this sexual orientation is determined early in life . . . . Some say boys as young as three years old may already be on a fixed path to a life of heterosexuality.

BRACE YOURSELF FOR ALL SORTS OF QUESTIONS

Your roommate may be very curious about your lifestyle. There are the inevitable questions about sex. He probably means no harm, even if the questions seem somewhat intrusive or come out muddled. One morning after I'd patiently explained to Josh what I knew about the fascination of S&M and leather for some gay men, he asked, obviously discomforted, "Well, then, what about fist-fucking? How can people do that?" I nearly choked on my Wheaties. One doesn't have to be an expert on everything.

Josh went through an intense period of AIDS-anxiety, constantly concerned about my health and the people with whom I was coming in contact. I didn't help his peace of mind by working at the time at a health center serving the gay community. "Now if you meet any people with AIDS," he pleaded, "you won't shake their hands, will you?" Bear in mind that Avowed Heterosexuals can and often need to be educated.

BE PREPARED TO DO SOME LEARNING ABOUT THE HETEROSEXUAL LIFESTYLE

I came home from a date one evening eager to chat about the handsome man I'd had dinner with. I rapped on Josh's bedroom door, and there was a muffled noise which I naively interpreted as an invitation to enter.

I opened the door and found Josh and his then-girlfriend, Lisa, lying in bed.

"Josh, this guy was incredible," I blurted out. "We had such a great dinner together and afterward we took a walk down Boylston Street down to the Boston Common, and—" sniffing, I asked suddenly, "Josh, what's that smell?"

Josh smiled at me sheepishly.

Grimacing, I continued, "Can't you smell it? It's all over the place. It smells—hey, it smells like tuna fish."

Josh giggled, and Lisa slid lower into the covers.

"Where's it coming from?" I demanded, stepping around his desk, his bookcase and the pile of dirty clothes on the floor. "It smells like fish, like a big tuna sandwich," I chattered. "Josh, you're a vegetarian, what would you be doing with tuna fish in your bedroom?" Josh started to convulse with laughter as Lisa threw the covers over her head.

The next day Josh provided me with some invaluable information about the nature of heterosexual relations. I also learned not to knock on his door after 11 on weekend nights.

THERE ARE SOME THINGS YOU SHOULD NOT DO WITH AN AVOWED HETEROSEXUAL

We traipsed out merrily one night in pursuit of potential partners. I was shocked by what I perceived was his derogatory attitude toward women ("Oooh, she's wearing an FM blouse," he whispered. "What's an FM blouse?" I asked, bewildered. "A fuck-me blouse," he answered), and he was amused to learn that men can react to one another on blatantly sexual terms. ("Mmm, I'd really like to get into that guy's pants," I said. "C'mon, you really don't think like that, do you?")

We spent the rest of the evening bickering about the kind of club to go to. It was a squabble out of a bad Abbott and Costello movie. "But you don't mind dancing with girls," he coaxed. "Yeah, but look at it this way—at least in a gay bar you can dance with me," I argued, figuring my logic was irrefutable. We finally just went home and we've never cruised together since.

DECIDE WHO WILL DO THE WINDOWS

You still have the same issues of living together that any two people have sharing a home. You have to decide who'll take out the trash, who'll vacuum, how you'll divvy up the cooking. There isn't any one perfect way to run a household, so be willing to negotiate.

DON'T TOLERATE RUDENESS

You may not get much support from some of your gay friends. They may be puzzled by your decision to move in with a straight guy, a "member of the oppressor class" as one separatist said accusingly. But just as you'd expect your roommate to treat your friends with respect, your friends should be expected to be at the very least civil to your roommate. If they can't understand that this is an important person in your life, then they're not very good friends.

AVOWED HETEROSEXUALS HAVE THEIR VIRTUES

My roommate helped me overcome my fear of broccoli and taught me how to make quiche. (!) He's also been one of the most supportive people in my life. Whenever I begin to complain that Mr. Right probably went and died in 1947, he perks me up and urges me right back into the dating fray.

Our living arrangement has enriched more people than simply the two of us. Josh feels quite comfortable now being an advocate for gay rights anywhere—in the workplace, within his own family and within his own circle of friends. As editor of a suburban newspaper in western Massachusetts, he's used his clout to make sure that gay people are treated fairly, and that news affecting the gay community is not ignored. His friends have learned that gay people are just like everyone else, and his family appreciates the degree of happiness and stability our living situation has provided.

IF THE LIVING SITUATION SOURS, END IT

You shouldn't be living together just to make a political statement, or to prove you're so butch you can share space with a heterosexual man. If you're not getting the support you need, end the living arrangement. You may be the best of friends yet incompatible as roommates; don't feel bad if it doesn't work out. And always remember, don't judge an entire class of people by one difficult straight man.

III

LOVE

How to Find a Husband

by Craig G. Harris

IT WAS A YEAR AGO ON A CRISP, CLEAR NOVEMBER AFTER-noon that I sprinkled rice on yet another newlywed couple. For me attending weddings has become a sort of pastime, if not a hobby, but until that autumn day I was under the impression that all marriage ceremonies looked pretty much alike. My opinion drastically changed when the grooms, Phillip and Freddie, exchanged vows and kissed at the altar of the Metropolitan Community Church in Greenwich Village.

Whether or not the other guests and I approved of this blatant imitation of a heterosexual ritual—in a church setting, no less—we had to admit the men looked handsome in their contrasting tuxedos as they taxied off to a tasteful champagne reception at their Brooklyn home.

By my third glass of champagne I'd begun to like the idea of gay men getting "married." After all, straight people shouldn't have a monopoly on Bloomingdale's bridal registry. I'd love to have a few place settings of Fitz & Floyd china on my breakfront. Why shouldn't gay men have the option of making a public declaration of commitment? Granted, it isn't something that we're all looking for, but on the other hand if you do have a hankering to be formally bonded, don't be ashamed. Go for it! Chart out a game plan, find that man of your dreams and claim him.

WHEN IS IT TIME TO SETTLE DOWN?

Cooling out and settling down are very different concepts. If you're a gay man and have any exposure to the media, you may have some concerns about becoming a member of an endangered species. If you're sexually active, you might want to cool out. That means cutting down the number of your sexual partners and practicing safe sex guidelines. It doesn't necessarily mean this is the time to find that one special man and flee into a monogamous relationship. Fear of ill health is no reason to get married.

Likewise, the fact that you've hung up your dancing shoes and packed your Patti LaBelle albums in the closet doesn't necessarily indicate that you're ready to settle down. It just means that you've yet to learn how to breakdance and don't want to expose that extra fifteen pounds you've recently gained to a cadre of discomaniacs who'll laugh in your face. You're just cooling out.

You're not ready to settle down until you're willing to spend your days living and loving in a genuine partnership. The act of coupling demands the maturity that allows you to discuss, plan, compromise and set the barriers on your relationship. When you're ready to settle down you're ready to be accountable to another individual, not because you have to, or because it's the "right" thing to do, but because you want to.

Some people never get the urge to settle down and it means nothing more than that. It doesn't necessarily indicate a lack of maturity or a Peter Pan complex. Open relationships and serial monogamy require a lot of effort and hard work. It boils down to a matter of choice and what lifestyle suits your needs best.

HOW TO ANALYZE YOUR NEEDS

Now that you realize that mere boredom is not sufficient reason to go on a manhunt, you'll want to take some time to seriously consider your needs. It may sound juvenile, but the best way to do this is to take a pen and sheet of paper and list in three columns: 1) the things you want from a relationship; 2) the things you can offer a partner; and 3) the aspects of your personality that might cause a lover to hide a small bottle of arsenic. Don't cheat. You don't have to share your findings with anyone.

Take a careful look at your list. In the first column you may find that many of the things you're looking for from a romantic relationship, you can easily acquire from other interpersonal relationships—friends, for instance. Maybe you need to develop a plan to nurture friendships. You may have included the benefits that you think accompany a domestic partnership. Be aware that these benefits are primarily emotional. While sharing an apartment with a lover will cut some costs, same-sex marriages aren't legally recognized, and when it comes to spousal benefits (anything from a family plan at the local Y to insurance packages) you'll lose out. If you've written that your needs include sharing your accomplishments and defeats with a special person whom you can come home to, comfort and be comforted by, you're probably on the right track.

Go to the second column. What is it that you can offer a partner? Money? A seaside condo? Travel? If these were foremost on your list, you're in trouble. Goodtime Charleys are a dime a dozen, so don't flatter yourself. These are the things sensible men look for from a trick. If you're looking for a relationship, it isn't a good sign to list such material items among your assets. Personal qualities that indicate an ability and willingness to offer emotional support, cooperate in a partnership, and give of oneself are what's needed here.

Onward to the third column. At some point in your life you've probably shared your living space with siblings or roommates. In those situations most people are acutely aware of the traits of others which drive them up the wall, but this is a two-sided coin. If one of your favorite pastimes is watching late-night Mary Tyler Moore reruns while eating crackers in bed, you have to understand that not every man is willing to accept Mary's early morning effervescence or bring a Dust Buster to bed. The fact that you have a fetish for seasoning your dishes with cumin, curry, or garlic and force-feeding your guests may also present a problem. Making the transition from a single lifestyle to that of a married man is not easy. If you find the man worth doing it for, you'll find a way to make concessions.

WHERE TO LOOK

Now you know what you're looking for. If you're looking for a similar eligible bachelor, I'll supply you with a few tips. If what you're actually looking for is a compatible trick or a sugar daddy, stop reading. There are tons of good places to look for a husband. One friend of mine spends his lunch hours sipping tea in the Plaza Hotel's Palm Court in New York in the hopes that some mildly attractive, very rich man will take note. To date none have, but he's still hopeful. Another friend gave up on prospects in New York and moved to Washington, D.C. (where there seem to be fewer straight men than native Washingtonians). Granted, he and his husband now share a condo with a view overlooking the Potomac. His game plan wasn't as outrageous as I thought.

I'm not suggesting that relocation is the solution (though I might not feel that way if I were in Snowville, Utah). Chances are there are eligible gay men wherever you are. In some cities they're easier to find. But if you're not in a large urban center, don't give up hope. There are pockets of us all over the world. Consult the *Gayellow Pages* directory and find out where gay men gather in your area.

Local gay publications supply listings of establishments and events which will also be helpful. These may even tell you what types of men you can expect to meet. For instance, there are listings of special interest clubs for chubby men, pretty men, political men, apolitical men, iron-pumping men, men who are into drag, butch men, femme men, literary men, ethnic men, ethnic men who don't want to be ethnic men, men who are into S&M, B&D, M&Ms, etc. The possibilities are endless. Once you've decided the kind of man you're looking for, you can readily find out where he'll be.

While you're looking, do some of the things you enjoy doing. If you're athletic go to the gym a few times a week. More than a few couples met over the nautilus machine. Besides, even if you don't find Mr. Right, the runners-up will certainly be worth a second look. If you're a runner, or play tennis or basketball, or any other sport, don't just socialize with the old gang, get out and meet new people. Keep your eyes open, there may be a potential husband on the team.

Odd as it may seem, places of worship are also a spot where many men have met and fallen in love. The Universal Fellowship of Metropolitan Community Churches has branches all over the country. The Union of American Hebrew Congregations also has gay synagogues around the country. These and groups like Dignity and Integrity even offer services for gay men and lesbians who wish to worship among themselves, as well as socials and dances where one can meet other men with spiritual interests.

Getting involved in the gay community by volunteering for an organization is one of the best ways to meet men, as long as that's not your only reason for lending a hand. Beware, you'll meet lots of politically correct types, many of whom are so dedicated to the cause of fighting for gay rights they don't take the time to enjoy themselves. Don't let this discourage you. With a bit of ingenuity you may be able to change their perspective.

Here's a list of ten novel ideas for finding a husband: 1) Spend a weekend camping at a national campground. The campsites are free and other costs are minimal, so you'll have a wonderful vacation if nothing else. 2) Do some research on gay history— imagine the men you'll meet in the stacks while you increase your knowledge. 3) Plan a fundraiser for a local gay organization, and keep your eyes open. Need I say more? 4) Get your hair styled at the most chi-chi salon in your city—if you don't meet the man of your dreams *while* you're getting your locks sheared, you'll look fabulous after you do. 5) Volunteer at your local hospital. Medical schools *do* accept gay applicants and you'll make your mother happy. 6) Dine alone at an exclusive restaurant, making sure to get a table where you're in full view. 7) Take a night school course in gay literature. 8) Ask your mother for a list of her friends with single sons. 9) Ask your father for a list of his friends that he always wondered about. 10) Spend your Saturday afternoons shopping at Saks, Neiman Marcus, Bullock's, Marshall Field, etc. Don't buy, just shop.

Friends may also be helpful to you in your quest to meet compatible men. In many cases your friends will know things you may not see in yourself. Don't be afraid to trust their judgment and meet people at their suggestion. You may luck out. You also may not.

If you don't feel like putting a great deal of energy in this hunt, you still have options. Local gay and progressive publications offer personal ads where you can specify the kind of man you'd like, and have him contact you either by phone or mail. You can even request that he send a photo with his response. Don't be surprised, however, if the photo was taken ten years ago and the accompanying letter ghost-written.

WHERE NOT TO LOOK

If you're a non-smoking vegetarian who doesn't drink, chances are you won't find the man of your dreams at the cigarette machine in a gay bar that's noted for its steak tartar. You have to use common sense. Some people employ consistently poor judgment when trying to find a boyfriend. You might be told to patronize a glitzy dance club because it's popular and the clientele is comprised of drop-dead gorgeous men. If you're a closet nerd or into quiet strolls in the country and home-cooked meals, those clubs aren't for you.

Don't look at the traditional meeting places such as bars and discos as your only option. While these are tried and true pick-up spots for many gay men, many men who are marriage material aren't hanging out there. They're probably at a benefit for AIDS research while you're spending your last two bucks on a Budweiser.

Among the places where some have actually met husbands in the past (though the likelihood admittedly is not good) are: cruising spots in public parks, bathhouses, tearooms, piers, X-rated movie theaters and book shops. Most marriageable men are spending their time in less controversial spots these days. That's not to say you won't find a husband in any of these places, just that it won't be easy.

PLAN OF ATTACK

Whether you decide to sit in the Palm Court, join Girth and Mirth (a social club for full-figured men) or move to Washington, D.C., you'll find that your plan of attack is not foolproof. You can place yourself in the right locations at the right times and no matter how hard you try, you may not achieve the desired results. At the same time you'll see your friend who just ended a five-year relationship meet the man who will change the course of his life. That's life.

Don't stop trying! The hunt is as much fun as capturing your prey, but in the long run you'll probably realize that the man you've been out there looking for—spending ridiculous amounts of money and effort—is the man that you made no effort whatsoever to meet. It could be at a bus stop on a rainy night or in the zoo, or any number of places. And before you know it, people will be sprinkling your heads with rice and wishing you the best, just like Phil and Freddie.

Sexual Arrangements
Between Lovers

by Phil Nash

YOU MET HIM AT A PARTY THREE MONTHS AGO AND YOU went to bed for the first time a week later. Since then you've ignored—or just avoided—all other "invitations." He spends two nights a week at your place, you spend weekends at his. He never has plans that interfere with your calling or just dropping by for an unannounced smooch. You even start ignoring the man at the gym that you've been trying to make for the last year, and your bar buddies have called to see if you're okay. You haven't bothered to renew your lapsed membership at the baths.

A few times (always during a mad embrace) he's said he loves you. You've sent him a few cards that essentially said the same thing. You idly check the want ads for a suitable apartment you both could move into. He's taken you shopping to buy matching plush terry robes.

He comes back from a week out of town on business—a week you felt more alone than you remember. Over dinner he tells you he got laid three nights in a row by a bartender from Albuquerque.

You don't show it—you're devastated. He needs to confess, so he gets it all out of his system by describing hair color, body type, size and range of motion. Masochist that you are, you let him. After all, there's nothing to forgive. You aren't married.

But your flaccidity later in the evening—even after a week of saving yourself for him—betrays your nonchalance. It's time to talk.

Sexuality is one of the most versatile components of our being. As mutable as a face, as telling as a voice, the very nature of sex allows us to convey the range of emotions: love and hate, tenderness and rage, indifference and curiosity, security and fear, conquering passion and sweet surrender.

Peculiarly, even social scientists have done little to extricate sex from the moral dilemmas that plague this most magical of human characteristics. Anthropologists may tell us that the potent rules that govern the use of sex resulted from certain tribal needs for propagation or inheritance. But in an enlightened culture to confine sex to procreative heterosexual monogamy is archaic.

Gay men know better. For us sex can be physical relief today, adventure tomorrow, Friday night's ritual, or an expression of profound tenderness when a beloved friend visits next month. For gays, sex can pave the way to friendship, help establish important social connections, relieve momentary loneliness, affirm love, vent contempt, or just be a way of showing off.

When gay men pair into loving companionships, it's most unlikely that either person will fully satisfy the range of emotional or social needs of his partner. Contrary to popular assumption, having a lover doesn't guarantee that one will never be lonely, bored or horny. Lovers don't always neutralize cravings for a favored fuck buddy, placate desire that erupts for a youthful hitchhiker, or stifle adventures in the streets of an unfamiliar city during an otherwise tiresome business trip.

In heterosexual marriage assumptions of fidelity are manifest. Because courtship is a sexual game with its primary objective being to find the ultimate mate, sexual exclusivity is often mandated—and even practiced. But between gay lovers there is frequently a tacit assumption of flexibility in their sexual ethics. Unfortunately, the matter is not quite so simple as declaring the relationship "open" or "closed." Sexual arrangements between lovers require a sophisticated level of diplomacy and willingness to negotiate and renegotiate from time to time. Arrangements can be as many and as varied as the people who form them. Personal introspection and honest communication about sexual needs and expectations between partners is crucial to building a foundation of trust.

A s of this writing, my lover and I have been together ten years and ten months. Our relationship has been "open" for ten years and five months. One day in the springtime of our love, we attended a gay liberation conference. Bob found himself conversing with another participant about some hot political topic, and for some reason they moved the discussion to the other guy's bed. My lover told me all about it that night. He broke the news gently, but offered no apology. I was a little bit hurt, but delighted at the same time. I'd had my eye on someone else at the conference—a student who'd just returned to town after a long study trip.

The next day I retaliated by asking a mutual friend to fix me up with the student. Bob left town for a few days, and the student and I had mediocre sex on the first night of his absence. I contracted gonorrhea and of course had to tell Bob all. Fortunately, my lover has a sense of humor. But other lovers might have found more emotional peril lurking in the situation.

Since the day our relationship "opened" quite unintentionally, our arrangements for outside sexual encounters have been more deliberately orchestrated. They have changed considerably over the years, influenced by our own changing emotional and sexual needs, levels of maturity, and environmental factors beyond our control.

Usually our experiences with outside sex have been easygoing, fun and very satisfying—independently and together. Other times they've been frustrating, emotionally draining, even destructive.

Perhaps others might profit from asking themselves some honest questions we've learned to ask ourselves when we've discussed how outside sex fits into our life together. Here are a few:

Which of my sexual and emotional needs does my lover fulfill? Security? Availability? Romance? Shared fantasy fulfillment? Release of tension? Uninhibited display of affection and gratification?

Which sexual and emotional needs are not fulfilled by my lover? Need for adventure? A desire for sex acts my lover dislikes? Earning self-esteem by attracting other men? Enjoying sexual gamesmanship? Intimate socializing with others?

Once these questions are answered, or perhaps even after they're asked, a foundation exists on which to base guidelines on how to deal with outside sex. Rules agreed upon by both prevent shattered expectations and destroyed trust. Here are some questions to consider:

Will outside sex be limited to specific times? Perhaps when

one partner is out of town? Only when the partner isn't expected at home? Would it help to plan to spend one "no questions asked" night a week (or month) apart?

Do you want to know the details of your lover's escapades? Will you divulge everything about your own to him? Would you both rather hear nothing at all about it?

Is it all right for your lover to share your bed with someone else when you aren't there? Will he mind if you bring others to your home?

Would you both benefit from occasionally picking up a partner for a three-way?

How do you feel about his having sex with your friends? With someone you also want to seduce? With someone with whom you've also had (or are having) sex? What would happen if you went to bed with his best friend? His worst enemy?

Will you agree to limit your outside sexual activities to "safe sex" to protect each other's health?

Will outside sex be limited to impersonal or one-time encounters, or will you tolerate ongoing affairs and romances on the side?

I f one uses only the rational faculties, these questions may be easily answered. But in practice lovers may learn things about themselves they never knew or suspected. Even after discussing all the issues and agreeing to abide by mutually acceptable guidelines, there will come a time like this:

For no special reason Apollonius, infused with romantic feelings, will spend all day fixing a special dinner to surprise Bruce. As he cooks he imagines serving dessert and sipping cognac in front of the fireplace, then making love until they collapse exhausted in each other's arms.

But Bruce will fail to show up at the usual hour. At bedtime he will call, only slightly relieving Apollonius's anxiety (who by now has called all the hospitals and police headquarters). Bruce will tell Apollonius that he met someone at cocktail hour who made him an offer he couldn't refuse. Whatever needs to be discussed can wait until morning, says Bruce, before hanging up.

When Bruce rolls in the next morning, cheeks pink and cheerful as a cherub, he is greeted by a weak, devastated Apollonius. Apollonius hasn't slept a wink because every time he closed his eyes he could see Bruce in the arms of someone else who, at least for that moment, was more desirable than himself.

Bruce reminds Apollonius of their agreement that allows both of them to accept a sexual opportunity if it's too good to pass up. Being reminded of the agreement is little consolation to Apollonius, who is too emotionally gutted to fight. He just cries. Apollonius is profoundly hurt and disappointed; he may also feel guilty for burdening Bruce with his emotional baggage. Or he may be plotting revenge. Or part of his heart may turn cold and never let him fully trust Bruce again.

Whatever their arrangement, this incident clearly points up its shortcomings. Bruce may have been within his rights, but he'll suffer the consequences of Apollonius's unanticipated pain. If they both try to understand what went wrong and assure that it won't happen again, they'll learn something about themselves and add new dimensions to their life together.

Lovers' agreements on how to deal with sex outside the relationship may work wonderfully for years and then stop working. During an especially insecure period when I was struggling with both my career and finances, I asked my lover to not have sex with anyone but me. Even the slightest threat to the security I placed in him was, for a short time, intolerable.

In our first five years of living together, we usually disclosed the details of our outside sexual escapades to each other. Now we rarely do.

Once, I developed a romantic attachment to a man I saw several times. I recognized that the feelings I had for him would cause me to take time away from home, so I regretfully ended the romance.

On several occasions when my lover was out of town, I had men over to spend the night. If I ever mentioned having sex with these men, I didn't bother to say where it occurred. Once, in a discussion, my lover told me that he had never asked anyone to stay the night at our house because he felt our bed was "sacred space" and wouldn't violate it by having sex there with anyone else.

AIDS has forced a complete change in our approach to outside sex. Our jobs have given us both a front row seat from which to watch the epidemic unfold, and from the moment it was clear that AIDS is sexually transmitted our arrangement began to change. Deep fear was our initial motivation to change; neither of us could face the possibility of giving the other a fatal disease. But fear gave unto a more positive assessment: couples who plan to share their entire lives must be prepared to face great sacrifices. We've begun to see ourselves maturing and growing old together. That dream is not worth risking for a momentary pleasure.

Reluctantly, we've all but stopped sexual contacts outside our relationship, and safe sex guidelines have been rigidly applied to the very few times that it has come up. Sexual fidelity was difficult at first, but it gets easier as time goes on. Our sex life together, which has always been evolving, has become richer with experimentation. Some old friends with whom I've previously enjoyed sex are still in my life. New friends with whom I might wish to spend a tender night in bed still enter my life but differently.

So for now, sexual fidelity is a phase my lover and I are going through. I feel we are fortunate to have each other's warmth and sexuality to enjoy when others face much more anxiety when they seek sex partners. We hope for a time when scientific breakthroughs and gay creativity will furnish new ways to be freely and safely sexual with other men—and gay monogamy will be a freely-chosen option and not an act of self-preservation.

In Praise of Long Distance Affairs

by John Preston

I MET STEPHEN WHILE I WAS IN HIS HOME TOWN OF PHIL-adelphia on a business trip. On the surface the encounter was ordinary for gay men. I saw him walking down Spruce Street and I followed him for a number of blocks until he entered a gay bar. It was a Monday night and there was no crowd. A few sips of beer, a few looks and we were set.

But it wasn't ordinary for me to have done that, not at that time in my life. I've lived in large cities and I'd been as sexually active as other gay men my age, but five years earlier I had moved to Maine, a place where anonymous sexuality is difficult if not impossible. The gay population in Maine is too small to allow it to happen often. Tricking had ceased being a regular part of my life. Even if the geographic change hadn't altered my sexual style, certainly the health crisis would have.

We did trick (safely) and we did it awfully well. The next morning I was struck with a sense of nostalgia. I woke in a stranger's apartment, drank coffee with him and remembered that this used to be the norm. I wondered at the time if I shouldn't leave it there—just a pleasant event. But I decided not to. I asked a simple question, "If we exchange addresses, are you likely to stay in touch?"

He looked at me for a moment and answered, "Yes, actually, I am."

I wrote, he phoned (an ongoing pattern) and we arranged to date over the next few months. At some ill-defined point we became a couple. Neither of us is comfortable with a great deal of ambiguity, however, and it wasn't long until we acknowledged that we were in the middle of a significant relationship.

That, right there, was another change for me. I wasn't consciously looking for a relationship. My last attempts hadn't been successful. My writing career didn't easily accommodate a lover, especially since I have an absolute need for solitude while I work. I was too experienced in the possible damage that could be done by unchecked infatuation. Moving cross country to be with a new passion had been romantic when I'd done it twenty years ago. It was out of the question for someone who had moved home to New England to reestablish his native roots and who was staring his fortieth birthday in the eye.

N eeds have to be complementary for any relationship to work. Stephen's dovetailed neatly with mine. His own career goals and carefully controlled lifestyle leave little room for a fulltime person in his home life. But it doesn't mean that he wants to live without the benefits and intimacy that a love relationship can provide.

There's often a cultural tyranny which dictates that lovers not only be monogamous, but that they share a nest. Stephen and I reject that. Most people who look at us and know us seem to find our situation romantic and daring. We actually find it extraordinarily functional. I can look at us and coolly point to a number of advantages in having a lover who lives three hundred miles away.

The most basic advantage is that I needn't look for anyone else. The hours spent in pursuing a romantic involvement of one sort or another have been recaptured. I don't have to spend a great deal of time arranging my life to adapt to another person's daily needs and routines. I am able instead to indulge my personal eccentricities and tastes in music, use of time and eating habits.

Yet there is always someone there now. Stephen and I are in constant communication. After our first months we naturally fell into regular daily phone conversations and frequent letter writing. We meet at least one weekend a month—the minimum I, at least, need to nurture our commitment. We're usually together more often than that.

Our situation has underlined for me some of the most elemental and human needs I have for a lover. I am amazed by how much difference it makes in my life to have someone to share holidays with, to brag to about triumphs and to go to when my ego's been bruised. There's a trust that I've always known comes from time spent together, but I hadn't realized that it needn't have a joint checking account and a shared lease to go with it.

The single most important benefit of our arrangement is the quality of time we do spend together. Since it's limited, we automatically strive to make it count as much as we can. We overlook the trivial and highlight the enjoyable.

We don't waste time worrying whether the other replaces the top of the toothpaste tube. We each have habits that might become irritating if we lived together. The knowledge that we're going to separate in a few days keeps those annoyances in perspective.

In order to accomplish all of this, Stephen and I have had to organize a great deal of our lives around our affair. There is some real expense involved in all this. Don't think those phone bills are any laughing matter, for one thing. There's travel expense as well. Since we always want to have our time together be something special, we've cut back on our personal expenses at home and instead save for our visits. Almost all of our discretionary income now seems to be spent on our shared time. In addition to journeys back and forth between Philadelphia and Maine, we've gone to New York City for Gay Pride, a summer weekend in Provincetown, a unique art show in Montreal and a good friend's party in Boston.

We most particularly invest great care and reap great benefits in our sex life. We save up for sex just as we save for luxuries like expensive champagne. It seems as though the anticipation of another one of our creative love-makings is more than compensation for transitory assignations.

The reality is that we have obligations which tie us to our home cities. It's true that we're also personally protective of our privacy, and our individual lifestyles aren't things either of us is anxious to alter. But ours isn't a situation that's based on a lack of ability to relate or to experience passion. Like most other people, we're trying to meet our relational needs and also continue our careers.

This isn't a uniquely gay situation. Whenever two people are involved in their work and relationships there are bound to be times when the two will be in conflict.

Recently a heterosexual couple I know well were forced to live apart for an extended period by their separate job requirements. At first it seemed an onerous task. It involved maintaining two households, frequent travel and much more time apart than they were used to in over twenty years of marriage. But after a year had passed they reported it was one of the most exciting periods in their life together.

They discovered the benefits that Stephen and I are using to build our relationship. It had been easy to settle into routines and ill-considered compromises. It's easy to forget to go out together, give one another presents, let irritants overshadow the attraction they'd felt for one another all along. Far from hurting their relationship, living apart and rediscovering how much fun they could have with one another left them in better shape than they'd been before.

While my relationship with Stephen shares many parallels with this couple's, there are ideas where being gay *does* make it different. The idea that we're still courting one another is the most distinct.

The pattern—whether it was revolutionary or culturally enforced, doesn't matter—has often been for men to meet, have sex immediately, and then figure out what relationship, if any, they want. While the rest of society was building up to sex, many gay men were starting there. We rarely figured out how to construct healthy relationships with that given dynamic.

Those straight people who are my peers will spend years dating, living together without commitment, and only after exploration might finally marry. My gay peers are often ready to start shopping for china after their second night together.

Living separately has forced Stephen and me to create a courtship. I suspect that if I felt as strongly for someone as I do for him, and that person lived in my home city of Portland, I'd unconsciously begin seeing him five or six nights a week, quickly allowing a much more involved relationship to evolve than would be healthy for me. Stephen, I suspect, would start to become defensive and withdraw if a person in Philadelphia began to assume that they'd spend that much time together. . . . We've made it past that point now.

Our relationship is not defined by distance. Our agreement includes one clause that leaves our options open: "Never say never." If we were for whatever reason to find ourselves in the same city now, we'd be infinitely more prepared to undergo the more traditional lover relationship. If as we continue to explore one another we were to decide this relationship isn't functioning, I'm sure there would be great pain in the separation. We would be dealing with the feelings in their bare bones. We wouldn't be arguing over who gets the rent-controlled apartment or the china.

I've seen other people use geographic distance as a vehicle for courtship as well. Some have done it more directly as they consciously moved towards their own personal goal of that "nested" monogamy. One friend here in Portland began a relationship with a New Yorker. It took a year before the other man finally moved to Maine. They spent almost every weekend of that period together. By the time they'd agreed that Maine would be their mutual base they were very well prepared to undertake buying a house together, sharing their finances, splitting up their resources.

The time they spent was highly romantic. They, too, indulged one another with the effort to make their weekends as valuable as possible. They've experienced the best of each other, but they also have had a chance to examine each other's weaknesses. There'll be few surprises in store for them in their future, but there'll be lots of knowledge of each other's makeup.

What are the dangers in long distance affairs? Where can there be problems? Of course they exist here as well as in any other form of relationship. I've said that Stephen and I are able to avoid the "trivial." I'm convinced that in our case, after a considerable amount of time, that's a healthy choice for us to make. But I've also seen where the avoidance of potentially annoying habits has become playacting to such an extent that the sudden appearance of a hidden character trait is really devastating. One man I knew years ago, for instance, controlled his alcoholism carefully during a couple of first dates. I wasn't around to see the way the disease so completely controlled his daily life, and when it finally did manifest itself it came as a true shock.

There's also no question that the expenses can get out of hand. Luckily Stephen's an accountant and watches over us like an eagle. But I could easily imagine the ways in which the travel and phone bills could become unmanageable.

I know that it took me quite a while to really learn that

Stephen is utterly trustworthy. Those people who have difficulty *trusting* another person are going to go through personal hell spending their time apart. If someone has difficulty believing that his nearby boyfriend isn't going to the bars or tricking on the side, just imagine what paranoid delights that person could entertain about another who lives hundreds of miles away!

The major choice about having a relationship of any sort is to *decide* that it will work. You also have to be willing to stand by that decision in the face of people who don't believe it. We can be a shockingly unsupportive community when it comes to relationships. "Your lover lives in Philadelphia? . . . Well, that doesn't count, let's give it a try."

The goal of a relationship isn't necessarily nested monogamy. There are other creative forms gay men can explore. I know of two men who maintain separate residences during the week then share a common one, their "real" home, on weekends and vacations. Others have discovered that actually living together was something they didn't enjoy, and opted instead for separate apartments in the same building.

There are moments in my own relationship with Stephen that are less than perfect; of course there are. I can become very lonely, I often wish for more sexual contact, and there are times when the phone just doesn't seem to be enough. But there are more benefits. They are wonderfully satisfying to me. If this situation goes on for years, fine. If it alters then we'll have to see what we can do with our choices. The longer we go on, the more options there seem to be. And we have yet to change our one rule: "Never say never."

The Care and Feeding of a Friendship Network

by Joseph R. De Marco

I WAS ALONE WHEN THE CALL CAME. PATRICK'S VOICE WAS its usual tinny self.

"I just called to tell you about a decision I've made . . ."

After fourteen years of enduring Patrick's stewing for three days before confronting a problem, I knew what followed would be ominous. Bearing in mind that Patrick is a diva, without the traditional girth but with more than a fair dose of the dramatic, I pulled out my largest handkerchief.

"It's all over between me and Hans." He managed a slight flutter in his voice when he said "all over."

I couldn't speak for a moment, trying to figure out what could be all over between this man and *my* lover. True, they had been toying with the idea of a relationship fourteen years ago when I came along. But *that* aspect of their lives was "all over" then.

"Remember when I said that I couldn't see how I could ever get along without you and Hans in my life . . . that we were friends forever?" His diva voice hinted at a lump in his throat.

Still I could not respond.

"Well, I'm just calling to say it's all over between me and Hans. I don't want to talk to him after the other night. The friendship is over . . . finished. I just don't want to take that kind of treatment any more."

What followed was a recounting of the events of the other night and the reasons they caused this breakup. The real discussion and the real problems were still to come.

Patrick was causing tremors in more than his relationship with Hans. That friendship stands at the center of a network of friends. Patrick's little scene undoubtedly would cause ripples and affect everything.

What was this friendship network? Where did it come from? How would this latest problem affect things between the rest of us? How could I keep things from spinning apart?

Gay friendship networks, like other primary groups, are places of special significance for their members. Those who belong feel most comfortable here. All screens are down and members act without pretense. Members share secrets and jokes, memories and feelings. They are insiders to their own little world; in fact, I like to think of our group as the "Insiders." These insiders form the core of a network of friends. Consisting of no more than ten people, this group acts as a family of sorts. There is frequent interaction, and little is done without including everyone. Essential to this group relationship is caring and love, concern and mutual aid.

When Hans and I moved from our apartment to our home, Patrick was there with his van. Load after load was hauled from one location to another. Patrick lifted heavy items and hauled cartons. Diva though he is, he managed it without a scene. And all on Thanksgiving morning!

Another of our oldest and dearest friends, Milo (the male equivalent of a Southern Belle) helped me out day and night for months when Hans suffered an extended bout of hepatitis. More than anyone else he was there and was understanding of the particular fears that shook us both.

How a network arises is one part chance, one part magic, and one part hard work. Usually friendships happen when you're not looking. Hans and I were busily engaged in the work of Gay Liberation when some of our most important and long-lasting friendships came about. It was done without thinking. That's the one part chance.

There is also that strange chemistry that draws people together. Friends, lovers, tricks, you name it, all of them will testify to an inexplicable crackle that happens when they meet that someone special. That's the one part magic.

The rest is hard work. First of all, if you want a friend or a lover it's a good idea to put yourself where they might be found. Remote locations aren't the best places to start up a friendship network unless you're fond of rocks and trees. And if you don't seem to be tripping over those you'd like to meet, do something about it.

Take a hint from Dean and Donnie (an Insider couple). They place personal ads for friends who meet specific needs in their lives. Dean is an inveterate game player and advertises for the like-minded. In this way he met Hans, my lover, who has an addiction to bridge (a game for the stout-hearted). And that, as they say, is how it all happened. We all met and hit it off immediately. However, before you rush out to your local gay paper, even Dean will tell you that you're likely to have more misses than hits. In the long run it's worth it.

The second rule of hard work is, "Ya gotta work at your friendships, or they ain't gonna work for you." Once you've met someone through chance and that special magic has brought you together, then keep the action going. Call them, invite them over, go out to movies. Work at it. Friendship doesn't survive on air. The substance of love has to be there.

Two more groupings are part of the friendship network: Tag-Alongs and Outsiders. Tag-Alongs are quasi-members of the group though not as close as Insiders. They aren't always included when group activities are planned. They may be particularly friendly (even close friends) with one or two Insiders but only acquaintances of the others. But they're accepted as friends of the group and share some confidences and inside jokes. Tag-Alongs are, of course, prime candidates for entry as an Insider should an opportunity present itself.

Outsiders are any others who may be present at group activities for one reason or another. It refers to those who have no desire or hope of being a part of the group. This group can include acquaintances of Insiders or Tag-Alongs who are only temporarily on the scene. It may include those who "must" be included in a particular activity for any number of reasons, again the condition being temporary.

A friendship group is a loving relationship like the relationship of any couple or family. There are good times and bad, problems and pleasantries. Over time a communal bond that may be stronger than blood binds the group together. The two analogies used so far, families and couples, apply very well to friendship networks. Even without the blood connections of the family or the religious/political/economic connections of marriage, the friendship network acts like both. The complexities of family life and the caring and love that go into a couple are all present in the friendship network. But as with families or couples there are burdens that accompany the benefits.

One of the burdens has to do with the old bromide about familiarity breeding contempt. The more you know a person, the closer the contact, the easier it is to get ticked off by idiosyncratic behavior. All of us Insiders have habits that at one time or another have driven some or all of us bananas.

Giovanni, one of my closest friends and an early Insider, is a schoolteacher who's become the Mr. Chips of his workplace. He has devoted his life to his work and has caused trauma in the group because of it.

"I can't come along because I have to attend the Junior Prom," he says meekly but adamantly. It doesn't matter that we've been planning something for weeks, or that he doesn't really "have" to attend the prom. The job comes first. Of course the song he was singing just the week before made us wonder about his sanity.

"I don't know what I'd do without any of you. I love it so much when we can get together. It's the only time I have any fun." His vacant look punctuates the statement.

Behavior of this contradictory sort has made him the conundrum of the group. But no one tries to figure him out any more. Unfortunately Giovanni at one time became the target of several fang and claw sessions, which led to a confrontation of another sort.

A ritual developed among the Insiders. On each member's birthday the rest of us would get together and take him out to dinner. For the first few times this was enjoyable. Hans and I, Patrick, Milo the Southern Belle, and Dean and Donnie all had fun. But something happened after the first year of these birthday gatherings.

How it started or when isn't clear, but on one of these occasions someone made tatters out of Giovanni. He was a laughingstock. And uncharitable though this was, he seemed to ask for more by his acceptance of the situation.

Hans, my lover, though he had participated in these sessions, never really liked them. When the insults and taunts began to spread first to me then to him, then to everyone else (with the possible exception of Milo, because who can attack a Southern lady?) things began to change. Hans grew more and more uncomfortable. Patrick, under the influence of spirits, became more and more vicious and his weapons were usually aimed at Hans.

Basil (a relatively new Insider), though seeming to be silent, would encourage conflict by one or two well-placed comments usually unheard by the group as a whole. Donnie was usually reduced to tearful laughter, thus providing an audience for the malevolent spirit of the group. I was as guilty as the rest and usually succumbed to the bizarre transformation that would occur whenever the Insiders gathered. We all seemed like miniature versions of Jekyll and Hyde.

This new condition only seemed to exist when the entire group was together. It was like a heavy veil. The same thing never happened when only part of the group was in session. There was a dynamic at work which we couldn't figure out. And we seemed helpless to do anything about it.

Hans, owing to his Teutonic capacity for bullying, was the one to puncture the veil. At one final confrontational meeting, a New Year's dinner with Outsiders and Tag-Alongs present, he and Dean had a scene. Epithets like "Nazi" and "racist" were thrown about. Phrases like "Let me tell you something we've noticed about *you!*" and "Who do you think you are?" rang out across the restaurant dining room.

No violence, just voices. Then a silence settled over the table; so thick I thought it was another course to be cut and served. No one breathed a word and only the clinking of silver against dishes was heard.

After the pall of silence lifted, and someone was able to smile again, I knew that a rift of epic proportions had been created. We were teetering on the edge; the life of the network was perched there and anything could end it.

Later that evening Hans declared, "I refuse to deal with them as a group." I was skeptical. Outbursts like that had happened aplenty. But he was adamant.

Birthday parties were suggested, even held, and he didn't attend. Sometimes I did, sometimes I didn't—Hans made me feel that my loyalty to him was involved. Eventually the birthday parties came to an end. Without the entire group of Insiders there the group, it seemed, didn't care to meet. Another point is that Hans and I were the hub of this group, and it hadn't cemented itself into place enough to fully operate without us.

Gradually gatherings were held again. Two or four would go

to dinner. Rusty made frequent visits to our home. We made our peace with Dean and Wilkie. Patrick, as always, made his appearances.

Two occurrences brought the group back together again in full swing. Patrick reestablished a friendship with an old friend, Nibby, a straight woman, who had recently moved next door to him. He asked us whether we thought Nibby would fit into the group. And we told him to bring her along and find out.

Nibby was an unqualified success. She had a sense of humor bigger than the rest of us put together and an accepting nature that made allowances for any quirky behavior we might exhibit. She was an Insider in no time.

The other event was a Dessert Gathering planned by Giovanni. He was languishing for the old group activities and flew, like a bee in a rush to pollinate, from one of us to the other. He tried more desperately than any other to sew us back together. And his little party did the trick. That and the presence of Nibby.

Patrick's friend Nibby is only one example of how a new element affects the group. A more telling story is what happens when one of these Insiders finds a mate and introduces him to the group.

Milo the Southerner was actually part of a tight little core group when we first met. He and Mack and Basil were seen together more regularly than salt and pepper. After some time Mack and Basil had a divorce. Mack winged his alcoholic way to San Francisco and Basil found refuge in the South. Milo was left to his own devices and found his way into our hearts.

Eventually Basil made his way North and into Milo's life. Milo naturally brought him into the group. He was a natural. Quiet, even tempered, and a good audience for the pranks and pratfalls of the others, Basil was in. But then romance reared its frilly head, lipstick smeared and mascara running. Basil had found Carlos.

He was duly introduced around and seemed acceptable. Most of the Insiders were a little uncomfortable. After all, this was no mere new Applicant. This was a Romantic Interest. Basil was counting on us to approve. But Carlos had a quick wit and the tongue of a Queen who's been around. He would have made an acceptable addition. Except that Basil wasn't satisfied. I think Carlos talked too much for Basil's taste.

But Basil didn't give up. The silent ones are stolid and persistent. On a trip out West, Basil met Jerry. They immediately hit it off—both of them were fond of silence and home cooking. Basil made the rounds with Jerry by his side and the procedure began again. This time it was different. Jerry wasn't like Carlos. He had no voice in the group and he made few attempts to become a real Insider. He seemed aloof and distant. Not really interested.

As for Basil, he was in Love Heaven. Home-bodies, both, they cut themselves off from the Insiders. Most of us were old hands at the romance business and knew they needed time alone. So at first it didn't seem strange. But as the time stretched from month to month and there was no sign of Basil or Jerry, the group began to feel estranged from them.

At this point Basil and Jerry would no longer be considered Insiders of the first rank. They get invited to large parties, but owing to their reluctance to participate in other activities they don't get invited to much else. If there should be a change in their behavior they would certainly be accepted back, no questions asked. But it would seem that their choice is to distance themselves. And that can only mean a withering of friendship.

Though new romance can change the shape and tenor of a network, sex can rip a group apart. The Insiders of our group have never been bothered by sexual intrigue amongst and between each other. We have all confided little sexual secrets and small indiscretions to each other. But as for sexual interest in each other, not a chance. The best reason for this is time. Once a group gets beyond a certain time wall, sexual interest wanes to nothing. The familial feeling interferes too greatly with any possible sexual fantasies. As with couples, sexual interest and activity decrease with time—even if there were sexual feelings these fade with the years.

Other groups I've known, however, have been devastated by sexual folderol. Dwight, along with Paul and Tiny (a couple), were all close friends, the center of their own network. But as soon as Dwight allowed his sexual feelings for Paul to take over, the group fell apart. Now Paul already might have been ready to leave Tiny and simply just used Dwight to do the trick (so to speak). There might have been any number of other factors. But sex is a definite crisis point in the life of the network.

More mundane problems, such as Patrick's dramatic statement, are the rule in these networks. Resolving a problem such as this can be instructive.

Patrick and Hans had a falling out. Not unlike their other arguments of times past, they both pig-headedly refused to recognize the validity of the other's arguments. Then things got out of hand. Hans began to cut deeply with remarks about Patrick's incipient alcoholism; and Patrick made Hans feel that his life's work was a worthless pursuit. At that point Patrick and Nibby left, and there wasn't a hint this would be different than other times. Then came Patrick's call.

Why did Patrick call me and not Hans? Why did he feel the need to call at all? When a situation like this arises, many questions need to be asked. Patrick, diva though he is, also has a clever streak wider than a skunk's stripe. He thought that I'd immediately report to Hans and the situation would clear itself out. But I didn't follow his game plan—always a hazard when you're trying to manipulate people.

I had learned from past experience. Patrick and others have had their differences with Hans. I was always in the middle, being his lover and the one closest to him. In the past I fell for the bait. I'd bring the case of the "injured" party to Hans, and he and I would more often than not end up arguing. All because someone wanted *me* to do the job of settling differences with Hans, instead of facing it himself.

By the time Patrick called I'd resolved never to be put in the middle again. After a couple of weeks Patrick realized his ploy hadn't worked. He then began bringing his case to others, moaning and crying that this wonderful longstanding friendship was "all over." Some thought he was being a little too dramatic; others reported to me trying to find the "truth" behind the story.

I became more firm in my resolve not to do his secret bidding. Perverse, but what are friends for?

Then, four months into the conflict, Nibby intervened. She asked me to have a private talk with Patrick. "That'll soften him up. He wanted you to tell Hans. You've got to see what you can do to get them back together." She was feeling the pressure because she'd been kept from interacting with the Insiders as a whole for some time.

I felt angry but realized that four months of juggling group events, of not seeing Patrick, of only a few telephone conversations with Nibby, had made me tired of the whole mess. So, swallowing my pride (and believe me that's quite a gulp) I arranged a meeting. Feeling a little like a State Department peace negotiator, I sat down with Patrick and tried to sort things out.

More than half of Patrick's bluster was due to his sense of the dramatic. He had been offended by some of Han's comments; but then, when a friendship develops and lasts fourteen years, you should settle for the best of it and chalk up the rest to life. What's needed here is a mature attitude, not the sensitive hide of a diva. Friendships are founded on tolerance.

Right now only a tenuous treaty exists. It's rather like sitting atop a powderkeg in a room loaded with pyromaniacs. But the long-term nature of the group, and the knowledge of what's caused problems in the past, will undoubtedly help keep things going smoothly for some time.

S o what does this all mean? It means that finding a friendship network is one thing, keeping it running smoothly is another matter entirely. There are, however, some basic guidelines.

If you're ready to develop a network, but feel lost, what can you do? There are all kinds of bromides that one can drag out at this point. Some of them are so old that mold refuses to grow on them. Here goes anyway:

Basically, go out of your way to meet people. Don't leer like a sex-thirsty nympho while you're in the process of looking. And, when you find them, don't latch on like a leech in heat. Let things grow naturally. There's always a tendency to push, but the most reasonable course is to make your friendship offers and then relax. Some will be returned, other people need a little more encouragement. Use your common sense. Don't push and don't force, but by all means act friendly! Invite people over. Share yourself—it will definitely be a reciprocal activity.

Once you're in the midst of a group situation, that's the time for some real work. Don't feel entirely responsible for the venture, but do your part. Keep the group fluid and exciting. It's a lot like marriage: People can grow tired of one another if there is little that's new to stimulate them. Try new things, new places, even new people. If there aren't any group traditions, no matter how informal, try establishing some: birthday celebrations, anniversary parties for the couples, holiday gatherings, Academy Awards Night, an annual picnic. Think about it and you'll find that there's probably something specific to your group that would do nicely. And, don't be afraid to be sentimental. Half the Insiders are unabashed public criers. More tears flow in this bunch than from a group of professional Greek mourners.

If your network is on the rocks, or if it's a group that just doesn't seem to gel, what's the solution? This is more complicated. First off, what's the problem? If it's just crossed signals, that's easy. If it's a matter of emerging personality conflict (remember Patrick and Hans) then you've got your work cut out for you. Some one of you will have to play the role of peacemaker. The "offending" parties will have to settle for some compromises. If all else fails, then a realignment of the network may have to be made. Let's face it, not all problems have the solutions we're looking for.

Of course, if sex has wiggled its way between friends, the group's in real trouble. There's no accounting for taste, but one of the ground rules for keeping a network friendly is to keep it sexless. The one exception to this rule (don't they all have one?) is if two unattached members of the group should happen to fall for each other. Love is strange and, incredible though it may be, things like that do happen. That should only serve to tighten the group's bonds.

Ultimately you will see what works and what doesn't. The trick is to try to see things before they happen and avoid the problems before they get out of hand. In general the best advice is: while staying away from sex, secrecy, and being overly judgmental, you have to keep the group fresh, honor commitments and keep people talking to each other.

As one sage remarked, "Sayin' it is easy; doin' it is tough."

Loving Friendship

by H. W. Seng

A FRIEND OF MINE IS FOND OF TELLING THE STORY OF HOW we met twelve years ago almost to the day. Briefly, it goes as follows.

I was leaning, suggestively I've been told, against the facade of a movie theater in a small university town in Ohio. The friend, and his new roommate, deciding to be friendly to the new faggot in town, approached with an invitation to join them for coffee at the doughnut shop across the street. I explained that I was waiting for some friends of mine (a straight couple) who were due to come out of the theater, and graciously declined the invitation. I waited until the theater emptied, but my couple didn't emerge. Somehow I had missed them. Fortuitously.

So off to the doughnut shop I went, rather sheepishly. The faggot welcoming-committee of two seemed delighted with my delayed appearance, but somewhat skeptical of my story of the disappearing couple. To this day I'm not sure that I was telling the truth. I was painfully shy and they seemed so terrifyingly friendly. One of them invited me upstairs—where they lived. I can't remember which one, but at this point in time I assume it was the one I call a dear friend today. The other I later came to dislike.

I can't remember much of the discussion which followed, whether or not sexual innuendo was in the air, but it seems we might have ended up in the sack but for the looming presence of the third party. This at least is the version of that evening that my friend tells. I do not object to the telling, though I'm not sure *absolute* truth resides in his narrative. We once tried to resuscitate the sexual possibility that was put on hold that evening, and ended up in giggles.

What I was left with then, and now, is a question which I don't think is uncommon among gay men. Are one's closest, most intimate friends passed-over lovers? In our rush to mimic the straight world's insistence on romantic fantasy as the only guideline in choosing the form our love will take, do we over-look those men who might have made us less deliriously happy, and instead more consistently at ease with ourselves? Perhaps we were heading in the right direction before the onslaught of AIDS by confining our lust and passion to less domestic settings. Domesticating desire may not be all that desirous.

There may still be in all of us gay men, post-gay movement, a residual self-hatred that does not allow us to say yes to the one who could love us less as a possession and more as a companion; always free to stay or leave at any moment of the night or day—less a commercial transaction than a hand-in-hand adven-ture. The chemistry of attraction has a perverse element that we talk about endlessly but don't pay much attention to. We keep secrets from our friends, and sometimes from ourselves, those betrayals of our soul that occur daily under the guise of a happily "married" life. In the long run what is the difference between compromise and denial? The longer together the more blurred the line becomes. All in the family. Don't let the neighbors see. We are happy, damn it.

There are choices involved in being a gay man beyond whom one takes to bed. Other forms and ways of loving that can diverge from established patterns. It's crucially important to always remember that we didn't establish the cult of the exclusive couple. All of us forget that the moral imperative sustaining that institution is imposed from without. It didn't grow out of our more numerous ways of expressing desire. If we came from a deformed family intent on deforming us in its mold, should we want to duplicate such a distressing atmosphere?

Our notion of family can be in terms of substitution. It might be inclusive rather than determined to shut out that which is not itself. Children and grandchildren represent a reproductive process that, in the strictest sense, we're excluded from. The world makes it difficult for us to get in on its act. Why we should want to is something I've always found difficult to understand. That we have to contrive to breed is the fundamental difference that separates us from the heterosexual majority. This is the sense in which we are revolutionary, and it is from the healthy alienation that grows out of such difference in sexual function that we should be constructing our alternative social units. The energy that might have gone into children—could it not instead be focused on our friends? Lovers of a different nature, sometimes just as dependent, and perhaps chosen more out of reciprocal feeling than neurotic need.

Need there be a difference in the intensity of love one has for a lover and that one has for a friend? We all know there are things we can say to a friend that we'd never whisper to a lover. Is the reverse true? Who is the confidante? Who is the interloper? Why all the hissing and hysteria if a friend takes his friend's lover to bed—once? Does the discord afterwards ultimately prove there are limits to friendship deriving from the inviolate nature of the couple?

Choosing a friend is a great exercise of freedom, for one doesn't need friendship in order to be approved of by society. We're forced to check the box "single" or "married" on most forms; next we're asked how many children. Never are we asked how many friends. No one ever has to know if you have any or don't. Friendship is often most intense when unadvertised. It often can come into conflict with other priorities. No matter how hard I tried I couldn't get across to my sister why I had to cut short my Christmas visit, because a friend was in the hospital with pneumocystis. "Well, his lover's there, isn't he? You only visit once a year, and now you're ready to run off for a friend. We are family, after all." My sister is not a selfish woman. I don't expect her to fully understand. It's sufficient that I do. But sometimes I'm afraid to act upon such knowledge.

I have a remarkable friend who said no to me a long time ago when I desperately needed a traditional lover relationship. I have three friends of twenty years who are staunch Reagan supporters, and whom my present friends recoil from when I speak of the progression of their lives. These men of different political and temperamental stripe are the boys I huddled with at college in the presence of the persistent, if sometimes undeclared, hostility of the straight world. We didn't even know we were gay then, three of us at least. Our friendship has survived because we helped each other survive.

There is a sense, however, in which friends of long standing can become a hindrance, an accumulation of safety valves and habits that become tedious while still giving comfort. The element of surprise, of delight and common sensibility, those chords which were struck when the friendship began, can become dulled by time and proximity. There are also acquaintances, which some of us have many of. They can be helpful; they are often seen when we're bored. They are in no way like friends. Sometimes, though I suspect not frequently, friends devolve into acquaintances.

With clothes off and mouth shut every gay man is a possible sexual partner; but every gay man is not a potential friend. Sometimes in our rush to accumulate affection, to build up an arsenal against the volley of abuse that we still have to fight on a daily basis—particularly now—we choose badly. But even in a wrongheaded choice we're exercising our freedom as gay men in the spirit of a formidable gay male network around the world that sustains us when in a strange land. That bond grew out of a sexual *menage* that was powerful, uninhibited, and not afraid to advertise itself as an alternative to settling down in the suburbs.

I've been told I have a special gift for friendship. I've never had a long-term lover relationship in the traditional sense. One case does not prove the rule. Some gay men seem to be able to manage both, though there are usually snags in the balancing act.

The guy from the doughnut shop, the man that got away, now has a lover who, while not like me in any way, might have been instead his friend. It could have happened that way. I talk to my friend about what a prize he landed, and often wonder how. I also continue a very affectionate, sustaining relationship with the other man in my life that most would say had gotten away.

Draw your own conclusions. At the least, admit that gay men have choices.

Getting the Colors Right: Making Interracial Relationships Work

by Charles Henry Fuller

THE BIGGEST MYTH SURROUNDING INTERRACIAL ROMANTIC involvement is that somehow these relationships are completely different than those between lovers from the same racial background. This is just plain foolishness. People meet, they fall in love, and given the right circumstances they're able to establish nurturing, fulfilling relationships. Race has very little to do with loving someone. Both members of the couple have to reconcile their romantic fantasies to include their partner while each must learn about the other's likes and dislikes as well as his struggles and triumphs. In short, they must learn those things which will enable them to endure. For the interracial couple the process of enduring will be considerably harder if they aren't able to negotiate some of the "booby traps" their physical difference may impose on the relationship.

In this essay I speak from my own experience—nothing more. The story of a black man who only sleeps with white men is not my story. The inherent racism and self-loathing expressed by that lifestyle fills me with a dull sense of pain and betrayal. Though the tale of a black man who only sleeps with other black men holds considerably more interest for me, my story has little to do with that one, either. I know that having had interracial relationships is no guarantee I've understood them; each was so different, the strengths of one often becoming the weaknesses of another. Still, to me much of what happened with each of these men in my life remains clear. Patterns do emerge as hindsight reveals which roads should have been taken and those which must be avoided next time.

FANTASY, REALITY AND HISTORY

Given the small number of black homosexuals in the Boston area where I live, my never having been involved romantically with a white man would be very queer indeed. However, the fact that my lover of almost four years is white still surprises me. Though my erotic fantasies don't limit themselves to any one type of man, I've always imagined myself being carried away by a beautiful, black Adonis at that penultimate moment when all of my physical and intellectual needs are sated. A white partner was never involved in my happily-ever-after fantasies.

Some years ago I went out with a man who loved to talk dirty once he was sexually aroused. This wasn't something which appealed to me, but since he didn't seem to have nearly as much fun when I asked him to be quiet, we agreed that he could indulge in this guttural chat as long as I didn't have to listen or respond to what he said. This worked out fine until one evening he said something which disturbed me.

"Oh, baby, I love your beautiful black skin—every inch of it."

Objectively I knew he meant this as a compliment, but deep inside something began to itch and I couldn't scratch it. His "beautiful black skin" was like poking a stick into a pile of mildewy rags—I couldn't be sure what memory he'd disturbed. The psychological bruises all blacks acquire as children—the taunts of "black Sambo," "liver lips" and "nigger"—don't go away because we're adults and can intellectually understand those hurts. I would have dismissed my uneasiness as knee-jerk paranoia if he hadn't immediately added, "Let me have it, black boy. Let me have that big, black dick, now!" Needless to say, the party was over and I started some dirty talk of my own.

In the weeks that followed, those two comments came back to trouble us again and again. I was never able to make him understand that stereotypes are exploitative. "What everybody knows" about this group or that one hurts people who are uncomfortable with those distorted, confining images. What he saw as a playful fantasy was for me a degrading reduction of our lovemaking to some black-white power struggle.

As we talked I learned for the first time that he only dated black men. To me this explained in part why all of his past relationships had dissolved. I didn't feel his erotism of my physical and emotional characteristics was a bad thing in and of itself. My difficulty arose when I realized his exclusive projection of these positive characteristics onto black men was every bit as racist a behavior as the refusal of many white gay men to see anything positive about their black counterparts.

The uses of fantasy and reality in a relationship are complex. We all dream, we fantasize, we put the soft focus on whatever aspects of reality need retouching at the time. No harm done. If anything, the occasional use of fantasy, particularly in a romantic setting, is preferable to constant doses of undiluted reality. But the interracial couple has to be careful that the use of fantasy in their relationship doesn't become mired in stereotypes which perpetuate the acting out of unhealthy racist scripts.

The relationship between white and black men is a historically ambivalent one. The power struggle of this country still supports the economic and psychological battering of men of color. We are objectified, trivialized and brutalized with alarming regularity. Pernicious stereotypes cling on year after year, and frequently the only legacies blacks are left are those of disenfranchisement and emasculation. Power and self-confidence are not givens in our lives, but must be reclaimed daily. I've learned that if I do not say "Enough!", if I don't show white people how to treat me, they'll treat me any way they want. This isn't right. Anyone who is going to share in my life has to have a sensitivity to the effects of societal oppression on me, and support my struggle against it.

Days exist when I can't bear the sight of another white person. Full up with the reality of my place as a black homosexual in white America, I need to immerse myself in things that have black or brown or at least non-white roots. I pull a little away from my lover when this mood is upon me, if not physically then in an emotional way. I consider very carefully the choices I've made.

At those times when I catch myself watching my lover across the room or studying his photograph in my wallet, when I am ashamed of being so keenly aware of his skin color and the privilege I perceive it affords him in this society, I examine my reasons for being with him. Whether this curiosity grows out of my own internalized racism or from some other source, I don't know. What I do know is that this sort of scrutiny, this coming to terms with the physical difference between us, is very important.

I have to be sure that what I love about him is involved with who he is as a person, not the color of his skin. It is one thing for us to enjoy our contrasting skin tones on a sensual, aesthetic level, and quite another to focus on it as the reason for our sexual attraction—one is highest praise, the other thinly-veiled racism.

DATING

In many ways dating is the most exciting time for couples. During this period they try to learn enough about each other to decide whether they want to continue as a couple. If they're paying attention, this is the time when interracial couples will look for those additional signals from their partner which let them know whether or not their relationship is going to survive. These include: where they go and where they don't go when they want to have a good time socially, how they address racial incidents, the blending of their differing cultures, and most importantly, how they resolve disputes.

The first issue the couple faces is that they *do* look different on the street, and people notice them. If you're not the "straight-acting and appearing" gay white male who frequents the personal ads of so many publications, you've already adjusted to being stared at on the streets. This goes with being different in America. What is surprising for interracial couples is that this voyeurism now follows them around both the straight and gay worlds. They've come to expect being leered at in the supermarket or on the subway, yet many are completely unprepared for the often disapproving stares of other gay men.

The restaurants in Boston's North End are the final word in exquisite Italian cooking in the area. Before we met, my lover used to enjoy going there for meals. When he suggested we go to the North End for dinner one evening, I told him that I would neither feel comfortable alone nor as an interracial gay couple in that neighborhood. A delicious meal wasn't worth the very real possibility of unpleasantness. This self-censuring on my part supports racism on some level, but I maintain an uneasy truce with political activism when I want to go out for a romantic evening with my lover. We went somewhere else.

The same sort of decision faced us when we decided to live together. Where would we be comfortable on the streets, both alone and as a couple? In a curious way this question has to be asked even when we're going to a gay club. If we're coming from different locations we can't assume that I'll be able to get in. Will they let me in because I'm obviously over twenty-one, or will I have to produce several forms of identification because I'm black?

These discourtesies are nothing new to black homosexuals, but for my white lover they were an irritating surprise. We both refuse to involve ourselves with businesses, events or neighborhoods where the man we love would not be welcome. Identifying this limitation on our life together is infuriating, and made all the more annoying because so often we cannot simply choose to ignore it.

An issue many interracial couples go round and round about is when to let racist comments or behavior go and when to draw attention to them. For example, are we being seated in the back of the restaurant because we're an interracial couple, because we're gay, or because it's the only open table? Of course we have to evaluate the situation and decide what response, if any, is required. Racist behavior is often more subtle, more the product of inattention than anything else.

My lover and I spent a wonderful day with some friends a few summers ago. The four of us drove up to Ogonquit, Maine, and ate, swam, did crossword puzzles, read and reread the same pages of politically correct novels, watched dreamily as the young men walked by—did all the things four gay men do on a lazy Sunday afternoon at the beach. When we got back to the city we decided to have dinner together. The talk moved easily until these three, all social workers, let it settle on the negative self-image among their clients and the difficulties my friends had as white, gay men working with predominantly non-white client populations. These friends are extremely bright, articulate and politically astute so the conversation was stimulating.

As the discussion developed I became increasingly aware that I was having trouble getting into the conversation. Every attempt I made to enter was ignored. Finally, one too many sweeping generalizations about black people forced me to speak up. Though they denied they were conscious of my being excluded from the conversation, we all wondered why they'd talked around me as though I weren't a person of color who would know something about what they were discussing. Racism and its effects on an individual's self-image are problems with which all blacks have to deal, regardless of their class background.

My point is this: each member of an interracial couple has to defend *himself* when he feels it's justified. He can't expect that his lover is always going to be aware of the racism lurking in the bushes. On the one hand we want our friends to be comfortable enough with us as people that they act naturally. However, we mustn't be afraid to educate them when they forget that we're not exactly like them, that we have experiences that in some ways make us wholly different.

In planning social activities, elements of the two cultures have to be represented in a percentage that is satisfying to the couple. Though our racial and ethnic backgrounds are different, my lover and I share many of the same interests. I enjoy opera, he enjoys classical music. We both love literature and dancing. These points of juncture in no way prevent us from taking pride in our own ethnic and racial heritage. Of course the oral histories of black Americans are of more interest to me, and the lives of Finnish and Italian immigrants in this country will always be of more importance to him. What is significant is that we recognize the necessity of staying in touch with our origins and sharing these experiences with one another. Most importantly, we don't assume that being involved in an interracial relationship guarantees we understand the other's culture. In our efforts to appreciate these differing influences in our lives, we've been drawn closer together.

Finally, learning how to fight with one another is almost as important to a couple as learning how to make love. If a couple doesn't know how to resolve conflicts it's unlikely that they're going to establish an enduring, nurturing relationship. Interracial couples must decide what role name-calling will play during their arguments. Will they accuse one another of being "selfish bastards" or "selfish black or white bastards"? One category affords dignity, the other lowers the relationship to a particularly narrow, racist plane. No place exists in a healthy relationship for this sort of verbal abuse. When either member of a couple uses racial epithets against the very person he's relying upon for love and understanding, he has no right to expect either.

FAMILY AND FRIENDS

At some point all couples realize that neither their individual families nor each of their friends necessarily will understand or support their relationship. Of course the reverse is also true for the lovers themselves, as they regard the new pack of strangers to whom they're expected to be nice. This is one of the awkward but undeniable truths of human existence: we can't like everybody, even when it would make things easier. The added burden for interracial couples is dealing with the racism of those we love in relation to our partner.

Clearly, my lover and I are not the "in-laws" for which our families had hoped. Even once they'd made their uneasy peace with our homosexuality, neither family expected their child would get involved in a long-term interracial relationship. We add insult to injury by being both gay and racially different. Though we emphasize the ways in which we are similar when dealing with our families, their feelings of betrayal, fear and bewilderment are not uncommon.

When my lover's mother first learned I was black, her reaction was one of fear. She was genuinely afraid for her son's safety on the streets, knowing full well that two white gay men or two black gay men might pass undisturbed on the street, but the combination of being interracial and gay clearly presented a problem of safety. Where would we live? was it safe? and other questions raced through her mind. She saw us as targets, potential victims of the homophobic violence she'd heard about. Her ability to articulate this fear is ultimately what made her take a closer look at our relationship, to assess its strengths and weaknesses in terms of survival, commitment, love. What she needed to know was whether I would take care of her baby, no matter what. Everything else was secondary to her. If she grieves at the loss of the grandchildren my lover might have given her, she does so in silence.

My family's reaction was quite different, or I should say indifferent. In their attempts to make sure I didn't feel uncomfortable about my sexuality or my choice of lover, they never bring up either topic. They've given me their approval and that's that. What's annoying about this blanket acceptance is that I'm still invited to family functions as a single person. I haven't been a single person for almost four years! When I confronted them on this point, they insisted that I bring him along if I wanted to. The problem then became where we would stay since my family lives quite a distance away. My parents conveniently don't have enough room and my siblings are uncomfortable about how they'll explain my lover to their children. "Tell them he's my special friend and leave it at that," I say. "Hmmmmmmm," they say. The bottom line is we either stay at home or at a motel. So far, we have stayed at home—our home!

Friends, as a general rule, are easier for the couple to include in their lives than biological family members. When complications do develop in terms of friends and the relationship, it's often because some of our friends have their own internalized racism which slips out at the most unexpected times.

When I was first coming out, I dated a man who was nine years older than me. He was the interesting "dirty talker" I mentioned earlier. This man had a group of friends, who were quite a festive bunch of guys. Whenever my lover was out of the room they'd make sexually suggestive remarks to me and openly speculated about my sex life with their friend. When I told my lover this sort of behavior bothered me, he countered by saying, "Can you blame them? You're so attractive, it's only natural they'd be curious. Besides, they think because you're black you're more open about sex. You mustn't let them upset you. They don't mean anything by it."

His friends were sniffing around me like a Virginia ham and he said I shouldn't let it upset me. In retrospect I still don't understand why he didn't see that sort of behavior on the part of "friends" as completely disrespectful of our relationship. The next time it happened I called them on their behavior. For the remainder of that relationship I had the reputation among his friends as being touchy. My lover could let them treat him any way he wanted, but I refused to put up with racist nonsense.

Though infinitely more subtle, the friend who always offers qualified praise can also be extremely annoying. My lover and I know an older white man who always extols my virtues in a racial context. When I'm away from the table he leans forward and says things to my lover like, "He's such a wonderful black man," or, "How lucky you are to have found such a decent black man." The point he repeatedly misses is that his praise immediately calls to mind the opposites, that is, indecent black men who aren't wonderful. I experimented by calling him a wonderful white man. His rather crestfallen response was, "Why do you put it that way?" My point exactly!

We don't have to stop seeing a friend because our lover doesn't care for him, but we do need to understand the reasons for the discord and decide what the implications are for our relationship if we continue to see this person. Naturally, both my lover and I have friends and family members that the other doesn't care for; however, neither of us sees any person on a continuing basis who disapproves of our partner for racial reasons.

Many interracial couples lose sight of the fact that they're in the process of becoming one another's family unit. They eat together, they sleep together, they cry together, if they're together long enough they'll even cheat on their taxes together—what is this if not a family unit? Their rights as a couple within their biological families should be just as important as those of their siblings who are leading more traditional lifestyles. Though it's important to avoid "us" versus "them" scenarios, the couple's needs must not automatically be sacrificed for the sake of family harmony or the personal limitations of friends. The couple's happiness is just as important as that of their immediate and extended families.

Everyone should broaden their frame of vision to see all the places where affection, love and intimacy may be found. These three things are so fleeting in life that we must learn never to close any door which might lead to a fulfilling relationship. I don't want to think of a time when my lover and I won't be together. We've learned not only to see more than a single way of getting from one place to another, but also to make whatever adjustments are necessary because of our ethnic and racial differences. The act of surviving as a couple has to do with verbal and physical communication, with respect, and with a strong sense of commitment to one another. Race has very little to do with loving someone.

Seven Deadly Questions

by Arch Brown

I HAVE LIVED WITH THE SAME MAN FOR TWENTY YEARS. Whenever someone finds out he immediately sees me as an expert on personal relationships, and the questions start coming fast and furious. At a party recently someone I met began to ask those same relationship questions I've answered time and time again. Tossing off my usual replies wasn't enough for him. After three years together he and his friend were having serious problems. He wanted answers . . . *fast!*

Of course there are no answers that work for every couple. The problems seem to be quite universal, however, because the same questions keep coming up again and again.

At that same party a group of us became involved in playing "list" games: Who were the seven dwarfs? What were the seven wonders of the world? The seven deadly sins? We never really completed these lists, but the next day I checked out my trusty dictionary. It didn't list the dwarfs and the seven wonders were pretty obscure, but the sins *were* listed and I was immediately struck by how they related to that typical set of relationship questions. Perhaps the early theologians who catalogued these "vices" knew the universality in questions of living and loving. Perhaps things don't change much after all.

COVETOUSNESS

Ninety-five percent of the people who ask me questions start out wanting to know how Bruce and I deal with tricking and outside affairs. More than anything this seems to be the crucial problem in most relationships.

And it is actually one of the simplest to solve. The solution is honesty. It's very difficult to say—and even more difficult to hear—"I do love you; but you're not enough for me and I must have others." If one or both partners feel this way then it *must* be verbalized . . . and confronted early in the relationship. In the glow of new love it's very easy to pledge undying fidelity. We know ourselves pretty well, however, and deep down we're aware what eventually is likely to happen.

If both partners believe they're going to be "true" to each other, that too should be discussed. Should signs of straying appear then both partners must confront the issue then and there . . . not next week!

Bruce and I were lucky. We were almost thirty when we met. I'd been through several affairs where we both had been unable to talk about sleeping around, and in all cases this inability brought otherwise viable relationships to a quick death. When we met in the summer of '65 I'd recently ended an affair and Bruce had been dating a man for several months. We both had nice apartments of our own and no immediate desire to live with someone else. *Being secure with yourself and liking who you are may be the single most important aspect of succeeding with a new relationship.* A person reaching out in desperate need for love sucks too much from a potential partner and destroys what might have been wonderful. Almost casually we began to see each other. I knew about his other friend and he knew I was dating other men. As the months went by we found ourselves seeing more and more of each other. Our love grew slowly. It was not based on a single hot night of mad sex. This slow and easy beginning was not planned. It simply happened.

When we started to talk about living together, I made it clear there were going to be times when I played around on the outside, and he said he would too. We agreed it was acceptable to enjoy sex outside our relationship, but not acceptable to come home and talk about it. As the years went by, however, we found it easier to be open about that as well. The more secure we were about each other, the easier it became to deal with outside boyfriends.

We know couples who limit "extramarital" activities to three-somes. They were never very successful for us. We are both too much focused on one-to-one sex to be comfortable with extra body parts bouncing around the bed.

The real threat in all of this is the "other affair" . . . that second date that suddenly turns into a relationship. We've had some bumpy times during these periods. We try to be cool and honest and talk out the situation, but it isn't always easy. All of the outsiders fortunately have been primarily sex trips and, when they end, we remain together.

In twenty years there has been no serious threat to our relationship. Such a danger remains a possibility and there isn't a damn thing we can do about it. If a couple wants the freedom to explore the outside world then they must be willing to deal with the consequences.

LUST

"What do you do when the honeymoon is over, and the passion starts to fade?" The first years tend to pass easily as two people discover the erotic pleasures of each other. For most couples this tends to slow down eventually. But even if the passion never subsides and sex continues to be wildly exciting year after year there still has to be something more if the relationship is to continue. We've known couples who've managed to stay together for quite a while simply because of the sex, no matter what they thought of each other outside the bedroom. But eventually sex, no matter how hot, proves not to be enough and the affairs "peter out."

One of the forces that brought Bruce and I closer in the first months of our relationship was our enjoyment of each other's company. We liked the same kinds of music and theater. We could take walks in the city and ooh and aah over the architecture and the crazy people in the street. He laughed at my jokes (a sure sign of a good person!) and, most importantly, my cat liked him.

Most straight marriages have children on which to focus. Most gay couples do not. But I think we need something . . . or some *things* to satisfy those same needs. For us the first "baby" was a little cottage on a lake. It was something on which to work together. Almost every weekend we'd take off in our little car and head for the country to paint or plant or sit quietly by the fire. Before getting together neither one of us had ever had a chain saw in our hands or replaced a window screen. We learned together. Creating a country home together brought a new kind of love between us that neither of us had ever experienced. . . . A deep satisfaction in knowing the two of us had shared an experience we could never have experienced alone.

Our second great shared love is travel. Neither one of us had been out of the country when we met. Before we lived together we took a week's vacation to Puerto Rico. I'll never forget standing on the parapet of an old fort over the sea with Bruce's arm on my shoulder. Something almost magical was happening to us both; discovering history, other peoples, other sights and sounds gave us an indescribable kind of gratification. Since then we've frequently traveled together and shared Italy, Spain, England, France, Morocco, Mexico, Tunisia, Jamaica, Bonaire, Greece and several journeys within the United States.

We always return exhilarated, exhausted and eager to plan the next trip. We spend months perusing guide books and maps. We learn as much as we can about our destination. As the next vacation approaches the excitement grows until we barely can wait to get to the airport.

I know some folks hate to travel and I'm not suggesting that leaving the country has saved our relationship. Every relationship needs some outside stimulants. There must be something new to anticipate and something wonderful to remember. Travel works for us.

ANGER

Bruce and I both like to avoid major confrontations. If someone starts an argument at a dinner party, one of us will try to smooth things over quickly. Likewise, we both tend to hold in things, let them stew and then—when the pressure gets too great—explode.

Usually the other person has not been stewing and, to avoid more screaming, he simply says, "Let's talk about this calmly."

Over the years we've tried to work out a pattern for dealing with frustrations. If Bruce is upset about something (and the something can be very important or quite insignificant) I try to be cool and set up a "date" to talk about it . . . Saturday at breakfast, perhaps. This gives both of us time to think through our frustrations and what we'd like to do about them. It's amazing how rational two people can be if they want to be. If the problems are very complex, it may take several "dates," but usually one session starts us on the road to a solution.

This isn't easy. It's much easier to answer a scream with a louder scream. Usually that goes nowhere productive.

ENVY

One or the other of you tells better jokes, has a nicer smile, makes more money, has more friends, works shorter hours, has a bigger dick or anything else you can compete over.

Envy perhaps is worse than anger because it's omnipresent. One is constantly reminded that he cooks better or you screw better. Day after day these little differences slap you in the face. It's very hard not to revert back to a "my daddy has a better job" attitude.

We try to turn these negative little jealousies into positives. After all, he is doing his wonderful cooking for ME. I'm honestly pleased when his funny story is the hit of the party. He is honestly excited when one of my plays gets a good review.

This boils down to developing an appreciation of the one you're with. If you were better at all things than your lover, you might not want to keep him around. For example . . . I'm usually more gregarious than Bruce at a party. I tell a good story. He is quieter, but has a simple straightforward charm that I lack. Therefore, some people think I'm "great" but end up really "liking" Bruce.

So? That's who we are. I'm glad they like my lover and I hope he's glad they thought I was "fun."

SLOTH

Most of us would be very happy to have our partners do all the cooking and cleaning and window washing and laundry while we take care of the work and play. Laziness is easy to fall into if someone else picks up your dirty socks.

Most straight men, including those with working wives, seem to have little to do with the upkeep of the house. Two men, however, usually have to share the chores (unless the relationship is based on a master/slave or husband/wife role model). Some couples may never need to discuss these responsibilities and just fall into certain jobs. But there were areas for us that needed to be talked through, or the garbage might never have gotten taken out. Over the years we've found the chores we do best (or hate least). I cook better than Bruce but he washes dishes better than I do. I dust and he vacuums. He does windows and I do bathrooms. He leaves papers and magazines all over and I drop socks. It works out.

GLUTTONY

Many of the relationships we've watched disintegrate over the years have fallen apart because of too much booze or dope or food or money or sex.

Two men with two incomes and comfortable lifestyles may easily fall into the trap of . . . one more cocktail or one more piece of cake.

What do you do when you realize your lover is an alcoholic or is compulsively overeating and beginning to look like a beached whale?

You talk about it. Anyone sliding towards an addiction is seldom willing to talk about it, much less deal with it, so don't expect miracles.

One man can't solve another man's problems. Freeing oneself from dependence on drugs or alcohol can be a long lonely process. Having someone's support helps enormously. Try to be loving and understanding and make him see you want him back again . . . whole and healthy and alive. And get help for yourself, too.

PRIDE

This was the only "sin" that no one mentioned at the party. Pride, however, surfaces all too easily. When your lover has a date or wants to go out for the evening and you feel hurt, it's your pride that's hurting. When he gets compliments on his dessert and no one mentions your soup, your pride is what's itching. When he complains because you didn't scrub out the sink carefully, pride must be dealt with. When he's "too tired tonight, dear," your pride is being insulted.

Having a lover . . . and keeping him, is hard work. But it's work that takes place in your fickle little brain. Every time something is said or left unsaid and you feel hurt, you must make a little decision. Am I gonna take that sitting down? Am I gonna let him get away with that? What did he really mean by that? Did he just mean to be so mean?

Sometimes it's not even a conscious decision that is being made, just a flicker across the brain waves. But they add up . . . bit by bit, every day of your life together.

In some cases I've had a great day writing and the energy is flowing and I want to go out with my lover to dinner or to a movie. He comes home exhausted and wants to watch television, then crash. Someone has to rearrange plans. Someone has to give in, although I don't really consider it giving in. If I stay in tonight, maybe we can go to a flick tomorrow. It's just a minor compromise.

We know a gay couple who I'll call Joe and Jim. Joe is completely helpless around the house. He finds it impossible to wash a dish or do the laundry. He can't change a light bulb. Jim does everything. He complains all the time . . . but he continues to make these compromises after ten years together because he wants to keep the relationship alive, or he has a martyr complex and this is the kind of relationship he truly wants. I could never live like that, but I'm not Jim. Jim and Joe have worked out their own system of pride-swallowing and it works for them.

Another couple we know thrives on mutual insults, especially in public. A third couple takes on the roles of star and audience whenever they appear in public. These relationships seem to work for these people. They have found their own way of dealing with pride.

So I don't go to the movies tonight or we have chicken instead of steak . . . again. We are together. We share a life that we both love. He has made me very happy for a very long time. I'll continue to make those little compromises because he loves me and, although I don't say it often enough, I do love him!

A Parable on Sex

by Gregory Miracle

Perhaps the best exemplification of my attitude toward sex is the parable of the man who lived in a city where jobs were scarce. He could scarcely make ends meet, and he would tell himself from day to day that although everyone should try to excel and be the best in some specific endeavor, he was worthless, like the unemployed masses, because no one appreciated his own efforts at excellence. The bricklayer was happy because he did his job well and was rewarded with a good salary. The mailman took pride in delivering all the mail on time each day, and people showed their gratitude by giving him cash at Christmas. The musicians at a local pub were popular enough to make a living at what they did, and they enjoyed a certain artistic notoriety. It seemed that everyone had a place in the scheme of things except him. This man was a wise old philosopher, and what he said concerned no one. He labored day and night to produce convincing theses on moral subjects and insightful essays on the conquest of happiness, but no one understood the products of his labor and he went to bed each night unappreciated, alone and unhappy because unfulfilled.

Then one day as he was walking to the market to spend his last dollar, more depressed than usual, he saw a man in the gutter whose long hair was knotted and tangled and whose raiment reeked of urine. In his hand was a bottle of cheap wine that had cracked, releasing its contents into the sewer near where he lay among the rubbish and vermin of the street. His hand bled as he still clutched the broken glass. "Help!" the poor man cried out as the melancholy philosopher walked past. "There is no justice in this cursed world!"

The philosopher halted his weary stride, and upon hearing this malediction from the gutter began to weep. "No justice? Indeed there is none! God help us!" he cried, ingeminating the derelict's plea. "But I have suffered more than you," he expatiated, "for my disappointment stems from a lifetime of wasted effort, not from a broken jug of wine. You might bleed to death if only you slashed your wrists with a loose shard, but I must go on, striving to achieve what no man but I conceives as worthwhile, for I have declared in my philosophy that suicide is immoral, and that surrender to the elements is sin. How trivial is your case in comparison to mine, how insignificant your lot, and how easily may it be resolved!" With that the philosopher kicked the bottle from the poor man's hand; but a loose shard shot out as he did so and slashed the drunken ne'er-do-well's wrist by accident, causing great gouts of blood to spew forth into the gutter.

"What have I done!" cried the philosopher, for the taking of another's life was in his mind as much a sin as suicide, and he bound the poor man's wrist with a tatter from his stinking raiment to stop the bleeding and dragged his unconscious body to the hospital.

Since the poor man had no money, the hospital would not keep him after dressing the wound, and the philosopher took him home out of a sort of moral obligation. But when the poor man came to and wanted wine, his host became angry and admonished him, saying, "I took you in out of kindness. Now you are sober, and I maintain once again that, now the emergency is past, my troubles are great enough without you, and I will throw you out unless you can provide some useful service for me." To which the man from the gutter replied, "I do not wish to remain in bondage to you. I have been a guttersnipe all my life, a hoodlum, but as a boy I could prostitute myself and earn enough money to get by on, sometimes even to enjoy the pleasures of life with. Now that my beauty is fading I can no longer make my way in the world. The satisfaction I have known is no longer possible. Once men wanted me for my body, but I have lost my bargaining chip, and I want nothing more than to drink myself to death. Which is more tragic, to have experienced the affection of other men and lost that opportunity, or never to have been appreciated at all? At least I can say I have been desired."

To this the philosopher knew not how to respond. He shook his head slowly and uttered a mournful reproach: "Then my estimate of you was correct, my poor victim of all that is wicked in this world. You'll never amount to anything, and I must discard you. My life will continue as it has always gone on, and I will have the pleasure of knowing that my work is the best work I can offer." He resolved to wash the man's garments, dress him and set him free, after which he would return to his treatises and essays. He looked the poor man in the eye and declared, "As I am, so might you also be."

But when he removed his house guest's fetid apparel and saw the emaciated body beneath that had once been sought after for its beauty, he knelt down and kissed the poor man's breast. "You are my savior," he sobbed, "who have revealed my greatest flaw and shown me that I could die without knowing what it is to love anyone but myself, and that my solitary life, this misery without charity, is more awful far than the mediocrity engendered by redemptive self-sacrifice. I will make love to you."

And the philosopher climbed onto the bed where the poor man lay and to lave his putrid skin made of himself a fountain of kisses, licking the sores on his poor friend's feet and the bruises on his swollen joints, for this was the holiest of bodies: it housed a saint, whose life was dependent on that of all others and had never known the cruel subversion that ensues when the ego becomes the sole proprietor of a man's creative efforts.

Whereupon the poor man clutched the philosopher's neck in a death grip, strangling him and leaving him dead upon the bed, his blue face imprinted not with agony, but with surprise, even delight, his features fixed in an expression of wide-eyed rapture. One cannot know for sure, but it appeared as though he had died just as his soul met with a divine ecstasy for the first time in his life. The poor man, of course, proceeded to rob the dead philosopher of what little material wealth his sorry life had afforded and went out to buy a new bottle of wine.

And so the next day the poor man returned to the philosopher's house and moved in. By selling his dead benefactor's belongings he was able to buy enough wine to slake his thirst for a time and enough nourishment to retrieve some of his health. After a week he bathed and cut his hair and looked at himself in the mirror. He saw now that he had resuscitated his beauty from its deteriorated state. "I can still hook for a living!" he laughed, and he donned alluring attire and went out into the street to make his fortune once again, rejuvenated, confident, his physical desirability enhanced as much as possible.

The first trick he encountered only offered to buy him dinner and put him up for the night, but the poor man declined this invitation, thinking that he could do better. The next man who propositioned him showed him enough money to keep him in wine for weeks, but this customer's face reminded him too much of the philosopher, whom he was now trying to forget, and so again he turned the offer down. Then he was approached under a streetlamp by a respectable-looking man about his own age who said, "Take me home with you and I will be your slave, Mr. Hustler, sir. I want you to tie me up and treat me like the filth I know I really am, sir." And the poor man accepted this offer, knowing that he would probably not get a better one that night.

When they arrived at the philosopher's house the poor man said to the respectable-looking man, "This is going to cost you plenty," and the respectable-looking man said, "I am prepared, sir" and produced a bill of large denomination from his pocket. The poor man snatched it from his customer's trembling palm, thinking, "How gullible these idiots are!" and barked, "Get down!" after which he made the stranger to undress and tie himself to the bed where the philosopher had once slept. While the poor man finished tying his patron-slave's wrists and ankles to the bedposts, he was again reminded of the philosopher, this time by something the naked man spread before him groaned: "Tell me what human garbage I am. I'll do anything you say!" Upon hearing this the poor man could tolerate no more and began shouting the strongest obscenities and severest commands imaginable at his servile client. This, of course, was just what the respectable-looking man wanted, and after the gush of rancor had subsided, he felt he had got his money's worth and left, hoping to return for even harsher treatment another day.

But the poor man was very unhappy now and went back to his bottle, unable to console himself in any other way. He lay and drank till he was unconscious, and when he awoke he continued drinking until nothing remained of his spirit or his financial resources, and in the depths of despair and destitution he perished, leaving nothing behind but a hulk of skin and bones in the gutter, drenched in urine, among the rubbish and vermin of the street.

And it came to pass that the philosopher's old home was renovated as part of a gentrification project in that section of the city, and a good-looking couple moved in who were haunted by the ghosts of the poor man and the philosopher. This couple were two men just graduated from college who fared well together as roommates, each taking an interest in the other's hobbies and career plans, so that they complemented each other in the most well-mannered, constructive fashion and functioned together as a pair in wedlock, although they desired no children. Each told the other in the most charming and consistent manner how fond he was of his partner and how glad he was they were together, and one would stroke the other's dark locks or new growth of beard and say the sweetest things for hours on into the night.

So fond of one another were they that they kissed each other ever more affectionately and made love with less and less effort each night. But not long after they entered the philosopher's dwelling to set up housekeeping, though the house was unrecognizable in its present form, the spirits of the poor man and the philosopher began to haunt them. Slumbering, as they were wont to do, in a frozen embrace of happiness, they would both wake up suddenly and ask each other, "Of what did you dream?" And the reply of one of the lovers would be, "I dreamt of a wise philosopher, embittered with age," and the other would say, "A man in the gutter with tangled hair and a putrid stench," and none could decide what this meant.

But it never altered their innocent love, and they were still so enamored of each other that in their love-making they scarcely thought of anything sexual apart from the sweet caresses and tender emotions they shared as a result of their doting affection for one another. Then one day, after they had both come home from work, one of them turned to the other, frowning, and said, "Why is it you can't appreciate anything I do?" And the other felt possessed also and, scowling balefully, shouted back, "Because you are human garbage, that's why!" And they fell upon each other, the one pleading incessantly to be understood, and the other barking orders and chiding his mate. And in the middle of this chaos, both of them ripping one another's Brooks Brothers' clothing to shreds, they both climaxed, and the sweet smell of ejaculate, spoonfuls of it, filled their nostrils, signaling that they should stop their fighting, and they told each other, "I didn't mean anything I said." For they had never had sex before without the words, "I love you."

IV

CULTURE
&
LEISURE

How to Be an Opera Queen

by Ivan Martinson

G AY OPERA LOVERS CAN BE DIVIDED INTO TWO GROUPS: the first are those who merely like the music and would probably be just as turned on by a good string quartet. They show a suspicious tendency to frequent lieder recitals given by singers who never made it on the big stage. They wear shirts in last year's tartan that clash with their running shoes. They appear satisfied with a single decent performance of a favorite opera and will be unable to recall who sang it two years from now.

The opera queen, however, is a civic institution, like the cop on the corner. He serves an important function, like that served at the gladiatorial games by Caesar's thumb. No singer who hasn't won her faction among opera queens can be said to have arrived, regardless of how often she's been on the Johnny Carson Show.

Far too much that is outrageous goes on at the opera. The audience claps their palms simply because it's "the opera" and because somebody has just stopped singing.

Well, someone must be willing to point out that *that woman* has *no business* singing Norma. Mind you, one never asserts this by so vulgar a method as booing—that only makes her slog harder at the defenseless music. It is the sneer that, like the patrolman's billy-club, identifies the opera queen, guardian of vice-regal authority and the moral order. It is not necessary to use it. Merely twirling it in plain view reminds everyone—divas and directors, conductors and comprimarios, board members and hoi polloi—that a higher authority—unbribable and un-ignorable—hears all. So, if you aspire to be an opera queen, hone your sneer. Give it a cutting edge.

A major point: *never be satisfied.* Except in the most ex-ceptional circumstances, never even be pleased. "A worm in every apple and two at matinees" should be your motto. Consider making these statements:

"*She sang better once.*"
"*She'll be ready in about five years.*"
"*The voice is good but not placed properly—maybe she'll have it on Tuesday.*"
(On Tuesday) "*She's been working too hard—she was better Friday.*"
"*If she could only act.*"
"*What an actress! But her technique's ghastly.*"
"*She's fine for* bel canto, *but—why is she singing verismo?*" (These terms, of course, can be reversed.)

The ultimate hurdle is Mozart. Be sure to say the company's not stylish enough for him. No one ever is.

For credibility's sake, toss a crumb: "Oh, the whole production sucked eggs, but the Second Prisoner was fantastic. Never heard it better."

Be offended by the out-of-place. Too much applause for a lousy high note should hurt as much as none for a perfect recitative.

"You call her a Turandot? Barely a Lauretta. Now I have an acoustical disc from 1908, and *that's* a Turandot! *Turandot* wasn't composed yet in 1908? Well if it had been, *that* would have been the ideal Turandot."

Never apologize, never back down, and don't worry if you contradict yourself. To be an opera queen it's not necessary to know what you're talking about. What is necessary is sincerity. Feel deeply. What true devotee would sacrifice enlightened amateurism for a benighted professionalism?

Have your criticisms at the ready. Be succinct. Be colorful. Be vindictive. Nothing you hear nowadays is ever as good as Maria was in Berlin/Havana/Mexico City/John Ardoin's shower (you've heard all the pirates). Season any admiration with cool perception: "Beverly can still manage the light coloratura; she goes skittering over the notes like a cockroach over garbage." Be personal. "Renata was diddling herself with the scepter and fondling her breasts—which I suppose no one else has been doing lately." Gently chaff their flaws: "What language *did* Joan sing that in? How could you tell?"

Don't fear sounding shrill, unless you have a nasty register break going from chest voice to head. And make merry—opera should entertain, even during intermissions and while waiting on lines: "Boy, if anybody in the music business needs cocaine, it's Kiri." But don't stand for irrationality from anyone else: "What do you mean, 'Leonie was off pitch'? That's like saying, 'Leonie sings Strauss.' Leonie's *always* off pitch. Was she or wasn't she the most exciting thing you ever heard of or saw on any stage?" Be flaky, but incorruptible.

Spreading the word about the past is hardly less pleasurable. A true lover of opera seldom lives in the present. Each moment must be rigorously examined—you must ask yourself, is it up to snuff? Is it *worthy* of your presence? Only very special moments make the grade: Montserrat's descending chromatic scale in *Vespri*, Regine's "ja, ja" in *Rosenkavalier*, Leonie leaping . . . off anything . . . anywhere. These are the moments when the heart stops and the world stands still.

The opera lover lives principally in the past and in the future. The past includes, but is not confined to, the "Golden Age" when they knew how to do it, as opposed to today when they don't. The Golden Age always came to an abrupt end about three years after whoever is talking started going to the opera, which can be fifty years ago, or twenty, or, less credibly, five. Memory cures all technical problems, rough spots, bad placement, lousy stagings. "But Galli-Curci was always off pitch," says your grandmother. Nonsense. Anyway, your grandmother isn't an opera queen. She refers to female singers by their last names.

Never refer to a female singer by her last name. Only her business associates do that. It's vulgar. In cases where two singers have the same name, such as, oh, Renata, inflection should imply distinction. Nicknames are often appropriate: "Did you hear Jackie and Flicka in *Donna del lago?*"

The future is, if anything, even more romantic than the past. Inconceivable repertory with dynamite casts pave the schedule as stars adorn the Milky Way. "Hildegard's doing Isolde and Donna Anna next year." "Oh, I can just imagine—" And you can: no flaws, no sudden indispositions, no Klara at the last minute. Be a bearer of tidings, both good and ill: "You *know* who's the new Brunnhilde/Elektra/Norma, don't you?" (Be inventive.)

"It must be true. Lois told me." "Impossible." (Don't be too credulous. You have a reputation for cynicism to maintain.)

Be loyal. The opera queen is a modern knight errant. Choose your diva wisely. The less popular the better—Leontyne has a million devotees, but to be Leyla's or Virginia's cavalier is a distinction.

The opera queen, like many others, judges his love by the beauty, the expressiveness, the sheer size of a single organ, frequently to the shallow, if natural, exclusion of the charms (or lack of charms) of every other part of the body. For the opera queen this part is the larynx. Of course the directing intelligence *behind* the organ deserves a good deal more credit, in a great throat, or, say, a gorgeous pair of gams, than is usually allowed.

Never miss an event. There are operatic events more important than the music. The Bing Gala was an event. Birgit's last round of farewells were events, though she sounded like hell. The infamous *Gioconda* in October 1982 where the tenor ran off stage and locked himself in his dressing room, missed his cue, had to be coaxed out, only to be mugged on the Venetian piers by Eva (all business, *dessa*, and in fab voice)—that, too, was an event. If you are an opera queen, you were there.

Always insist you were there. Recollect it distinctly. "How was Elyena's Amneris?" "It was like being in a taxi accident with Jackie O—*terribly* exciting, but it wasn't precisely pleasant."

Much of the opera queen's life is vested in electronics. Not a few would prefer to avoid live opera almost entirely in the unassailable conviction that the present is a hopelessly dreary epigone of the nigh-obliterate past. No opera queen worthy of the name knows any higher pleasure than cornering a group of friends with his collection of one-of-a-kind tapes, out-of-print discs, obscure piracies and rare 78s of the immortals—immortals whose true rites are as forgotten and as mispracticed nowadays as the Eleusinian mysteries. This is the opera queen in his element, his lair, his holy of holies—alone with his hi-fi, a few impressionable friends, and every note Georges Thill, Conchita Supervia, Giannina Arangi-Lombardi, or Heinrich Schlusnus ever recorded.

Fall into the drama, but don't lose your head. Many opera queens feel instinctively for Amneris, that regal creature, too noble to stoop to murder her rival, and yet what thanks does she get from that inane but gorgeous hunk she loves? Or Tannhauser, who knows perfectly well what's good for him . . . the pure Elisabeth is what's good for him . . . but who invariably drifts back to the soulless sensuality of Venus.

Reality pales beside opera. Opera can become your means for enhancing the joys of existence and alleviating its pains. Reality may be perceived through opera, its hues noted not as subtle variants of a uniform gray (as life presents itself to most of humankind), but in stark, decorator shades, black in the bedroom, vermilion in the study. We are swept away by heroes and villains, lovers and friends, sudden delights, abrupt hostilities and turnabouts of every kind, as when the Queen of the Night suddenly becomes a witch or your true love reveals his long-concealed rank, marital status and other undesirable traits of character. It's hell on the nerves, yes, but an opera queen has neurons of titanium, and the life he lives is vivid beyond all songless telling. Learn how to concentrate while in the grip of monomania. Take time off at an otherwise desperate moment to croon to your furniture, to apostrophize unhearing deities, to plan a little dinner party. Never mind how it feels—if it sounds good, do it. After all, which is the worthier ambition, a life in the opera or the reverse?

Why is opera so gay an art form? Is its flamboyance subconsciously homoerotic? Ballet can be just as flamboyant. Is opera more visceral than other arts? But straight people have viscera.

Theory: The emotional extravagance of the characters appeals to us. Straight folk, with the constant release of tension granted them by public display and the harping on their lifestyle in every branch of life and art, have had their responses lulled and dulled. Gay men, even the most liberated, have lived part of our lives in a vise, a tension between what society urged and what our needs demanded. In each of us a tendency was born to hold back on certain types of self-expression, at least in the company of the general public. Few of us entirely outgrow this. Hence much gay creativity, inspired by the long repression, bubbles up. We thrill at opera's explosions of bare feeling, the sublime musical metaphor for passion. Those fat and foolish people on the stage, raucously yelping and cavorting in their anachronistic motley, are a symbol of the freedom and release we long for.

On Identifying With Judy Garland

by Gregg Howe

I N 1970 WHEN I "CAME OUT" (MEANING SIMPLY THAT I MET another man who was an avowed homosexual and who was all too willing to prove the fact in a manner I shall never forget), Judy Garland was involved. In the heady afterglow of that first legitimate experience I was lying back, smoking a cigarette, and Bob got up and put on Judy Garland's famed Carnegie Hall album. I shrieked (shrieking was quite permissible for queens in 1970), "*I LOVE JUDY GARLAND!!!*" Bob, nonplussed, turned and said, "Of course you do, you're gay."

To this day I've never fully trusted a gay man who doesn't love Judy Garland. Loving Judy Garland and being gay aren't mutually inclusive, but in my mind the two are definitely related. Judy was larger than life, Judy was brilliant, Judy was vulnerable, and most importantly, Judy had a voice unlike anyone else's.

While growing up in a very small town in America in the 1950s and 60s I knew I didn't quite belong. I was all too guiltily aware of the reason for my outsider status, though I was unable to articulate it for fear of dire reprisals. This was compounded by the fact I was fairly certain I was the only person on this planet *like that*. I had a great need for a fantasy life. Most of the people with whom I identified were women, and, while I shan't bore you with those I encountered in my everyday life the famous women included Marlene Dietrich (cool, calculating and almost otherworldly in her beauty), Bette Davis (hard, brittle, witty and strong) and Elizabeth Taylor (beautiful, rich, at times brilliant and always outrageous).

O f all these ladies, Judy Garland outdistanced the others. Judy was a woman with whom I'd grown up, or so it seemed because each year *The Wizard of Oz* was broadcast on television. From my first glimpses of her on the yellow brick road—frightened, excited, ingenuous—I knew I loved her. And Judy was also quite socially acceptable, unlike playing with dolls. Though his devotion can't compare with mine, even my father liked her, and there were many of her albums in our home.

As I grew older Judy's appeal became intertwined with her public persona, her ability to bounce back. Of course she, like me, was tragic. Yes, tragic. It is not by chance that all great drama—until the century in which we live—revolved around royalty (i.e., persons larger than life who weren't concerned with getting the dishes washed or earning a living). Nor is it surprising that with the decline of royalty (there is very little left and that's not tragic), screen stars and performers became a new royalty. They too appeared untouchable—they couldn't be hurt as we mere mortals could. For a queen like myself, who was hurt everyday at being called "sissy" and "fag," it was a relief to retreat into the idea of being one of the untouchables—Bette, Marlene, Liz. But Judy transcended all the others because she wasn't untouchable; she seemed accessible, she wasn't beautiful, she wasn't impervious to the world around her. Judy didn't seem to feel as if she belonged, and neither did I. In her music she gave dimension to that heightened emotional awareness borne from the pain of rejection. That link initially bound me tightly to her.

Obviously a great deal of my identification with Judy was posthumous. She had already been dead for a year when Bob turned and matter-of-factly explained that I loved Judy because I was gay. About two weeks after that, Bob also explained just as matter-of-factly that sex and love are not one and the same thing, a concept totally beyond my grasp. As I was getting my feet firmly planted on the yellow brick road of gay life, assuming that all my fears and problems would evaporate, I was confronted with yet another complex interpretation of reality.

Judy had suffered on a grand scale and so did I, with the aid of her legend. I spent many long evenings listening to Judy singing about exactly what I was feeling, or at least about what I thought I was feeling. There wasn't much of a middle ground in Judy's songs; they tended to be either ecstatically happy or unendurably miserable. As I voraciously read everything written about

Frances Gumm/Judy Garland it became apparent that, like her songs, there wasn't much middle ground in her personal life either.

With a minimal effort I was able to inextricably confuse Judy's talent with her personality, using the latter to illuminate my own lackluster day-to-day trials and tribulations. I read with horror of Louis B. Mayer's treatment of her, of how she'd been hooked on speed at the studio as a child, of how she'd been forced to try to fulfill an image that was beyond her ability, and of how she'd been humiliated when she'd failed. I understood this final horror all too well. I read about her setbacks, her triumphs, her bouts with alcohol and drugs, her suicide attempts, her acts of magnanimous kindness, her acts of irresponsibility, and finally her death. I accepted them indulgently, without question, for none were her fault. In my eyes she was the ultimate victim: the tragic queen who, despite the insurmountable obstacles placed before her, was able to rise again, and again, to startle, to overwhelm, to overcome. And—most importantly—each time she completed this act of amazing willpower she received massive ovations, spectacular notices, and outpourings of pure love. What more could a young queen ask of an idol?

Self-indulgence is both a virtue and a vice. It can reveal an habitual need to avoid reality, or it can be a necessary release. With Judy I indulged my need to avoid reality for quite some time. I wish I could pinpoint the moment it occurred to me that Judy was—along with so many other things—self-destructive. I'd like to be able to relate some dramatic moment in my life that caused the tragic aspect of Judy's charismatic appeal for me to wane. Alas, it's as impossible for me to pinpoint when I began to separate Judy's talent from her public persona as it's been for her biographers to distinguish Judy's public persona from the woman, and from her own concept of that image. Gradually I discovered that middle ground that exists between Judy's renditions of "Get Happy" and "The Man That Got Away." It's precisely that middle ground that Judy never discovered.

Much has been written regarding the fact that the Stonewall Riots occurred only days after Judy's death, and that the queens were the ones who turned on the police and said NO, NOT THIS TIME. Judy lived life on that cutting edge, which for so many gay men seemed the only available space for a very long time. Her life seemed magnificently tragic, whereas for many of the queens who loved her, tragedy came without this quality of iridescence. Judy's death inspired those Stonewall queens. Her death was not victorious, it was a giving in, an inability to walk the fine line she'd been precariously negotiating for so long. She'd finally been beaten and perhaps the realization that there would be no more comebacks, no more ovations, that she was—as she was so often reported to have dreaded—alone, served to inspire some of those queens who turned on their tormentors that night. John Richy writes bitterly in *The Sexual Outlaw*:

> In New York the weekend of her [Judy's] funeral, the first gay riot occurred.
> "Over the rainbow" was not good enough. Here, now. *That* was the reality. The acquiescing hurt was fucked. During what ordinarily would have been a routine mass harassment of gays in a Greenwich Village bar called the Stonewall, homosexuals resisted the cops for the first time. This time The Man didn't get away.
> Garland the symbol of gay oppression was truly dead.

Many aspects of Judy's public persona were not self-destructive. Her resilience, her exuberance, her sense of humor, and her ability to sing a song in a manner so that the words touched the listener as if she were sharing that part of herself that all of us wish we could share. That indefinable quality in her voice is what has endured for me.

I no longer want or need to seek refuge behind Judy Garland the tragic queen, but I do want to be vulnerable, to touch people's lives, to love and be loved. These too were things that Judy represented to me. These are the things I've carried away from my infatuation with Judy Garland.

Recently the Public Broadcasting System has been rerunning Judy's television shows filmed in 1962–63, and in some of those shows we see Judy at her best. It is time to watch those programs without remembering Mel Torme's book about that year called *The Other Side of the Rainbow*, in which he chronicles her paranoic outbursts, her overwhelming fear, and her demands that could never fill the void she believed would engulf her at any given moment. I want to watch those shows and see the performer who, no matter what her problems were, can still make me laugh and cry.

Still, when I listen to the Carnegie Hall album recorded live in 1961, and Judy breathes heavily into the microphone, and says, "I don't ever want to go home, not me, no not me, I'll sing 'em all and we'll stay all night," I get goose pimples and want to reach out and give something back to the woman who gave me so much pleasure, perverse as it may have been at times. I supplied the perversity in our one-sided relationship, not Miss Judy Garland. And I have learned from it.

A Dozen Women We Adore

by Gregg Howe

Tallulah Bankhead's deep guttural "Dahling" is all that's needed to bring this legend to life. She's now best remembered for her flamboyant, irreverent wit and her excesses. This Southern senator's daughter became one of the first bad girls of this century. She compromised her talent for her personality, but what a magnificent personality. When asked if a well-known playwright was homosexual she's reported to have replied, "I don't know dahling, he never sucked my cock."

Joan Crawford is the greatest of the tough women. Hard as nails, vain to a fault, her films both good and bad still pack revival movie houses. "Mommie Dearest" built a career on survival. She always seemed prepared for a good fight, particularly when climbing from humble beginnings to the top of the social heap. Her Crystal Allen in *The Women* is a role few gay men can resist. She exemplified the hard-driving woman who succeeded no matter what the cost, and stood there in her Adrian gown and furs as if saying, "Don't fuck with me, fellas."

Bette Davis has a style too irresistible not to imitate. The swinging of her hips, her cigarette attacking the air and her staccato delivery often overshadow Bette Davis the actress. *Indomitable* is the word that best sums up Miss Davis. She always seems somehow bigger than life, bigger even than the roles she played, and she's played some pretty big roles. Her Margo Channing in *All About Eve* has fueled many gay men's fantasies.

Marlene Dietrich's icy beauty and whiskey voice have made her a symbol of glamour. She created an illusion of beauty that bore no resemblance to reality. Beyond the grasp of the men who worshipped her in most of her films, she seemed quite content to go on about her own life without that man as well. Marlene often dressed in a tux and tails, a paradox perhaps, but one that's to be cherished.

Katharine Hepburn's independent spirit has served to place her as a woman who not only refused to knuckle under to the men who wished to control her, but as a woman who managed to maintain the upper hand. Her stature as an actress is unquestioned, and her refusal to compromise her personal life for public perusal has set her apart from so many of the women of her time. She's living proof that age need not diminish beauty or dignity.

Bette Midler seems to be one of our own. Is there a gay man who doesn't know that Bette started out at the Continental Baths in New York? Her bawdy wit, her outrageous antics and her frenetic energy level are shown in their best light by the way she makes fun of herself without compromising her self-respect. This heightened energy can also be focused to translate a ballad into a story whose meaning can't be missed. The first time I saw her live in 1973 at the State Theatre in Columbus, Ohio, she walked onstage, looked at the audience and shouted, "I bet you didn't know there were so many of you, did you?" Half the audience roared their approval, superior to those who sat stiffly mystified.

Marilyn Monroe is in a class entirely by herself. No one has ever projected such raw sexuality. Underlying it was a vulnerability that couldn't be denied. Marilyn was sensitive, a great comedienne, and begged for love so mercilessly that still, twenty-odd years after her death, she is a woman who requires no last name.

Diana Ross has made it, and hasn't the least desire to belittle that fact. She walks onstage draped in lamé, dripping furs, and then proceeds to proclaim her love for the world. The girl from Detroit became one of the Supremes and has spent the past twenty years becoming the only Supreme. She's managed to continue to produce hit after hit, no matter what musical style is in vogue. When it rained on her controversial concert in Central Park in 1983, she stood shouting at the half-million rain-drenched spectators, "I've waited a lifetime to get here and I'm not going anywhere." Only an act of nature succeeded in moving her.

Barbra Streisand sang "I'm the Greatest Star" in *Funny Girl* in 1963 and has spent the past twenty years trying to be just that. Not a glamour girl in the beginning, she quickly altered that. She's created an aura about herself that's almost impenetrable. Perfection is her goal, and she sees control as the means to that end. I still long for the Barbra who belted out "My Man" with the imperfection of spontaneous emotion. I miss the imperfection of Barbra, but can't help respecting her desire to be the greatest star.

Elizabeth Taylor is often called the last star. She's the last of the great stars who were nurtured, created, and controlled by the studio system. She's led one of the most public lives of any woman of our time. Her ups and downs are legend, and she laughs at them with that vulgar laugh that she employed as Martha in *Who's Afraid of Virginia Woolf*. She's been the most beautiful woman in the world off and on for thirty-odd years, and in that time has, as they say, "let herself go" on numerous occasions. But always she returns svelte and gorgeous again. Few actresses have had a career with so many brilliant performances and so many truly hideous ones. She is Liz, pure and simple—nothing more and nothing less.

Tina Turner's recent comeback was a shock so welcome that many of us were stunned. After her initial success in the late sixties with her husband Ike she's now returned on her own, and her power is undeniable. She's stronger than strong, with a voice and presence to match. She's inspiring. When she sings "You better be good to me," she means it.

Mae West was an image of her own making. She did more with an innuendo than could ever be done with a blatant statement. She exaggerated her femininity with a drag queen's style, but made herself suggestive rather than ridiculous. She hyperbolized sex and in so doing made it *fun!* She delivered a line like, "Is that a pistol in your pocket or are you glad to see me?" with a panache that stripped it of vulgarity.

In Defense of Erotica

by Samuel M. Steward

FROM THE VERY BEGINNINGS OF LITERATURE, EROTIC WRITing has run alongside the literary mainstream. It has always survived. Sometimes it has been very deeply buried; at other times it exists openly on the surface. Certain theorists claim that a permissive or matriarchal society allows it to flourish openly, but when the patriarchal or right-wing tendency takes over, erotica is condemned. Even the terminology changes and erotica—a word with a rather favorable semantic slant—is then called pornography, a word meaning "writing about whores." One of the great difficulties today has been the failure of anyone ever to define "obscenity" or "pornography" or even "erotica" accurately or successfully.

A great fuss is made nowadays over the ill-treatment and degradation that women are supposed to be getting in such writing, and pornography is roundly condemned. But after all, the detractors are talking about heterosexual pornography. What they have to say has absolutely no bearing on male homosexual erotica, or even on lesbian erotica—although the lesbian writing produced by the members of the female S&M organization Samois does treat women a bit cruelly. But those women like it and want it, just as male masochists desire it from their masters. As far as gay males are concerned, the current squabbles of women against pornography have no meaning at all. Women are not poorly treated in gay male erotica, they're completely absent from it, wholly ignored. It is only in heterosexual pornography that women are degraded, and pornography written by straight people is of no concern whatsoever to the gay male community.

The interest of male homosexuals, then, is directed only to the kinds of erotica that deal with males, whether they are gay or straight. Of all the forms of artistic expression, none better than erotica fulfills the basic meaning of "entertainment"—from *inter* and *teneo* [to hold (one's interest) between (beginning and end)].

The communication between the writer's mind and emotions and words, and the reader's response, is simple, direct and immediate—much more accurate and exact than in music or painting. Music must submit to the subjective analysis of the listener, and much of modern painting has to depend on the artist's explanations, or the viewer's background of experience. But erotica affects directly and immediately. There is no period of delay or of "emotion recollected in tranquility." The writer of erotica touches the nervous system of the reader with an electric finger. He stimulates the reader's juices, makes the eye sparkle, sets the adrenalin flowing, activates the sweat glands and finally creates the hard-on . . . or in classic example, the ejaculation.

The bible-thumpers complain that erotica is to be blamed for nearly all of the sexual crimes in existence. Poppycock. Nothing could be farther from the truth. After a reader of gay male erotica becomes aroused, chances are minimal that he'll go out looking for sex on the streets. For one thing his erection will usually impede his walking any farther than his bath or bedroom, where —yes, he will commit rape, hand-rape that is (manus + turbare = masturbation) upon himself, and then go peacefully to bed and to sleep. Thus erotic writing may be looked upon as one of the greatest forces for "good" in a community. It keeps wanderers off the streets, reduces rape of all kinds, lowers cleaning and laundry bills (much to the discomfiture of Eros, patron saint of the laundryman) and certainly wipes out child molestation—which is usually done by heteros.

Writing under the pseudonym of Phil Andros, some years ago I produced fifty or sixty soft-core short stories for European publications in Zurich and Copenhagen, and later—after the new freedom in the United States (granted following the Supreme Court's decision on pornography around 1966)—I produced seven hard-core novels under that pen-name, creating as the "hero" of the series a hustler whose name was Phil Andros. Nowhere in any of those novels or short stories are women ill-treated, subjugated or downgraded. In fact, they are notable in those writings only because they are entirely absent, or dismissed with such a sentence as: "She had the usual number of arms and legs and boobs, all in the right places."

An interviewer once asked me why I wrote the Andros novels, and I rather flippantly replied that I had done them for my own pleasure, and to bring happiness to lonely old men whacking off in their hotel rooms at night. But perhaps the purpose had another element that was more serious. One can hardly find credible the idea of "educational erotica," or erotica written with a humanitarian viewpoint, yet perhaps those motivations were at hand. Phil Andros worked his way through the seven novels from a meager understanding of himself, his hustling and motivations, up to a thorough comprehension of his inner self—denied in the early work—that he was completely homosexual. Furthermore, he accepted his nature without bitterness or complication, avoiding the strictures of biblical "morality," for morality was after all only a word to him, derived from the Latin *mores*, meaning "customs of the community." From his novels a novice might have picked up information on where to go, what to do in bed, how to meet others, how to avoid hepatitis or posterior prostatic urethritis, or worse. To have readers tell me many years afterwards how Phil helped them along the way comes both as a surprise and a gratification.

Some of the greatest names in English literature as well as those writing in other languages and cultures have produced their share of erotica. One scarcely needs to point out that even Plato peevishly wanted the *Odyssey* to be expurgated before it was read by the young. Ovid wrote *The Art of Love*; Aristophanes *Lysistrata*. The names of erotic authors Rabelais and Boccaccio are familiar to any literate person. The Old Testament contains *The Song of Solomon*, an erotic love-poem that the fundamentalists in general are hard put to explain away, the rabbis interpreting it as a piece showing God's love for Israel, the Christians as a dialogue between Christ and his church. Adolescent readers consider it pretty hot stuff, and it's been the occasion of spilling more semen than the church fathers ever suspected.

And literate persons are also familiar with the erotica of the Earl of Rochester, John Cleland, D. H. Lawrence, Henry Miller, Benjamin Franklin, James Joyce, the simon-pure James Whitcomb Riley ("The Passing of the Backhouse") and the beloved Mark Twain, whose hilarious *1601* is read to this day. "If there is a decent word findable in it," Twain once wrote to an acquaintance, "it is because I have overlooked it." By the 1950s there had been over fifty editions of 1601 published, in everything from the cheapest to richest bindings and formats—but you won't find this piece of scatological erotica in the standard sets of Twain's works. For musical erotica turn to The Sod's Opera by Gilbert and Sullivan—if you can find it.

Erotica differs largely from the muck that circulates today as pornography, written to formula by hacks, composed without skill or imagination, first drafts knocked off at the rate of a thousand words an hour. Contemporary publishers of this low-grade stuff demand from 50 to 75 percent—by actual page count—of steamy sex scenes in a novel of thirty-five thousand words. As in Denmark, the quality of American erotica diminished within a few years after the ban against pornography/erotica was lifted. And we may also look forward, if the trend towards these miserable publications continues, to the near-complete extinction of the genre. Then there may flourish once again the giddy sexual double-entendres of a James Branch Cabell, the sly whirlygiggles of a Ronald Firbank, the arcane and hermetic writing of a Gertrude Stein or the delicate cobwebs of an Anais Nin. Indeed, the elegant erotica—for both men and women—dainty and light-hearted yet profoundly stimulating, of "A. N. Roquelaure" in her Beauty trilogy, offers us more hope than anything recently seen.

Finally, in this day of darkness when a plague more mysterious and terrible than any of the Middle Ages spreads its horror over the world, it is not being frivolous to suggest that erotica has acquired a new and significant importance for gay men, and one which may eventually extend its meaning—in the straight world—even to heterosexual activity. Will it not keep you at home if you live without a partner, and help you to keep your fires smoldering? And if you live with a lover, may it not furnish a faltering romance or your tired bed habits with an occasional new quivering tingle, an incitement to a revival of passion and understanding?

In other words, kiddo, discard the phrasing that tells you to "ram it to him, shoot his asshole full of hot gyzym" in favor of "I watched his ivory body cleaving the greenly illuminated water of the swimming-pool; I saw his strong and muscled thighs and arms rise from the water, his handsome torso dripping with diamonds, and I knew that he was mine. Laughing, he climbed from the pool. I toweled him, rubbed his black and shining hair, reached up and kissed his dark full lips, and felt his naked body cool against mine. And took him home to my bed."

Gay Theatre Is Not Surviving

by Terry Helbing

GAY THEATRE IS NOT SURVIVING. HOW CAN I SAY THAT, you ask? After all, at this writing (June, 1985), Harvey Fierstein's *Torch Song Trilogy* has just completed a multiple-Tony-Award-winning three-year run on Broadway; the Jerry Herman-Harvey Fierstein-Arthur Laurents musical adaptation of *La Cage aux Folles* has been running for two years, also collecting several Tony Awards; William M. Hoffman's play about AIDS, *As Is*, has just moved to Broadway from the Circle Rep, garnering critical acclaim and awards; and Joseph Papp's Public Theatre, which for almost a decade virtually ignored the idea of gay theatre, has practically become a gay showcase this past season, producing Albert Innaurato's *Coming of Age in Soho* and Larry Kramer's impassioned agitprop AIDS play, *The Normal Heart*.

So how can gay theatre *not* be surviving? While commercial gay plays are enjoying unprecedented success, the small companies that have been the vanguard of the gay theatre movement for the past few years are greatly reduced in number, and those that remain are experiencing hard times. In part the very success of recent plays is contributing to their difficulties.

Plays with major gay characters or themes (like Marlowe's *Edward II*) have been produced for hundreds of years; but it's simpler to describe contemporary gay theatre from two watershed events in the recent past, each of which coincided with a similar sociological occurrence in the broader gay movement. The first was the appearance of Mart Crowley's *The Boys in the Band*, which moved to Off-Broadway in 1969 and ran 1,000 performances. While some would decry Crowley's negative depiction of gay male stereotypes, the play can be viewed as a historical record of the late 50s and early 60s. More importantly, it brought gay theatre out of the closet. At the same time the

Stonewall Riots launched the modern gay movement, and as a result of these two events hundreds of gay plays would be produced Off- and Off-Off-Broadway for the next ten years, often at newly-formed theatre companies throughout the country, dedicated exclusively to gay plays.

The other significant event was the favorable critical reception in 1981 to Harvey Fierstein's *Torch Song Trilogy*. The four-hour epic had been playing to empty houses Off-Off-Broadway until Mel Gussow's unprecedented rave review in the *New York Times* began a shower of critical accolades that helped the play move to Broadway in June, 1982, and win Tony Awards for its author-star in 1983. About the same time the dread spectre of AIDS began killing hundreds of gay men and permanently changing their social and political lives. After these two events gay theatre never again would be the same.

At first glance one might think the recent success of *Torch Song Trilogy* has only changed things for the better. It's definitely made gay subject matter more viable; New York's major resident companies now select at least one play each season that contains a gay character or a gay subplot. No doubt they hope to cash in on the current trendiness and commercial success of gay material. Small gay companies and independent gay producers suffer as a result.

The ultimate goal of gay theatre is to put itself out of business; when gay characters and subject matter are accepted and discussed as readily as one's hair color or occupation, there will be little need for gay companies to point up the worth and individuality of gay people. That time has not arrived; in fact, we are far from it. But the current acceptance of gay material may be a passing trend, like disaster movies or youth-oriented dance films are for Hollywood. The success of the two major AIDS plays, while clearly concerned with gay people and issues, is actually a response to a serious crisis and not indicative of lasting change.

How do gay theatre companies suffer at the hands of Broadway success? Theatregoers who wish to view gay plays don't have to go to a gay theatre when they can see gay material all over town. The ticket prices of Off-Broadway companies, combined with limited discretionary income, means that even the most avid theatregoers can see just so many plays. Furthermore, with so many cultural events competing for one's attention and dollars, many rely on word-of-mouth or the opinion of major critics before seeing a play.

As a result, while there is a core audience who will attend an ongoing gay company, God bless 'em, the company must prove over and over again to the general public that a particular play is a "hot" item. With many major daily newspapers unwilling to attend gay theatre it's difficult to get the message out to the public, and quality productions often go unseen.

Many of the people on the mailing list of gay theatre companies are not regular theatregoers, but like to attend an occasional gay event as an alternative to the bars and discos, and do not feel much commitment to gay theatre. Most gay men believe it's important for the gay community to have cultural institutions like a chorus, marching bands, or theatres. Unless such approval is put into practice by buying tickets, those cultural institutions can't continue to exist.

The success of *Torch Song Trilogy* and other gay plays has created audience expectations difficult for gay theatre to meet. Most gay productions in New York City are classified as Off-Off-Broadway theatre, but audience perception frequently ignores one of those "Offs." On shoestring budgets and in small theatre spaces, gay theatre can't possibly achieve the production values of Broadway and Off-Broadway shows, which have budgets of hundreds of thousands of dollars. Instead of appreciating and enjoying a different and important kind of theatre experience, many theatregoers still expect a big-budget production. A reviewer exhibited this attitude when he dismissed a gay theatre company's production because audience members had to walk across the stage to get to the public restroom. Somehow this made the entire operation not worthy of serious consideration. Most Off-Off-Broadway theatres are lucky to have bathrooms. This elitist outlook fails to consider the quality of work being done onstage.

Paying $40 for a ticket doesn't guarantee the viewer a good show, as anyone who attends Broadway regularly can attest, but paying $10 for a ticket at many gay theatres doesn't diminish the quality by three-quarters.

Funding is so scarce for struggling gay companies that they

can't (and should not) invest outrageous sums of money in trying to appease expensive tastes. A limited number of wealthy people are willing to invest their money in gay theatre and get a tax write-off. As with all theatre there is so little chance of any return on the investment that speculators would have much better chances for a return in the stock market or at the gambling tables. Meridian Gay Theatre—which I co-founded—has received grants from the New York State Council on the Arts and the New York City Department of Cultural Affairs; San Francisco's Theatre Rhinoceros has received money from the National Endowment for the Arts and their city's Hotel Tax Fund; but in both cases these grants cover only a small fraction of overall operating expenses. Gay theatre companies don't have the option of seeking private corporate support as do their straight counterparts. It's difficult to imagine Xerox or IBM rushing to lend financial aid.

Many who hear of the plight of gay theatres say, "Why don't you sponsor a benefit?" Because our government has been so unresponsive to the desperate straits of the gay community during the AIDS crisis with their resounding lack of funding for research and patient care, the gay community has had to make up the slack. We have done so quite admirably, with benefits of all sizes and descriptions, from New York's Gay Night at the Circus at Madison Square Garden to a neighborhood street fair. People are "benefitted out." Worthy as the cause of gay theatre may be, people can support only so many such causes before they overload.

The success of *Torch Song Trilogy* and other plays has encouraged the writing of more material with gay themes, but this too is a mixed blessing. While gay companies may be receiving more scripts, most who write plays can't be called playwrights; they're not versed in the exigencies of writing for the theatre. They wisely follow the maxim, "Write about what you know," and too often the cathartic plays that result may be cheaper for the author than seeing a therapist, but don't work very well as theatre pieces. They usually imitate what they see or what has been successful, so gay companies receive many scripts which in form resemble screenplays for TV movies or sitcoms; and the subject matter reflects the Broadway successes: trilogies, drag queens, AIDS. If writers are unrealistic about writing for the theatre, they write unproduceable plays—scripts with 35 characters and 15 sets written in cinematic style—simply not within the realm of an Off-Off-Broadway company's producing abilities. Unknown gay writers aren't likely to come out of nowhere to be produced immediately on Broadway.

Given this changed atmosphere for gay theatre, what can the handful of companies remaining nationally do to ensure their continued survival?

Find more high-quality scripts. This is not a problem endemic to gay theatre; all theatres face the problem of finding enough good material. Modern gay culture has been in existence so short a time that writers haven't had a chance to create a significant body of literature for the theatre. For a long time gay writers felt there was no place for their plays to be given serious production consideration, so why bother writing them? Lesbian authors felt they had even *less* than no chance, so they are further behind gay male writers. *Torch Song* has helped to change the situation, and gay theatre companies have been doing their share as well. Meridian sponsors the annual Jane Chambers Memorial International Gay Playwriting Contest, now in its sixth year (it was previously sponsored by the Gay Theatre Alliance), to encourage the writing of new gay plays; and Theatre Rhinoceros in San Francisco and Chicago's Lionheart Gay Theatre have also sponsored playwriting contests. Meridian's staged reading series give playwrights a chance to see their works performed before an audience, and Theatre Rhinoceros Gay Writers Workshop functions as both a support group for the writers and laboratory for new writing. These efforts may not bear fruit tomorrow, but their ongoing presence will help gay writers produce a significant body of work.

Mount high-quality productions. Severe financial limitations shouldn't be a hindrance to high-quality work. Imagination, ingenuity and a lot of elbow grease is necessary for gay companies to produce the best work possible, but the gay network is famous, so companies should use it to their best advantage. No doubt someone in the cast or crew knows someone who tricked with someone who runs an antique clothing store or fabric shop, so necessary materials can be procured inexpensively. Gay theatre companies must take themselves seriously if their audiences are to. Seriousness of intent will not solve all problems, but at least the commitment should show.

Keep it simple. One sure way to accomplish professional work is to be realistic about the capabilities of one's theatre company. If your staff and acting pool is limited, don't try to produce a multi-set musical extravaganza. For beginning companies, do an evening of one-acts or a single-set, full-length play with a small cast. It's better to start small and achieve steady, respectable growth than to set impressive-sounding goals and fall on your face.

Reach out creatively to the community. Gay theatre companies have been doing this for years, but a reminder never hurts. The idea is to produce plays in an already rent-paid situation to help keep costs down. For the past decade, theatres have been producing Doric Wilson's *The West Street Gang* and *Street Theater* in "environmental" productions—in bars during their early evening off-peak hours. Not only does this limit expenses, it's also a good way to reach gay audiences that may not usually go to the theatre. In some cities, gay theatre companies have aligned themselves with the local gay community center. While this can cause scheduling and logistical problems, it can also provide a recognizable locale as a means of attracting audiences. In New York City some producers have donated proceeds from entire runs of plays as benefits for the Gay Men's Health Crisis, which helped publicity. Don't be afraid to try some unusual strategies.

These suggestions may not save struggling companies, but they can serve as a springboard for those with the will, stamina and energy to produce gay theatre in the 1980s.

Gay Concerts

by Stan Leventhal

IF YOU'RE ANYTHING LIKE ME, YOU KEEP YOUR EYES WIDE and an ear to the ground to spot the "Next Big Thing" in music. Perhaps it's right in your own backyard or, if you're a city-dweller, right on your windowsill—and you haven't noticed. Sure, Michael Jackson and Madonna are popular, but let's face it, their routines are strictly for kids. The modern pop star is, to put it delicately, less than sensitive to the needs of mature homosexuals.

Which is one reason why gay concerts have become so popular. Whether they become the Next Big Thing is still uncertain, but what have you heard about lately that offers any competition? Mud wrestling? Pia Zadora? Nouvelle cuisine? Face the facts: when you saw Dolly Parton you almost got into a brawl with some marines. The Jackson's tour, though a joy to behold, took a chunk out of your bank account that necessitated peanut butter and jelly sandwiches for two and a half weeks. At the Van Halen concert some skinny kid puked all over your brand new shoes. Compared to these extravaganzas, gay concerts seem like sound alternatives.

The two types of gay concerts that have begun to attract large audiences are performed by gay male choruses and lesbian singer-songwriters. Polysexual marching bands have been known to remain stationary long enough to perform in a concert hall, but so far they've made about as much impact as handcuffs at a jack-off club.

The phenomenon of gay concerts has developed over the last ten years. Certain female singers who traditionally sang about peace and granola came out as lesbians and began extolling the virtues of womanlove. At about the same time all the gay men who had lead roles in high school and college musicals but never achieved Broadway stardom began to form choral groups. It didn't take long for the hipsters in the gay community to start spreading the word. Before you knew it, gay concerts were selling out Carnegie Hall. Walt Whitman and Gertrude Stein, even in their wildest flights of fancy, never could have predicted such activity. But just as yuppies, personal computers and tofutti have become endemic of our contemporary world, so gay concerts have become a magnificent part of the cultural scene.

Of course your enjoyment of a gay concert depends a great deal on the performers, but also on your expectations, those with whom you attend, what you wear and how you behave. As a veteran observer of this musical genre, I offer a few tips to the uninitiated.

Although children and parents are welcome at these concerts, extreme caution should be exercised. Impressionable youths, otherwise doomed to a heterosexual existence, may wind up seeking aversion therapy so they too can grow up to be a lesbian with a guitar or a clone in a tuxedo. These role models can be very alluring. Each child's personal psychological profile must be considered before allowing entry into the auditorium.

Parents should be invited only if they themselves are gay or if they've come to terms completely with their son's or daughter's gayness. The spectacle of one hundred and fifty men belting out "Mad About The Boy" leaves little room for doubt. Some parents like to let you think they know what's going on, but remain blissfully unaware. Their equilibrium could be undermined after two and a half songs. Be careful.

If you decide to bring straight friends to one of these events, some explanations beforehand may be of great value. You might tell them, for example, that if they've ever seen Liberace, David Bowie or Anne Murray, they've been to a gay concert. It might help also if you inform them that the term "gay concert" is not synonymous with "cheerful songs." Warn them, should a straight couple be your guests, that any flagrant displays of heterosexuality will be tolerated but not appreciated.

What one wears to one of these programs depends on what one hopes to accomplish. If one is seeking to meet the man of his dreams, the middle-of-the-road outfit is a good strategy—the radicalism of tank-tops with jockstraps and conservatism of three-piece suits both extreme. In a polo shirt, casual slacks and Topsiders one is on safer ground.

If you bring a straight woman to a gay concert and she looks too overtly hetero—pleated skirts, frilly blouses with circle pins and saddle shoes would be a definite giveaway—she may encounter looks of sympathy. She may even be offered help. Tell her it's best to consider a look that is butch—khakis or overalls might do fine. Even a pants suit. But caution her not to overdo it. A fraudulent lesbian can be spotted from as few as fifteen paces.

And straight men should be warned as well. A phony gay man, when confronted with the real thing, will rarely provoke violence. Feelings of embarrassment, shame and inferiority, however, may lodge themselves within the psyche of the imposter. Unless one can handle attitude dispersal like a seasoned gym queen, it's best not to impersonate that which one can never be. Leather drag, construction helmets and spaghetti straps are no-nos. Blazers, chinos and wingtips are probably the best choice.

But the main thing to consider when bringing first-timers is that gay men's choruses perform a lot of show tunes and lesbian singer-songwriters perform a lot of political material with a radical slant. It would be as unwise to bring someone who hates Broadway musicals to hear a gay chorus as it would be to bring someone who voted for Reagan to hear a lesbian singer-songwriter. Unless you desire to convert a non-believer. A noble deed, but I should warn you that you're taking a risk. If this is someone you wish to alienate, attendance at a gay concert may be the perfect solution. On the other hand, if it's a good friend why endanger a healthy relationship?

A few words on the subject of lobby etiquette will be helpful. You're bound to spend some time before the concert, during intermission and after the encores in the lobby of a respectable music hall. While there's nothing wrong with asserting one's gayness, it would be foolish to act as though you're in the back room of a notorious sex club. If you must, do your drugs beforehand or in the men's room. And while discreet cruising is not objectionable, hardcore sex acts will be looked upon as improper, even by the most liberated. Try to impose some self-control and save the sex for later. You'll be glad you decided to wait. Trust me on this.

And a word on your conduct in the auditorium. I know it's tempting to shout "Bravo!" every time something is sung well, but too much praise lavished on any performer usually results in too many encores. A bit of restraint will prevent the trauma induced by missing a moment of Joan Rivers or Saturday Night Live.

A little planning and common sense are all it really takes to enjoy a gay concert. If approached correctly the rewards will be numerous, the disappointments few. If, however, you're one of those who finds such fare to be rather tame and simply can't be bothered, don't get upset. There are alternatives. If you're willing to take the chance, you might find satisfaction in America's other gay spectator events—roller derby and opera.

Gay Bars, Gay Identities

by T. R. Witomski

IN THE WIDELY-READ BUT WOEFULLY INACCURATE EVERY-
thing You Always Wanted To Know About Sex But Were Afraid
to Ask, David Reuben wrote:

> The first visit to a gay bar is quite an experience. Superficially, it
> seems like any other cocktail lounge. Men and women sit at the bar
> and mingle freely at booths and tables. There is the usual background
> of conversation with male and female voices balancing each other.
> Then it slowly begins to sink in—the entire room is filled with men!
>   The feminine whispers, the high-pitched laughter, the soft
> sighs, are men's voices. The cocktail dresses, the tight black outfits,
> are worn by men. Even the trim, middle-age matron entering the
> ladies room . . . is a man.[1]

Now that we know what a gay bar is not, we may move on.

The history of gay bars is the history of the emergence of gay
identity. Gay identity is not synonymous with homosexuality.
Homosexual acts have always occurred, but a widespread, large
gay society is a relatively modern phenomenon. Though gay bars
are used to connect with sex partners, their primary purpose is
social, not sexual.

John Boswell, in his widely-acclaimed Christianity, Social
Tolerance and Homosexuality, makes a well-researched claim
that the origins of gay society may be found in the monasteries of
the early Middle Ages. Since many of the monasteries made their
own alcoholic beverages and were all-male societies, by a stretch
of the imagination, they could be viewed as the gay bars of their
time.[2] But not until the eighteenth-century were gathering places
established exclusively to cater to people with shared erotic
tastes.

The most notorious of these clubs was the Hell Fire Club,
formed in England around 1750. Here, all forms of sexuality
were practiced, tinged with Satanism and anticlericalism and
overtones of sadomasochism.[3] Today, in New York and Chicago,

two clubs use the name Hell Fire, but modern Hell Fire members are more likely to don leather for their sexual rituals rather than the garb of nuns and priests as their namesakes did.

In France in the late 1700s a group of nobles formed *La Saintecongregation des glorieux pederastes* (Sacred Fraternity of Glorious Pederasts).[4] Members were sworn to avoid women—except to produce heirs—attended formal orgies, and wore beneath their coats a cross with a picture of a man trampling a woman as a sign to those in-the-know of their sexual preference, thus making them forerunners of today's gays who sport symbolic arrangements of keys and handkerchiefs.

By the nineteenth-century recognizable gay bars were a feature of most large American cities. One of the earliest references reads:

> During the last decade of the nineteenth century, the headquarters for [male homosexuals] . . . of the upper and middle classes was "Paresis Hall," on Fourth Avenue several blocks south of Fourteenth Street [in New York City]. In front was a modest bar-room; behind a small beer-garden . . . Paresis Hall was as innocuous as any sex resort. Its existence really brought not the least detriment to any one or to the social body as a whole. More than that: It was a necessary safety-valve to the social body. It is not in the power of every adult to settle down in the monogamous and monandrous love-nest ordained for all by our leaders of thought . . . [Paresis Hall] was one of the "sights" for out-of-towners who hired a guide to take them through New York's Underworld.[5]

In *Sexual Inversion*, Havelock Ellis published a report from a correspondent on the gay scene in the United States at the beginning of the twentieth century:

> The world of sexual inverts is, indeed, a large one in any American city, and it is a community distinctly organized—words, customs, traditions of its own; and every city has its numerous meeting places: certain churches where inverts congregate, certain cafes well known for the inverted character of their patrons; certain streets where, at night, every fifth man is an invert. The inverts have their own "clubs" with nightly meetings. These "clubs" are, really, dance halls, attached to saloons, and presided over by the proprietor of the saloon, himself almost invariably an invert, as are all the waiters and musicians. The frequenters of these places are male

sexual inverts (usually ranging from seventeen to thirty years of age); sightseers find no difficulty in gaining entrance; truly they are welcomed for the drinks they buy for the company—and other reasons. Singing and dancing turns by certain favorite performers are the features of these gatherings, with much gossip and drinking at the small tables ranged along the four walls of the room . . . You will rightly infer that the police know of these places and endure their existence for a consideration; it is not unusual for the inquiring stranger to be directed there by a policeman.[6]

If the quaintness of the language is ignored, these two descriptions could be of gay bars today. While individual gay bars come into and go out of business continually, the gay bar system is remarkably stable. According to psychologist Evelyn Hooker, this stability is due to three facts: 1-Gay bars are highly lucrative for their owners; 2-gay bars meet the expectations and needs of a large number of people; 3-even homophobes believe unofficially that the elimination of the system is both undesirable and impossible; according to one policeman quoted by Hooker, "That kind of people has to have someplace to go and at least they are with their own kind, and you don't lose 'em—you just move 'em around a little."[7]

Just as there is no one type of gay person, there is no one type of gay bar. The diversity of gay bars at least in major urban areas was quite established by the 1950s, as Howard Brown noted in his memoir *Familiar Faces, Hidden Lives:*

Friends in Detroit had provided me with a classified list of more than fifty gay bars in New York: elegant bars, homely bars, dancing bars and so on. Gradually I was able to transfer my social life from the bars to the apartments and town houses of the men I had met there. My circle of acquaintances expanded in no time.

But perhaps we should slip back into those bars for a moment . . .

. . . In the summer of 1954 I walked into the East 55—a gay bar that took its name from its location on East Fifty-fifth Street in Manhattan—and found myself in a very posh place indeed. Everybody was well dressed; there was a fancy pianist jazzing up the air, and the restaurant served excellent food. Could a bumpkin physician who was also somewhat fussy afford to be seen in such a place? He could.

I met Mark at the East 55 bar one freezing winter night. He said

I was the first gay man he had met who had a graduate degree in anything. He, in turn, was the first gay man I had met who was interested in social causes. He was a graduate of the Wharton School of Finance and worked with a well-known liberal organization. Something of a *nouveau demi-riche*, I had rented a small penthouse on East Fifty-second Street overlooking the river and the United Nations Building. I invited him up, and we talked for hours. We did not go to bed together. Homosexuals can be just friends, too. Mark and I still are.

Meeting Mark—and meeting him, moreover, in a gay bar—helped me to see gay social life in a new way. I had learned that there were places a homosexual could go where it was even possible to meet his peers.

The Blue Parrot—a couple of blocks from my apartment—was smaller, more intimate, decidedly less elegant, and cheaper than the East 55. Since it was so close to home, I often dropped in. The men who hung out there reminded me of my fraternity brothers back at Hiram, getting on and growing chunky. Mark, like most of the men at the East 55, wore elegantly tailored suits. The guys at the Blue Parrot dressed casually and looked straight . . .

Shaw's—also in my neighborhood, at Third Avenue and Forty-ninth Street—was a gay bar for a special set: the supermasculine crowd. The men who frequented Shaw's dressed up as city cowboys, in Levi's and boots and as much leather (such bars are known as leather bars) as they could pack on one body. I looked almost criminally out of place in my blue business suit. I had come in part because I was intrigued by the thought of men who took such extreme measures to avoid effeminacy (no transvestite would have dared to enter Shaw's), but mainly to make a pickup.[8]

When post-Stonewall liberation brought droves of gay men out of their closets, they brought gay bars with them. Finding a gay bar used to be a major undertaking—the bars lacked advertising venues, were often located off-the-beaten-track, and frequently didn't post an identifying sign outside. But several years ago, when living in Florida, I saw in the local newspaper's weekend entertainment section a listing for the Parliament House that proclaimed the place a "gay club." Outside the club was a huge, brilliantly lit sign that told me "this must be the place." We had indeed come a long way, baby.

Unless you find yourself dead center in the Mojave Desert, you're never probably more than a few hours' drive from a gay bar. Oddly, outside of major cities they tend to be on the average larger than the typical New York or San Francisco bar. Bars in gay Meccas tend to be extraordinarily specialized: leather bars, serious leather bars, dance bars, chicken/chicken hawk bars, hustler bars, Yuppie bars, singalong piano bars, literary bars, bars which primarily attract a black or Hispanic or Oriental clientele. But outside of cities with very large gay populations the bars are more like "one size fits all." In Heartland, USA, you can find bars featuring drag shows in one room, a piano player in another and posturing leathermen in a third—a combination that attests to the diversity of the gay community throughout the country.

T hough bars are a staple feature of American gay life, they aren't centers around which most gay people build their lives. In a study by Martin S. Weinberg and Colin J. Williams, more than fifty percent of the respondents said they went to gay bars "about once every few months" or even less often.[9] But if everyone who has ever sworn "I'm not going to go to the bars anymore" were to uphold his statement, all bars would be empty.

For one gay minority the bars function as extended living rooms. For another minority the bars could as well be on other planets—these gay men have never been to a gay bar and have no wish to go. Most of us are somewhere in the middle of these extremes—attending bars, say, once or twice weekly or monthly, or when going out with a particular group of friends or on vacation.

After the thousands of hours I've spent in gay bars hither and yon, it would be unseemly (to say nothing of psychotic) for me to write negatively about them. I really do think your chances of finding a lover for the rest of your life (if that's what you're looking for) are probably as good in a bar as anywhere else. And your chances of finding a trick in a bar are somewhat better than that (though in this age of AIDS, casual tricks ain't what they used to be).

In some bars it is—or at least until recently *was*—perfectly correct to accost a complete stranger and introduce yourself with a detailed description of just what sexual activities he should participate with you to make you happy. (In a few bars it is/was perfectly correct to accost a complete stranger and introduce yourself with a detailed description of just what sexual activities he should participate with you *right then and there* to make you happy.) This ploy was successful rather more often than one would suppose, and undoubtedly many gay couples originally met as a result of this, er, direct approach, and now live together in suburban bliss in Toms River, New Jersey. However, trying such a path to nirvana in bars where it is disapproved of has been known to produce dire repercussions.

Since gay bar going is a social activity, being comfortable in gay bars is not unrelated to being comfortable with one's gay identity. Most gays live their daily lives "acting straight"; even gays who are "out" to coworkers and family conform to varying degrees to heterosexual norms of behavior. Paradoxically, gays may therefore find it more difficult to relate to other gays than to straights. In gay bars they may feel overly intimidated and unable to relax. Or fueled by alcohol and/or other drugs, gays may use bars as stages to act out heights of obnoxiousness.

Every primer on meeting new friends and winning lovers seems to intone *Be yourself*. I'm not sure that's such good advice. Better to go to a gay bar being the person you want to be. And then you can still do everything the learned advisors tell you to do: Look pleased to be where you are. Don't be afraid to initiate conversations; you *can* talk with people you have no sexual interest in. Have a positive attitude; if you keep whining about not having a lover, you'll never have a lover. Enjoy yourself. Be gay, damn it. *Gay*. Look it up.

Because much of gay socializing takes place in bars or at other gatherings where alcohol is available, and since homosexuals are bombarded daily with messages from the hetero world that tell them being gay is *not* OK, alcoholism is pandemic among gay men. Reliable studies estimate that more than twenty percent of the gay population is drinking alcoholically.[10] Alcoholism can be as incurable and progressive and as ultimately lethal as AIDS. If you think you have a problem with alcohol, you do: Calling Alcoholics Anonymous (listed in every phonebook) is a first step on the road to sanity.

Gay bars are not a metaphor. Though sad, self-destructive alcoholics and giddy, amoral disco bunnies are found in gay bars, these people do not epitomize the gay bar system. And neither do gay bars symbolize the decadence of society. The Jerry

Falwells see gay bars as evidence of the decline of Western Civilization, but gay bars are simply not *that* good. Gay bars are a phenomenon; they are *there* in the same way that supermarkets, laundromats, and movie theaters are there, as places to frequent if you find they fulfill a need.

THE INS AND OUTS OF GAY BARS: TEN OBSERVATIONS

1. Think carefully before you say: "Every year the crowd here gets younger."

2. No one out for a few, simple, quiet drinks and a single, simple safesex trick will be even vaguely impressed by your public articulation of any of the following bits of information: Joan Crawford's shoe size; your personal acquaintance with a well-known porno writer or nude model; where you once saw Truman Capote; how to care for African violets; a past which—even for a moment—featured a feathered boa; what your last lover did to you to cause the irreconcilable breakup of the relationship; the "important" names in your trick book; an opinion on opera (patrons of leather bars must be particularly scrupulously careful to avoid this one—no matter how overwhelming the temptation); a "divine" recipe; a novel use for wire hangers.

3. Though *All About Eve* is a wonderfully witty movie, do not use any of its lines in life—or in a bar.

4. The following opening lines are nevermore to be used in a bar:

    > "What time is it?"
    > "Got a light?"
    > "Isn't your name John?"
    > "Crowded, isn't it?"

    Instead, substitute:

    > "What year is it?"
    > "Wow! What great socks!"
    > "Are your teeth real?"
    > "Are you as superficial as I am?"

5. The Law of Gay Bars: The sleazier the bar, the higher the average income of its patrons. Corollary: The number of

broken toilets in a bar is directly proportional to the number of American Express cardholders present.

6. Terrible punishments are in store in the next life for those who think a bar designed as a jail cell is cute and for the inventor(s) of the licorice whip.

7. The ability to concurrently drink, gossip, cruise, and roll a joint is not a job skill.

8. No bar should have three bathrooms. The third bathroom will occasion "clever" remarks which are always out of place.

9. Yelling "Mary!" in a crowded gay bar will result in hundreds of sprained necks.

10. Despite the many and varied interesting experiences that have happened to you in gay bars, do not under any circumstances write them down.

Notes

[1] (New York: Bantam Books, 1971), p. 178.

[2] (Chicago: The University of Chicago Press, 1980), pp. 159–60, 187–88, 191–93, 218–28.

[3] Vern L. Bullough, *Sexual Variance in Society and History* (Chicago: The University of Chicago Press, 1980), p. 480.

[4] Ibid., p. 483.

[5] Earl Lind, *The Female Impersonators* (New York: *Medico-Legal Journal*, 1922) quoted in Jonathan Katz, ed., *Gay American History* (New York: Thomas Y. Crowell Company, 1976), pp. 366–67.

[6] Quoted in Katz, p. 52.

[7] "The Homosexual Community" in Ralph W. Weltge, ed., *The Same Sex* (Philadelphia, Pilgrim Press, 1969), p. 31.

[8](New York: Harcourt Brace Jovanovich, 1976), pp. 54–56.

[9]*Male Homosexuals: Their Problems and Adaptations* (New York, Penguin Books, Inc., 1969), p. 145.

[10]Gay Council on Drinking Behavior, *The Way Back* (Washington, D.C.: Whitman-Walker Clinic, Inc., 1981), p. 2.

Books and the Gay Identity—a Personal Look

by Jesse Monteagudo

BOOKS PLAY A MAJOR ROLE IN THE WAY GAY MEN COME TO terms with their sexuality. Even today most gay men grow up apart from other gay people. We lack the personal contact and role models which help other minority group members cope with being different. Without these role models many of us turn to books to learn more about ourselves. We search in books for information and reassurance, but what many of us find may be neither informative nor reassuring.

During the sixties, when I first became aware of my sexual attraction for other males, America's homophile organizations were already a decade old, and some books were beginning to reflect positive attitudes towards homosexuality. As far as I was concerned, however, they might as well not have existed. Most of the books available to me spouted the age-old negative stereotypes about "the third sex," often in the guise of "science."

Gay youth growing up in today's increasingly tolerant climate, with a vast and diverse body of literature at their disposal, don't realize how different things were only twenty years ago. At that time most books written about homosexuality—including those found in school and public libraries—treated the condition negatively, as a crime, a sickness or a sign of moral disorder. Sometimes these books were kept in a special section of the library. Young people could obtain them only with a special pass or their parents' consent. This reinforced the idea that homosexuality was something so gruesome it had to be hidden from impressionable children.

There was nothing to worry about. For most books at the time portrayed the homosexual lifestyle so negatively as to immediately discourage the reader from further interest. Most nonfiction authors dwelt on the sensational aspects of our community—like transsexuals—or concentrated on men who sought a psychiatric cure for their homosexuality. This biased and limited perspective was prevalent in scholarly works, like Charles Socarides' *The Overt Homosexual*, as well as in books written for a mass audience, like Jess Stearn's now-classic *The Sixth Man*. In *The Sixth Man*, Stearn wrote about the "Homintern"—a group of powerful homosexuals who sought to spread deviance around the country through various ways—and assured his readers that the "mod look" in women's clothes was a plot by gay fashion designers to make American women look ugly.

Fiction was no better. While James Barr (*Quatrefoil*), Christopher Isherwood (*A Single Man*) and Jay Little (*Maybe—Tomorrow*) produced positive novels about male homosexuals, most fiction authors sided with the majority in how they depicted "the third sex." Books with such revealing titles as *The Flaming Heart* by Deborah Deutsch, *Desire in the Shadows* by Joe Houston and *The Strange Ones* by Ben Travis depicted gay lifestyle as a fount of misery awaiting death. They gave us a world of miserable wretches who aped the other gender, were obsessed with sex, and whose sordid lifestyle led to ruin, degradation and, often, suicide.

I had no role models who could help me come to terms with my emerging sexuality. Growing up in Miami's Cuban community—then, as now, homophobic—the only (mis)information I had was my friends' fag jokes, my father's admonitions about being picked up by homos, a couple of swishy stereotypes who lived in the neighborhood, and a misleading television documentary which appeared in the wake of Florida's attempt to purge its schools of gay teachers in 1964. The view of gay life I gleaned from these founts of knowledge was a twilight world of drag queens, child molesters, and sex in public toilets.

Had I had access to a body of gay-positive literature, I would have had an easier time coming to terms with myself. After all, I was able to rise above my environment's reactionary political views by reading liberal authors. My local libraries' enlightened view, however, stopped at matters of sex. My reading on the subject was limited to a few dreary medical texts and hysterical popular accounts. The worst of these was *Everything You Al-*

ways Wanted to Know About Sex (But Were Afraid to Ask), a bestseller written in 1969 by Dr. David Reuben. Though Dr. Reuben's thoughts on heterosexuality did much to improve the public's attitude on the issue, when it came to homosexuality his book was a disaster. In Dr. Reuben's universe, homosexual men were pathetic neurotics constantly in search of a quick sex fix, whose sex drives often led to violence, and who were doomed to living lives without love, companionship, or even satisfactory sex. Though Reuben's idea of gays was certainly not unique, his book's popularity ensured that his views were widely disseminated.

It was the first book (after the Bible) to affect my views on homosexuality. Its influence was profound and entirely negative. It kept me in the closet throughout my high school years. I was determined, after reading Dr. Reuben, not to end up in a hospital, undergoing a sex change operation or having a coke bottle surgically removed from my ass. My high school years were a period of great personal conflict and sexual frustration. Only when I entered college in 1972 did I begin to indulge in sex, and even then I limited myself to brief encounters in adult bookstores and the cruisy campus library restroom.

During my high school years the only books I found which described male homosexuality in a positive light were pornographic books I found in adult bookstores. I recall reading quite a few of them at the time; not, alas, now-classic works by Phil Andros or Richard Amory, but tripe written by hacks writing under pseudonyms whose sole purpose was to get their readers' rocks off as often as possible. Their titles are forgotten, for they were hastily disposed of as soon as I finished reading so that my parents wouldn't find them (I was living at home at the time). These books presented a view of homosexuality a world apart from Dr. Reuben's. In the fantasy world of gay pornography, mansex was enjoyable, an act repeatedly performed by handsome, muscular young men free of guilt! While these books were clearly set in a fantasy world, they provided me with an alternative which, under different circumstances, could be a part of my life. In short, the one-hand pulp novels taught me that gay sex could be fun.

Fortunately my college years coincided with the wave of gay liberation which followed the Stonewall riots. While visiting relatives in Los Angeles in 1971 I spotted a copy of The Advocate in a vending machine; when I asked my cousin what it was, I was told, quite simply, a homosexual newspaper. Though too timid to buy a copy, the idea of a newspaper for homosexuals started me thinking. Shortly thereafter, I read Merle Miller's coming-out story in The New York Times (later published in book form as On Being Different), and learned there were successful people who were also homosexual. The appearance of movies with gay themes—like Midnight Cowboy and Myra Breckinridge—led me to read the novels on which they were based (by James Leo Herlihy and Gore Vidal, respectively). I eagerly began to search out books by and about famous gay men like Marcel Proust and Oscar Wilde, and I thrilled to D. H. Lawrence's Women in Love (also made into a movie), the nude wrestling scene giving me an instant hard-on.

Gay liberation caught up with me when I obtained a part-time job in the campus library. By 1973 books began to be written which reflected the emerging movement. Though many libraries still refused to carry the new gay books, my college library wasn't one of them. As a result of the library's openness, my college education proceeded on two levels: my formal academic program and my informal course in gay liberation. Needless to say, the gay books contributed more to my personal development than any college text.

The titles themselves were eye-openers: Society and the Healthy Homosexual (George Weinberg), Out of the Closets (Karla Jay and Allen Young), I Have More Fun with You than Anybody (Lige Clark and Jack Nichols). Though these books recognized the problems inherent in being a homosexual, they blamed such problems on homophobia—a term coined by Dr. Weinberg to describe the irrational fear of homosexuality. In addition, these books showed me the benefits and pleasures of a liberated gay lifestyle.

The best of these books was Peter Fisher's The Gay Mystique (Stein & Day, 1972), a well-written introduction to male homosexuality written with perception and wit. Fisher did not write as a "detached" heterosexual examining homosexuality through a microscope. Rather he wrote from a first-person perspective, combining general observations with personal experience. Fisher was a man I could relate to, who went through a period of guilt and confusion before learning to accept himself.

By coming out, Fisher was able to build a successful career as an author and gay activist, and to establish a satisfying and enduring relationship with Marc Rubin. Peter Fisher was the role model I was looking for.

The new gay books did more than build my self-esteem; they introduced me to a variety of gay lifestyles and institutions. No longer was it necessary to cruise tearooms or porno palaces in order to get my rocks off. These books told me where to go to become a part of the emerging gay culture, and gave me the courage and confidence to go there. After all, if these authors could be openly gay and feel good about it, so could I. I came out in 1973, and never returned to the closet. Inspired by my friend Mark Silber, who in 1973 helped start the Stonewall Library, I began to collect lesbian and gay books.

The importance of gay literature in my life has led me to introduce this literature to other gay people, in my work as a book reviewer and supporter of the Stonewall Library. The past decade has seen the publication of hundreds of books designed to help gay men and lesbians come to terms with their identities—politically, culturally and sexually.

A few titles deserve recommendation. In addition to *The Gay Mystique*, a good first book to read is *Coming Out Right: A Handbook for the Gay Male*, by Wes Muchmore and William Hanson (Alyson, 1982), which is full of information every gay man should know. Don Clark's *Loving Someone Gay* (New American Library, 1978) describes the pleasures of a gay lifestyle which might be useful during the coming out process. *The Christopher Street Reader*, edited by Michael Denneny, Charles Ortleb and Thomas Steele (Coward, McCann, 1982), is a collection of articles originally published in *Christopher Street* magazine, and covers a wide variety of topics.

Gay men looking for advice on relationships, religion, the law and other topics should read *Positively Gay* (Celestial Arts, 1979), an anthology edited by Betty Berzon. The best book for and about gay male couples is *The Male Couple*, by David McWhirter and Andrew Mattison (Prentice Hall, 1982). The legal aspects of being gay are dealt with in *The Rights of Gay People: An American Civil Liberties Union Handbook*, by E. Carrington Boggan, et al. (Bantam second edition, 1983), and in *A Legal*

Guide for Lesbian and Gay Couples, by Hayden Curry and Denis Clifford (Addison, Wesley, 1980). The *Advocate Guide to Gay Health*, by R. D. Fenwick (Alyson, 1982) is a useful resource on health matters which, unfortunately, was published too early to have much information about AIDS. The best books written about AIDS thus far are *The AIDS Fact Book*, by Ken Mayer and Hank Pizer (Bantam, 1983) and *How to Have Sex in an Epidemic*, by Richard Berkowitz and Michael Callen (News from the Front, 1983).

For those wishing to learn about their past, Vern Bullough's *Sexual Variance in Society and History* (University of Chicago, 1976) is the best general history. John Boswell's *Christianity, Social Tolerance & Homosexuality* (University of Chicago, 1980) is a fascinating history of gay people in Europe from the beginning of the Christian Era to 1300. Jonathan Katz's *Gay American History* (Harper & Row, 1985) is a collection of historical documents while *Sexual Politics, Sexual Communities* by John D'Emilio (University of Chicago, 1983) is a narrative history of the gay movement in the United States from 1940 to 1970. Finally, in *Another Mother Tongue* (Beacon Press, 1984) Judy Grahn looks at the roots of gay language and lifestyles, and persuasively argues for the existence of a centuries' old, worldwide gay and lesbian culture.

Black Men/White Men (Gay Sunshine Press, 1983), edited by Michael J. Smith of Black and White Men Together (an interracial gay organization), is a good but flawed introduction to black gay men and interracial gay relationships. *Now the Volcano*, edited by Winston Leyland (Gay Sunshine Press, 1979), is a literary anthology of gay fiction from Latin American countries, primarily Brazil. There is a larger volume of material written about older and younger gay men. The best in both categories was published by Alyson Publications: *Gay and Gray* by Raymond M. Berger (1984) and *Young, Gay & Proud!* (1980).

Gay fiction has kept up with nonfiction in both quality and quantity. E. M. Forster's *Maurice* (W. W. Norton, 1971) and Christopher Isherwood's *A Single Man* (Avon, 1977) are classics as readable now as when they were first written. Among the best contemporary gay novels are *Moritz!* by Bob Herron (Calamus Books, 1983), *Dancer from the Dance* by Andrew Holleran (Bantam, 1979), *Tropic Lights* by Gerald Lebonati (Knights Press,

1985), *Tales of the City* (and its sequels) by Armistead Maupin (Harper & Row, 1978) and *A Boy's Own Story*, by Edmund White (New American Library, 1983). *On the Line: New Gay Fiction*, edited by Ian Young (The Crossing Press, 1980) is a good collection of short stories. The best collection of gay poetry in print is *The Penguin Book of Homosexual Verse* by Stephen Coote (1983).

Though libraries no longer keep gay-oriented books in special collections, prejudice often determines the selection of books, especially if the library is located in a rural area or the Bible Belt. As a rule, libraries are more likely to stock a gay book if 1) it's published by a major press, 2) it's written by an established author (or a highly-acclaimed new author) and, 3) does not contain sexually explicit material. Only nonfiction books dealing directly with homosexuality are found under "homosexuality"; fiction, biographies and books dealing with history, the arts or other topics are found under their respective sections.

In some major cities gay activists have started libraries and archives of gay-related material, whether as independent units or as part of existing gay organizations. One of the leading gay libraries in the country is the Stonewall Library, located in Fort Lauderdale, Florida. Founded by Mark Silber in 1973, the Stonewall Library has over a thousand books and countless periodicals and documents, and serves as both a research center and lending library.

The same rule that governs most libraries' selection of gay books also applies to most bookstores, except the stores are more likely to carry sexually explicit material. While few bookstores have a separate "gay section," most place gay-related books in various sections according to topic. As a paying customer, you'll get better service at a bookstore than in a library; salespeople are always ready to help, and if a certain book isn't in stock, most stores will special-order a copy from the publisher.

Adult bookstores are often the first place where a gay man comes in contact with gay books. Porno bookstores are found in most urban areas, except where censorship movements have succeeded in closing them down. Books found there are sexually explicit and often of dubious literary value. While they might help one gain a positive gay identity, they're no substitute for better-written, quality gay books.

Located in most large cities, gay bookstores are often gay-owned, movement-oriented businesses that may also serve as community centers. In addition to providing a supportive environment, gay bookstores offer a wider selection of gay books, including books by small presses not found elsewhere. Many of them also provide a small order catalog service for out-of-town customers.

Among the gay bookstores which also provide catalog service are "Chosen Books," 940 West McNichols, Detroit, MI 48203, (313) 864-0485; "A Different Light Bookstore," 4014 Santa Monica Blvd., Los Angeles, CA 90020, (213) 666-0629; "Giovanni's Room," 345 S Street, Philadelphia, PA 19107, (215) 923-2960; "Lambda Passages," 3931 West Davie Blvd., Fort Lauderdale, FL 33312, (305) 584-6969; "Lamda Rising," 1625 Connecticut Avenue, NW, Washington, D.C. 20009, (202) 462-6969; "Outright Books," 901-C Duval Street, Key West, FL 33040, (305) 296-5356; and the "Oscar Wilde Memorial Bookshop," 15 Christopher Street, New York, NY 10014, (212) 255-8097. For the addresses of other bookstores check the *Gayellow Pages*, Renaissance House, Box 292, Village Station, New York, NY 10014.

Though major publishers are no longer reluctant to publish books dealing with homosexuality, most gay books are still published by small, gay-owned presses. Gay presses are more likely to take risks than major publishers to publish books written by new authors or that deal with sexually explicit or politically controversial material. They are also more community-oriented and thus more in touch with their readers. Though small press books are only found in gay or special interest bookstores, they can be purchased directly from the publisher, at the list price plus postage.

One of the most important tasks for gay men today is to create and preserve gay-positive literature. We cannot trust that the future will see increased acceptance of homosexuality. Germany under the Weimar Republic was relatively tolerant of homosexuality, but it was followed by the violently homophobic Third Reich. One of the Nazis' first acts was to burn all literature they did not approve of—which included all books which provided a positive view of homosexuality. *They* knew the power of

The AIDS epidemic and the rise of the Moral Majority threaten us with a backlash which could do away with the progress—and books—we have acquired since Stonewall. Though there are as yet no bonfires, the rise of anti-pornography laws and censorship of school and library texts could very well hearken a large-scale suppression of gay-positive literature. Our enemies know the power of books; that is why they seek to control them. We must work to keep the libraries and bookstores free, so that gay people in the future will have the options we didn't have when we were young.

Ride 'em, Cowperson: the National Reno Gay Rodeo

by Mike Hippler

T HE SIGN AT THE GATE MAKES IT CLEAR: "NOTICE—THIS IS a gay event. If it will bother you to see two men or two women together, please do not come in. If you're here to cause trouble you will be ejected. Thank you." If this were New York or San Francisco, such a sign wouldn't be necessary. But this is Reno, Nevada, and the event is the ninth annual National Reno Gay Rodeo at the Nevada State Fairgrounds. A little precaution goes a long way.

It is not the only gay rodeo in the country—there are others now in Denver and Houston, and elsewhere—but it's the oldest, the biggest, and, some say, the best. It was founded in 1975 by local rodeo buff Phil Ragsdale as an alternative to the bar scene, according to its founder. "We were trying to raise some money for a local charity. At the same time, we wanted to change the stereotype as to what gay people were supposed to be."

Ragsdale, who grew up on a farm in California's San Joaquin Valley and who had been involved in rodeo only in an amateur sense before, found the undertaking to be quite a bit more trouble than he had anticipated. His major problem was securing the livestock. Over 35 ranchers refused to rent him their animals when they found out the specific nature of the event. Only at the last moment, the day before the rodeo was scheduled to take place on October 2, 1976, did he obtain the livestock he needed.

That first rodeo attracted a grand total of 125 paying customers. The next year attendance grew to 400, and by 1982 over 10,000 people a day flocked to the Washoe County Fairgrounds for what had become by then one of the national gay community's most celebrated entertainment events. As the crowd grew, so did the scope of the rodeo. In 1982 visitors from all fifty states and over fifteen foreign countries jammed not only the main event but the weekend barn dances and country fair as well. Joan Rivers was the Grand Marshall, and celebrities present ranged from respected actress Nancy Walker to several international porn stars.

The Reno Gay Rodeo is open both to men and women, but unlike more traditional rodeos, in Reno men and women compete in each event equally. Women ride broncs and bulls as well as rope calfs. Men ride in barrel races. Although men still outnumber women, the number of women competing has grown each year. Most contestants are amateurs. Nearly all are gay. The rodeo is open to straight people as well, although Ragsdale is just as happy that few take part. "I didn't used to allow it," he admits. "I would hate to see the rodeo taken over by straights."

Fat chance.

It is early Saturday morning. So far, only a few cars have lumbered into the dusty parking lot of the Nevada State Fairgrounds (formerly the Washoe County Fairgrounds, but, like the rodeo, they've come up in the world). Ticket-sellers are arranging the money in their counting boxes. Vendors are readying their wares—cowboy hats, belts, buckles, buttons, T-shirts and the like. There is one booth for ear-piercing and another for tatooing. There is one advertising "Gay Jewelry" and another displaying license plate rims (one of these, however inappropriately, proclaims "2-Gether 4-ever, Mike and Debbie"). A hawker at the Dunk Tank practices her cry, "Dunk a Dyke, Sink a Sissy!" while off to one side, three men adjust the controls of a giant hot air balloon. They want to see if they get enough takers at $10 a ticket to justify bringing their balloon to similar events in the future.

Over at Command Central, located in a low, pre-fab building several hundred yards from the grandstand, Phil Ragsdale sits in the midst of a small cadre of workers, quietly talking on the phone. Most of the workers chew doughnuts or chat with one another. Ragsdale appears unhurried, at ease. Surely this is the calm before the storm. No, Ragsdale explains, it's simply that he has pulled his back out this morning and can't move. Summoning his lover on a walky-talky, he sends him out in one of the rodeo golf carts to unlock the press booth, one of the many details as yet left unattended.

In the exhibition hall behind the grandstand, Ron, 31, a part-time cowboy and full-time banker from Denver, is watching a group of cloggers practice while he waits for the rodeo to start. He will be a contestant today, competing in bulls, broncs, and barrels. It's his fourth year at Reno. He has also taken part in Denver's Rocky Mountain Regional and Cheyenne's Frontier Days, and in November will participate in Houston's very first gay rodeo. Sponsored by Poco's in Central City, Colorado, his number is 20. His major claim to fame, besides being chairman of events for the Colorado Gay Rodeo Association, is that last year in Reno he tied for first in cows.

Ron has no idea why he does what he does. "I just like it," he says. "I guess it's because I was raised on a farm in Ft. Collins, Colorado." Contrary to popular belief, he claims lots of gay people grow up on farms and ranches. For years they were an invisible part of the gay subculture, but sometime in the mid-seventies, when the Country-Western craze swept America's urban centers and its attendant gay ghettos, Country-Western faggots came into their own. "Dolly Parton made it easier for us," swears Ron, "as the first Country-Western singer who made it big in the gay bars." Without explaining he adds, "Joan Rivers did too."

"Riding in the rodeo is a positive statement," he feels, "much better than being in some drag show." In Denver he has been invited to benefits by his mayor and congressman. In his own family, however, that respect is harder to come by. Although his family has known he is gay since he was 23 and has learned to live with it, they don't like his involvement with the rodeo. "They say it embarrasses them," he offers. "They think I'm too public with what I do."

Mike, 39, is one of the oldest contestants in the rodeo. Born and raised in Dallas, he has lived for the last twenty years in Los Angeles, where he keeps two horses on land outside of town. He first became interested in the rodeo through his uncle, a professional rodeo rider, and attended professional rodeo school at Aurora Grande, California in 1971. He now rides for Floyd's Bar in Long Beach. When not riding broncs or cows, he's a purchasing director for a Los Angeles hospital.

Mike notes that opposition toward gay rodeo often comes from a formidable foe—professional rodeo riders. "They're very redneck against it," he states. "If you're a gay cowboy and they find out about it, your chances of staying on the professional circuit aren't great. They'll make it real hard on you." Consequently, Mike claims, most gays in professional circles maintain a low profile and avoid the gay rodeos altogether. This is one of the major reasons Mike chose not to become a professional.

Another reason Mike prefers amateur status is that the sport can be extremely dangerous. His friend Ron was trampled by a bull his first year at Reno and spent ten days in the hospital with internal bleeding. Nevertheless Ron fared better than one of the rodeo clowns gored by the same bull. Mike himself broke his arm in the ring last year at Denver. "I had the shit stomped out of me and woke up in an ambulance." Shortly after that he gained the nickname, "The Horse Killer," when his bronc ran into a fence and broke its neck. He felt sorry for the horse, of course, but was glad it was not his own neck.

So why does he do it? Mike shrugs his shoulders. "The thrill of doing it is incredible, the adrenaline going through you—it's great."

Cars are streaming steadily into the parking lot now, raising clouds of dust which slowly settle on license plates from a score of states. The drivers and their passengers sport brand-new cowboy hats and broad anticipatory smiles, but many of these smiles betray a hint of anxiety and guilt, for at the entrance to the parking lot a band of twenty animal-rights protestors beg potential spectators to boycott the event. "Gay rights yes, animal rights too!" they shout through megaphones. It makes little difference. The cars keep arriving and few, if any, turn away.

The opening of the rodeo sets the stage for what is to come. After riders carrying American flags gallop past the grandstand, the announcer calls for the rider carrying the California flag. The Reno Gay Rodeo flag is presented instead. Then the announcer bungles a few of the other introductions and forgets the Texas flag altogether. There are annoying delays and more than a little confusion on the field. The cowboys don't seem to know exactly what to do. But Grand Marshall Rose Maddox's hair is just the right shade of platinum, the sun continues to shine fiercely, and for a few, drugs are finally cashing in, so all is right with the world. Few people in the stands really care what goes on in the field, anyway. For them it's just another excuse to party.

Robert and John are fairly typical spectators. Lovers in their forties from Chicago (they met in a dirty bookstore there two years ago), they flew to Reno via Arizona, where they spent four days in the Grand Canyon. This is their first time to the Reno rodeo—to any rodeo for that matter—and they are having a ball. "We're already making plans to come back next year," says Robert, fondling the hoop in his ear. "It isn't just the rodeo. It's all the other things as well. Thursday's horse show was fun, and the boot-throwing contest was great to watch." At the dance festival he learned the difference between clogging and square dancing. But it's the barn dance at the Sands Hotel Saturday night that he looks forward to most. It promises to be the social highlight of the four-day weekend.

Near Robert and John a striking blond with bare, chiselled pectorals is hawking beer. He poses for a picture with a tall, dewy youth clad only in gym shorts, as giddy as a debutante at her first ball. As the debutante puts his arm around the beer seller, his genitals fall out of his gym shorts. He laughs, only mildly embarrassed, and rearranges his shorts. The beer-seller, however, asks the photographer not to print the picture, at least not publicly. "I'm a high school teacher, you see, and it wouldn't go over so well with the school board, I think."

On the field the barrel racing is under way. No one knocks over a barrel, and the most popular contestant is Inez, a hefty, fifty-year-old lesbian who loses her hat in the final stretch but who clocks a decent time nevertheless. Bull riding is supposed to be next, but the bulls don't cooperate (one contestant falls off her bull before it ever leaves the chute), so the judges move on to calf roping instead. When one poor, dimwitted calf runs smack into a wall and bumps his head, the crowd moans in collective sympathy. This is hardly a vicious, bloodthirsty bunch. In fact, most are pleased to see that when a contestant ropes a calf around its neck, he or she does not "throw and tie" it. Instead, the calf breaks away before the rope can yank it back. It's one concession rodeo organizers have made to please its critics.

There are eleven events at Reno. Nine of these are traditional, but two are "camp" events designed purely to amuse—steer decorating and wild cow milking. When it's time for the wild cow milking, all the confusion that has gone before seems somehow justified. This is a team event, with the team consisting of a cowboy, a cowgirl and a drag queen (a cowqueen?) brought in for comic relief. It's the lesbian's job to hold on to the rope securing the wild cow, the drag's to grab it by the neck, and the cowboy's to milk it. This is one of the few events in the rodeo where roles are strictly defined, although hardly according to traditional patterns.

When the cows are released all hell breaks loose. Most lesbians and drag queens manage to hang onto their ropes, but nobody gets a hand around a cow's neck at first. Instead, the cows drag their opponents around the field, much to the delight of the crowd but to the dismay of the contestants. A drag's wig is knocked off. Another loses her skirt. Fortunately no one loses a tooth, and at last a cowboy manages to persuade his cow to stand still long enough to give him what he wants, (he's tried this before with human opponents with varying degrees of success). The cowboy races to the judge without spilling his precious cargo, and the contest is over.

A s the rodeo winds to a close on the first day of competition, gay people flock back into the downtown area, invading the hotels and casinos of the normally unflappable community. Local residents view this particular invasion, however, with mixed feelings. Some don't mind a bit, like Susan, a desk clerk at the Wonder Lodge Motel, who was born and raised in Nevada. Says Susan, "It doesn't bother me any. They've got a right to live just like anybody else." Others appreciate the money it brings, whatever they think of their visitors' lifestyles. Perhaps that persuaded former mayor Barbara Bennett to include a letter of welcome in previous rodeo programs. There is no such letter from the present mayor. However, he's done nothing to block the rodeo from taking place.

One man, on the other hand, is doing everything he can to stop it. Last year a general contractor who is also a member of the John Birch Society, formed a group called the Pro-Family Christian Coalition and circulated a public-opinion petition expressing opposition to the gay event. In two weeks the group collected 8,000 signatures, which they tried to present to the governor, "but the governor snuck out the back door." This year he organized another petition drive, this one proposing a new county ordinance forbidding the use of county property by groups which "habitually violate . . ., advocate, and/or promote the commission of unlawful acts." The key word, of course, is "unlawful," and in Nevada, homosexual acts are a felony (NRS 201.190). The coalition did not collect the 9000 signatures necessary to force the county commissioners to review the petition (if they reject it, it goes to a direct vote of the people), but the contractor vows he'll be back next year.

Unlike the animal rights coalition, this man's group is nowhere to be seen at the rodeo or in town. On the phone he states, "We are not interested in direct confrontation with those people." Instead, he and his followers have fled Reno for the nearby beaches of Lake Tahoe. Nevertheless he is just as adamant as ever in his opposition to the rodeo, which he calls "an abomination and a blight upon the community." He continues, "It's really not the rodeo we're concerned with. It's the celebration of the homosexual community trying to gain legitimacy and justification in a state where this is regarded as a felonious crime. We regard it as a threat to the safety and the health of our children and our community."

Homosexuals take over the Sands Hotel Saturday night, transforming the parking lot and three floors of surrounding balconies into one giant, open-air barn dance with thousands attending. Tourists passing by on the other side of a low, temporary fence stop to gawk and wonder. "What the . . .",? mumbles one disgruntled soul. No one inside the fence even notices.

Gay Men and Movies: Reel to Real

Michael Bronski

I can remember Susan Hayward and Dana Andrews in *My Foolish Heart* and it is always tied up with the fact that I was sitting next to a sailor at the Trans-Lux. He was groping me and I was groping him and I was watching Susan Hayward pregnant in *My Foolish Heart*. That is part of my whole sexual experience.

I'm sitting there, identifying with Susan Hayward, of course, and she is in love with Dana Andrews and suffering these trials, and the song is "My Love, My Foolish Heart" and here I am with a stiff cock in my hand. I mean, that's just heaven!

—George Mansour

THOSE SENTIMENTS ARE FROM GEORGE MANSOUR, ONE OF the premier film bookers in the country who's worked in the industry for more than thirty years. Movies for him—and for countless other gay men—aren't something you spend two hours doing on a rainy Saturday afternoon. They're a way of seeing, understanding and dealing with the world—not only the outside world of conformist reality but also the inner world of the imagination, feelings and sexuality.

Gay men have always gone to movies, and according to various surveys make up an unusually high percentage of the movie-going public. More importantly, movies and movie stars have always maintained a very high profile in the mythology and collective unconscious of gay life. It may be the queen whose only claim to fame is his Debra Paget (in *The Ten Commandments*) imitation, or the all-gay claque who chant Bette Davis's *All About Eve* lines with her during the film. Many more are deeply interested in the serious work of such openly gay directors as Pier Paolo Pasolini and Rainer Werner Fassbinder.

Gay men were always attracted to movies for a variety of reasons. Told by the culture that men do not express their feelings, they went to the movies to have their emotions validated by the high-flown theatrics of a Bette Davis or a Joan Crawford. The intense feelings, glamor and sexuality of these stars were an oasis in an emotional desert. Gay male moviegoers also appreciated and lusted after any number of male beauties (many of whom the gay vine had it were "that way"). And finally there were many instances where movies would present a situation to which gay men could relate. These instances were most likely covert and subtextual (such as the all-male world of westerns or adventure films), or sometimes homoeroticism would rise to the surface as in the James Dean/Sal Mineo relationship in *Rebel Without A Cause*.

More often than not Hollywood portrayed homosexuals as evil or pathetic. The list of such films is long and peppered with top names as well as little-known films: *Advise and Consent, The Fox, The Detective, Cruising, Justine, The Children's Hour, Cleopatra Jones, The Eiger Sanction* (a complete and fascinating look at gay people and Hollywood movies is recounted in Vito Russo's *The Celluloid Closet*).

But if Hollywood wasn't great about dealing with homosexual characters, there are plenty of films that show a strong "gay sensibility" and are of interest to gay men. The following is a random list, in no particular order and with no claim to being definitive:

She Done Him Wrong, directed by Lowell Sherman, 1933. Mae West, in all of her wise-cracking glory, wears diamonds and helps crack a white slavery ring. After seeing this you'll understand why some have raised the question, "Did Mae West invent drag queens, or did drag queens invent Mae West?"

The Bride of Frankenstein and **Show Boat,** directed by James Whale, 1935, 1936. Whale was an openly gay director eventually blacklisted for not remaining in the closet. His handling of his characters as outsiders—both Helen Morgan's Julie in *Showboat* and Boris Karloff's monster in *Bride*—is exceptional. Equally graceful are Irene Dunne's better than usual acting in the musical and Ernest Thesiger's very gay, very mad, doctor in *The Bride*.

The Wizard of Oz, directed by Victor Fleming, 1939. No matter how you look at it—as a Judy Garland film or a fable of being different and wanting to escape—it's one of the alltime favorite gay films ever made. This childhood classic still brings grown men to tears. It's not for nothing that lesbian singer Holly Near has declared "Over the Rainbow" the gay national anthem.

Mildred Pierce, directed by Michael Curtiz, 1945. This is Joan Crawford in the flip side of *Mommie Dearest,* a mother so giving and unselfish she'll take the murder rap for her bum of a daughter. Also featuring the incomparable Eve Arden as "the best friend."

Red River, directed by Howard Hawks, 1948. John Wayne and Montgomery Clift star in what is probably the most homoerotic of all westerns. Half the time they carry on like father and son and the other half like lovers. But you can't beat the scene where Wayne looks fondly at Clift's butt and says "That'll do."

Rope and **Strangers on a Train,** directed by Alfred Hitchcock, 1948, 1951. Two examples from the English master on fine filmmaking and Hollywood homophobia. John Dall and Farley Granger play homocidal homosexuals who kill for effete kicks in *Rope. Strangers* offers Robert Walker as a dandified psychotic killer with a domineering mother and a penchant for men on trains.

All About Eve, directed by Joseph L. Mankiewicz, 1950. Not only the best written, and wittiest, filmscript to ever come out of Hollywood, it has Bette Davis as Margo Channing and some of the best one-liners to grace the American screen. George Sanders also gives a wonderful portrayal as a vicious gay gossip columnist.

Something for Everyone, directed by Hal Prince, 1970. A bitter black comedy of bisexual bad manners that was so before-its-time it hardly even became a cult item. Michael York is the interloper to Angela Lansbury's campy, rundown royal family. The best surprise is Jane Carr (seen earlier in *The Prime of Miss Jean Brodie*) as the very precious, teenage temptress.

Sunday, Bloody Sunday, directed by John Schlesinger, 1971. Beautifully worked out, and very British tale of heterosexual

Glenda Jackson and homosexual Peter Finch who both love Murray Head. Probably the best and most honest film about sexual desire and need to come from a mainstream filmmaker.

Yentl, directed by Barbra Streisand, 1983. Not only has Barbra Streisand held her own in the pantheon of gay male favorites for more than twenty years, but her directorial debut was a lovely fairy tale of transvestism and unspoken love.

While Hollywood was depending on the subterfuge of "camp" to convey gay content or sensibility, European directors were able to be a little more explicit. *Mädchen in Uniform,* a 1931 German film written and directed by women, portrayed lesbianism in a girl's school in a positive light. Although there aren't an overwhelming number of gay films in the history of European cinema, their track record is much better than their American counterparts. While Hollywood was determined not to allow moral leeway in their characters' lives (or their directors' subjects), Europeans seemed eager to approach and investigate all sides of life. Thus Ingmar Bergman was able to broach such topics as incest, lesbianism and rape in *The Silence* and *The Virgin Spring* years before they would be allowed in an American film.

A second reason why European films were able to deal with more adult themes—especially homosexuality—was that there was, and is, a much freer climate in which to live within the film industry. Hollywood has always demanded that everyone connected with it remain closeted. This rule was strict when applied to actors (although rumors do creep out), but even stricter when applied to directors. There are plenty of gay directors (and producers) in Hollywood, and not only don't we know who they are—we don't even hear rumors of who they are. When silence is this strictly enforced it has to affect the films that are made. Any director—gay or straight—who would make a film with overt, sympathetic gay content, runs the risk of being labeled or branded by association. European directors—Pasolini and Fassbinder are the two who spring to mind immediately—have had more freedom to live and create openly.

In the past ten years European directors have produced an amazing number of gay-oriented films ranging from melodramas to historical fantasies, autobiographies to situation comedies.

There are more and more each year as the American market expands to include a wider range of foreign films. Here are ten that have managed to become film classics in a few short years.

Last Tango in Paris, directed by Bernardo Bertolucci, 1973. This story of the joys and displeasures of anonymous sex was rumored to have originally been about two gay men, but was perceived by the studio to be unmarketable as such. But viewed with this fact in mind, its application to gay life (and loves) seems unavoidable (not to mention the fact that Marlon Brando gets finger fucked by leading lady Maria Schneider).

Arabian Nights, directed by Pier Paolo Pasolini, 1974. This was Passolini's third installment to a trilogy which began with The Decameron and The Canterbury Tales. Here are stories woven into stories, around stories and within stories. Of the three, Nights has the most gay content (and the most nude boys) as well as the most beautiful scenery. Pasolini's talents as a fabulist have never been better exhibited, nor has his eye for the discreet charm of sexual perversity been better exposed.

Fox and His Friends, directed by Reiner Werner Fassbinder, 1974. Fox is a poor, working class, German queen who wins the lottery only to find that he has a lot of wealthy friends who are willing to tolerate him for his money. More a tale about class than sexuality, it's one of Fassbinder's first films to deal with homosexuality in an objective and compelling way.

Salo, directed by Pier Paolo Pasolini, 1975. Salo is as frightening as Arabian Nights is charming. Updating deSade's 120 Days of Sodom to fascist Italy, Pasolini has created a powerful and (to some) repugnant tale of sexuality, power and corruption. It's a serious film with serious intent, but may still give you a lot more than you bargained for. Not for the faint of heart or intellect.

A Special Day, directed by Ettore Scola, 1977. Marcello Mastroianni is a homosexual about to be interned by Mussolini, and Sophia Loren is a working-class housewife neglected by her fascist husband and children. They turn to one another for one afternoon and both see things a little differently than before. A meticulous blend of the sexual, political and personal. Scola manages (for the first time in film history) to give a gay man a heterosexual encounter without compromising his sexual identity, integrity or making moral judgments.

La Cage aux Folles, directed by Edouardo Molinaro, 1979. What started out as a small French movie based on a Parisian farce has ended up being the most popular foreign film to ever be released in this country. Spawning both a sequel and a hit Broadway musical, this bit of fluff (and it's nothing more than a gay rewrite of Kaufmann and Hart's *You Can't Take it With You*) has shown millions of Americans that gay men can care for one another and have long-term relationships.

Nighthawks, directed by Ron Peck, 1979. Made by an independent director and producer, *Nighthawks* is a slice of life of a gay teacher in London. There are no great dramatic moments, but like small, minutely observed British films of the 1960s, it's both wonderfully detailed and moving.

The Consequence, directed by Wolfgang Petersen, 1980. A melodramatic love story that resembles a 1940s Hollywood *film noir.* The two men in love have never a minute to themselves as they run from one oppressive situation to another. But while the plot may be overused and tattered, the writing and directing is tight and taut. Downbeat, but a good film.

Taxi Zum Klo, directed by Frank Ripploh, 1981. This is quickly becoming a gay classic, like *The Wizard of Oz.* The autobiographical story of a Berlin school teacher who is a compulsive cruiser, yet wants a relationship, seems to hit home with everyone. Like Dorothy Gale, Frank yearns for something different and finds his "over the rainbow" in men's rooms across the city. It's candid and funny and has a whole lot to say about the way we use sex and love in our lives.

Querelle, directed by Rainer Werner Fassbinder, 1982. Adapted from Jean Genet's novel, Fassbinder's last film is a homosexual phantasmagoric spectacle. It's as though Busby Berkeley wandered into uniform night at the Mineshaft and decided to make a film. It's about oppression and identity, but is so outrageous and so gay that the visuals overshadow the plot. With Brad Davis, Franco Nero and Jeanne Moreau.

Old-fashioned queens may think they're Lana Turner and high-tone queens may want to discuss the latest semiotics on Pasolini's *mise en scène*. But the minute anyone says the phrase "gay movies" everybody thinks of porn. It may be four-minutes' loop in the peep shows or hour-and-a-half productions, but much sooner than later everybody's mind turns to sex.

And really, when you think about it, sex is really the basis for a lot of our movie going. It may be spoken of as emotions, or glamour, or a desire to see ourselves and our lives on the screen. But at the bottom of all of that is a need—and desire—to see some reflection of our sexual lives. And what better way than by watching gay porn.

Pornography has always been considered the stepchild of the arts. Like Cinderella, it has been shunted aside, considered utilitarian and made to do the dirty work while everyone else gets to look beautiful. Many people complain that all porno can do is turn you on—well, thank God for that. Porno—good porno—hits us where we live. It makes us respond (that's a nice way of saying "get a hard-on") in ways that other art doesn't. The problem with porn is that most people (and this includes even people who enjoy it) don't want to give it very much credence.

It's commonplace to say that porno really isn't very well done. And while this is somewhat true—there is a lot of badly produced, acted and directed porno in the world—how is it ever going to get better if no one pays any serious attention? Most gay male porn is conceived of, produced and acted by gay men. As such it's a purer distillation of the gay experience than all American and European films put together.

There has been a lot of porn produced in the past fifteen years. Whether or not any one piece will turn you on depends on what you like, so there is no hard and fast criteria as to what is "hot" and what is not. What follows is a simple list of some of the best porn makers and their titles. These may not be to everyone's tastes, but they are well produced, professionally filmed and nicely acted.

Jack Deveau founded "Hand in Hand" films in the late 1960s and was to produce and direct many of the best gay male porn films. *Left Handed* is a tale of love gone slightly wrong and was probably the first time that a gay porn film had real people with lives and feelings. *Drive* is a semi-surrealistic James Bond parody that features a crazed transsexual who wants to de-sex the world with a secret formula. There is plenty of tongue-in-cheek wit as well as lots of sex here. *A Night at the Adonis* is sort of a *La Ronde* in a porno movie house. The wit and sex are in perfect proportion and there are several sub-plots to keep those with narrative minds happy.

Artie Bressan's first porn film—*Passing Strangers*—won first prize at the San Francisco Erotic Film Festival in 1974. His newest porno—*Pleasure Beach*—garnered four major awards at the Los Angeles Erotic Gay Film Festival. In between he has done *Forbidden Letters* and *Daddy Dearest*. Like Jack Deveau, Bressan is equally concerned with his characters as people with feelings. He never stints on the sexual aspects of the films, but he never loses sight of the fact that he is making them to turn people on—real people with emotions and feelings. Aside from his porno work, Bressan has managed to turn out two excellent "serious works" (Bressan considers his porno to be serious, even if distributors don't): *Abuse*, about a gay, parentally-abused teenager and *Buddies*, concerning a man with AIDS and a stranger with whom he becomes emotionally involved.

Peter de Rome, more than any other gay porn maker, has received critical attention for his work. His first films were shorts, collected under the title *The Erotic Films of Peter de Rome*, and have been screened in museums. They are a diverse collection, but the standouts are "Prometheus Bound" and the outrageous "Underground" (yes, Vera, they really are having sex on a NYC subway car while it's on rounds). He next made the fanciful *Adam & Yves* (with its *homages* to *Last Tango* and Cocteau) which includes real footage of Greta Garbo walking down a New York City street. His last major film was *The Destroying Angel*, a dark meditation on Edgar Allan Poe and unfulfilling sex. It's dark and brooding and not all that sexual, a change from his first films that are filled with not only visual wit, but lots of hot fucking.

The Gage Brothers have made a trilogy: *El Paso Wrecking Corp.*, *The Kansas City Trucking Company*, and *The L.A. Tool and Die Company*. All three star top names in gay porno such as Richard Locke, Fred Halsted, Mike Morris, and Jared Benson. These are buddy films, pure and simple, although to paraphrase Oscar Wilde, they are hardly simple and never pure. Each film is a series of picaresque adventures in which both of the "buddies" go off and have a lot of sex. What the films lack in detailed script they more than make up in beautiful photography, precise, imaginative editing and lots of hot action. The whole series is not to be missed.

These are only four great names in porn. There are plenty of other porn films that are well-made and stimulating. *Centurians of Rome* is an old-fashioned epic with lots of sex. It's also the only porn film that has horses and authentic looking costumes. *Born to Raise Hell* is hard-core S&M. This is not the usual stuff that's faked in some hotel room, but pretty rough sexual abuse, shaving, piss and uniforms. Although sometimes crudely made, it packs a wallop that most other S&M films lack. *Al Parker is Wanted* is a gay remake of *The Defiant Ones* with a gay and a straight man chained together on the run. Well-filmed and thoughtfully scripted, it's quality all around.

In the past few years there has been a burgeoning independent gay film industry. Christopher Larkin's 1973 *A Very Natural Thing* tried breaking into the commercial market but failed to gain much attention. Such films as The Mariposa Film Group's *Word is Out* (1979) did break through this barrier and made some impact on what was deemed marketable and presentable in first-run theaters. In 1984 *The Times of Harvey Milk*, directed by Rob Epstein and Rob Schmiechen, won an unprecedented Academy Award for best documentary, and Greta Schiller's documentary *Before Stonewall* received considerable press attention. The fact that there are film makers willing to take the risks (both professional and monetary) to make these films shows that times are changing.

Gay men go to the movies for any number of reasons. One chooses films according to one's likes and desires. But there is always the wish to see that image, that fantasy, that flickering illusion which somehow represents a part of one's life. One can feel it when the lights go down, just before the screen lights up and the audience becomes hushed and quiet: desire and need.

Note: Most of the films discussed are available for showing on a VCR. The more commercial classics are usually found in any urban video store.

Many of the porno titles are also available, but if they are not, there are several mail order houses from which they can be ordered. It's very easy to duplicate video tapes, and not all mail-order companies may have the cleanest, clearest copies.

Some of the newer gay independent films are harder to come by but are becoming more accessible. It would be best to check gay magazines or bookstores to find out when and where they are available.

Sports, Anyone?

by Hugh Murray

MANY GAY MEN ARE BORED BY SPORTS. PERHAPS AS youngsters the other boys yelled "You throw like a girl!" or "Do it like a man!" Eventually many of us yielded the sports field to the bigots. They sneered with contempt at the weak, sissy faggots; the gay boys replied (at a distance) that the jocks were stupid, mean, and prejudiced. They were also somehow attractive.

For the moment, forget about the past and reflect on sport. Though we are uncertain about the relation between mind and body, surely there is some important connection. If you engage in sports you are likely to look better, and looking better, you'll feel better. Moreover, sport will strengthen you; if you feel stronger, you feel better. Developing the body soothes the mind. The old adage might be revised: sound body, sound mind—at least to a certain extent. For a healthier and stronger individual, and for a healthier and stronger community—consider getting involved in sports.

Sport helps one to appreciate another form of beauty. In sport one sees the beauty of action, skill, movement, grace, and power exerted.

There are some who play selfishly, always trying to be the star; there are those who sacrifice for the team. But everyone is sacrificing something. One can't make the volleyball tournament at ten A.M. and disco till four the previous night, or swim in a contest after drinking all day. One can't catch on the softball diamond at noon after pitching on the bed all night. For five years I've played soccer at least once a week. There were some sacrifices. But I have played with over one thousand people from everywhere—gay and straight. Most of time I held my own; occasionally I did quite well. I'm proud to have made this sacrifice.

You say you've never engaged in sport. So? I was an intellectual employed as a university professor in Europe when, at age 32, I was practically forced into sport. My first attempt at soccer was laughable, for I kept grabbing the ball with my hands. My colleagues finally put me in the goal, where hands were legal. I worked hard and I improved. Then I returned to the U.S. and stopped playing for nine years. When the Ramblers Soccer Club was organized in 1980 as a gay soccer club, I immediately joined, even though I was 41 years old and beginning all over. My game was terrible, but I kept at it and eventually won a medal in soccer at the '82 Gay Games.

Once I feared pain. I recall having a dormitory job when I was in college. I nipped my finger and refused to wash dishes because of the tiny cut. My involvement in sports has given me a new attitude. Today I may get minor cuts on my leg during a game but am unaware of them until the game is over. I worry less because I'm more confident about my body. I can be oblivious to cuts, ignore blood, overcome pain. I generally feel better—physically and mentally. And I feel especially good during Gay Pride Week. In 1985 I partook in the Front Runners 5 Mile Run in New York's Central Park.

Where should you begin? Listen to your body. What do you think you might enjoy doing? Arms, legs, feet, hands, trunk, what does your body tell you that it is good at? Different sports stress different parts of the body. Think to match your body's desires to the proper sport. If you're tall and agile, basketball might be ideal. But there's swimming, racing, surfing and other sports that might better suit you. Weak ankles, for example, should influence your choice of a sport with less running over hard surfaces. If you have good arms, bowling, pitching, volleyball, tennis, basketball are possibilities. One good and one bad arm might eliminate volleyball, but none of the other sports. If you are generally big, football and hockey and weights are possibilities. What sport did you like as a kid? Which have you always wanted to play? Watch a game on TV and ask, could my arms do that? My legs? Since you're watching professionals, remember, you don't have to be as good as they are to be good.

Once you have decided on a sport, read a book on that sport. Study the rules and the tips on playing the game. Reading is not doing, and some of the book will make sense only after you attempt to practice the sport. There are also general books on sport that I recommend: Yukio Mishima's *Sun & Steel* (Kodansha,Int.,1970) and John Hoberman's *Sport and Political Ideology* (U. of Texas, 1984). Hoberman's work covers the twentieth century and thus contains nothing on "the golden age of gay sport," the ancient world. But it's interesting to see Auden, Brecht, Mao, Lenin, Nietzsche, Meyerhold, Mussolini, Freud, Sartre and others reflect on sport. Mishima's small book is more mystical, but moving.

There are also excellent sport films. Some of my favorites are "Personal Best," "Pumping Iron," and "Pumping Iron II," as well as numerous Olympic films. In each, bodies and muscles are prominently displayed. "Personal Best" deals realistically with some of the pain and sore muscles of sport, and "Pumping Iron II" asks the viewer, "What is a woman?" Once that question is raised, you soon delve further—"What is a man?" "What is a human?"

If you want to participate, how do you find out about a gay sports group? Well, how do you discover any gay organization? The answer depends on your community. In some large cities you can call your gay switchboard. There are local gay newspapers, community centers, churches, bars. You might try the local phone directory for a gay information number. If you can find nothing, consider founding a group.

A major decision one must make is whether to play an individual or team sport (or both). If you're extremely sensitive to criticism, perhaps you should begin with something individual, join a gym, learn to swim, etc. You can build confidence and muscles. You might join an aerobics class. Tennis anyone? What about doubles? And with doubles you'll hear criticism, occasionally curses, from your partner. And sometimes, get hugs. With baseball, volleyball and other team sports, both the curses and kisses are more numerous. One point must be stressed—gay teams are usually more supportive and less critical than straight ones. So even if you do err, your teammates won't stone you.

The first day of a new sport is the hardest. "They'll laugh at me," you may say. "I won't be able to do anything right. I'm too old to make a fool of myself like that." Such thoughts are natural. But you'll be surprised how friendly and helpful your teammates are. Remember, however, on the first day your mind isn't accustomed to listening to your body if you haven't been exercising regularly. Consequently, you may overdo it and the next day suffer sore muscles.

The second time you may find yourself confused. More is expected of you, by others and by yourself, than on the first day, yet you'll probably perform with less skill and energy. Your mind may remember some of the pointers from the previous practice, but your body still hasn't grasped the coordination. You become frustrated under the greater pressure. You realize that your performance the other day had indeed been "beginners' luck." Keep trying!

By the third session you may be almost too embarrassed to return. This time you have no high hopes. Yet you also begin to note the first signs of improvement. You finally manage to hold your wrist properly for the swing, or keep your arms together when the volleyball slams against them, or grasp the finger position to get the best pull in the water. You feel good. You're learning.

After a few more sessions, you've got the hang of it, somewhat. Moreover, you hear your body when it begins to speak: "We can do more," or, "This is too much for now." Listen to your body. You begin to be considered a good player. If the game is cancelled, you find yourself missing it. You begin to love the sport. You decide it's worth the struggle.

And the sooner you begin, the more valuable it is. I started late, but am so glad that I finally started at all. Surprise yourself and amaze your friends by giving sports a try.

V

GAY
IDENTITY

Seven Heroes for Modern Gay Men

by David Williams

GAY HEROES? NOW, REALLY! ONE CAN PROBABLY COUNT them on the knuckles of one's pinkie. The notion seems slightly amiss, one might say—as absurd as effeminate brutes, or mincing soldiers, or lisping cowboys. Heroes don't wear makeup, and fairies don't conquer continents. A homosexual rescuing a woman in distress? *Please!* The closest any queen will ever get to bravery, my dear, is the dictionary.

Stereotypes are always with us, unfortunately, and none more so than the nell, or queen, the poor sucker who takes the brunt of abuse directed against homosexuals by nervous juveniles and goose-stepping Bible eaters. So it should come as no surprise that these "obvious" gay men have been upfront through much of our history. That they are still considered weaker than so-called macho gays and less heroic than their heterosexual counterparts says much about the quality of our schools, and the decadence of organized religion.

The seven individuals listed below may be the most outstanding members of that most exclusive club, the gay hero, but there are millions of gays and lesbians across this country and throughout the world who perform heroic acts each day simply by walking out their front doors. To be gay in Falwell's brave new world has become synonymous with courage. Not to have two kids and a dog in the yard is considered an illness, and taxed accordingly; showing affection for a member of the "wrong" sex has become a crime. But despite the disapproval and abuse of parents, siblings, teachers, preachers, employers, fellow workers, heterosexual friends who learn the awful truth and fall away, and taunting strangers in passing cars, the homosexual has passed the truest test of courage: to be oneself when all around are people who say one can't.

Richard Cornish is more a symbol of heterosexual repression than a red-blooded gay American. Although earlier executions of men for the crime of sodomy have been recorded, such charges were usually thrown in with witchcraft, blasphemy and heresy. Homosexuality was simply another inverted value which, before our modern Age of Enlightenment, was routinely connected in the public mind with the work of the Devil. Cornish's case is unique in that it's one of the first instances of a man hanged solely because of his sexual tastes.

Cornish was master of the *Ambrose*, a ship lying in anchor off Jamestown, Virginia, in the summer of 1624. One afternoon after imbibing, he summoned young William Couse to make up his bed. When the bed was made, as Couse later testified, Cornish coaxed him onto the fresh sheets, began lavishing hugs and kisses on him, and Cornish buggered him (anal intercourse). Throughout the following days the captain showed increasing fondness for his mate, but Couse, dredging Scripture, demurred. Couse finally reported his boss to the Virginia Council, which found Cornish guilty and sentenced him to death.

There is some doubt today, however, that Cornish ever took Couse to bed, although he does seem to have frolicked with other sailors. The records are murky. We do know that several men were pilloried for calling Couse a liar. Cornish's brother never believed he was guilty. Couse himself is described as "scurvey" and "rascally." Was he a latent homosexual on a guilt trip?

Whatever transpired, Cornish paid the ultimate price. Thus, as a symbol for all gay men and women who have been publicly disgraced by the courts, and the thousands of others who have been murdered or driven to suicide by self-righteous members of society, Cornish, though far from perfect, ranks today as our first gay American hero.

What more can be said about **Oscar Wilde**? Quintessential gay martyr; disgraced at the height of his fame by his lover's father, the Marquess of Queensberry (of boxing fame); publicly sacrificed (as at least one writer whispers) by a few gay members of Britain's Liberal Party to block further snooping into their own sexual extravagances; imprisoned for two years at hard labor for the "love that dared not speak its name" (a phrase he coined); unable to regain his creative powers after release; finally wandering to Paris and a premature death, at age 46, and burial in the same soil that Jim Morrison, the rock singer, would later enrich.

Is it too much to presume that, had he not been brought to trial, his fame would not be as great? Certainly his gifts are evident, but his major works are minimal, his minor writings pretty trifles with no life beyond the last witty twist. He was more a master of the art of conversation than the printed word. But because of his martyrdom Wilde has become immortal. His plays are still read widely and performed occasionally. And his one novel, "The Picture of Dorian Gray," about a man who retains his youthful looks by transferring the aging process to a portrait of himself painted in his early years, remains a classic of late Victorian romance. His accuser's name is fading, but Oscar Wilde in death has become Dorian Gray; for this most unfortunate artist has now achieved what so many gay men long to be: ever-young, ever-fresh . . . ever-Oscar.

Dr. Alfred C. Kinsey, though heterosexual, ranks high in our gay pantheon. Kinsey, a zoologist at the University of Indiana in Bloomington, early became an expert in the mating habits of the Mexican gall wasp, but when he started asking students and fellow faculty members about their own sex habits—on a strictly scientific basis, of course—his real life's work took wing. His studies eventually led him to Chicago, where he uncovered the existence of a 300,000-member homosexual subculture of which non-gays were previously unaware.

Kinsey's two books, *Sexual Behavior in the Human Male*, (1948) and *Sexual Behavior in the Human Female* (1953) covered the total spectrum of American sexual activity, but his comments on homosexuality created an especial sensation. Kinsey claimed that 37 percent of post-adolescent American males had had at least one sexual encounter with another male which led to orgasm, and that 50 percent had experienced erotic responses to members of their own sex at some point in their lives. The statistics for women were only slightly lower. He went on to defend homosexual activity as a natural expression of human sexuality.

At a time when McCarthyism was creeping into American life, religious leaders were quick to revile him. He was accused of promoting world communism, and a 1954 congressional committee singled out his work as an example of scientific research producing "extremely grave" social consequences. Kinsey, however, who was just as startled about his conclusions as anyone, stuck to his guns, and the American public tittered through 500,000 best-selling copies.

Kinsey was the first brave public figure to insist that same-sex encounters were perfectly normal. Were it not for his unique research, millions of liberated homosexuals might still be cowering in their closets today.

I t seems nothing short of extraordinary that **Henry Hay** came out to his fellow students at Stanford University in the prehistoric year of 1931. Even more extraordinarily, he survived to tell others. The reactions sound familiar: most friends drew away, leaving a few now liberal souls who couldn't have cared less. Hay eventually joined the Communist Party during the Depression, where he learned organizational skills but was also advised to suppress his sexual inclinations. His idea of forming a homosexual political group didn't take shape until the summer of 1948, and it was another two years before his efforts gave birth in Los Angeles to the Mattachine Society, the first major gay organization of the modern era.

The original impetus for organizing was the witch-hunting charade of Senator Joe McCarthy (who may actually have been a closet case). Concerned about the growing number of gay people forced out of government service because of their sexual activities, the group proposed reforms of sodomy laws and an end to police raids on gay bars and public cruising spots. It also initiated discussion groups, another novelty.

Despite initial enthusiasm, the Mattachine Society lumbered through obscurity until one of its cofounders was entrapped by a police officer. When he decided to fight the charge (unusual for the time), the society took up his defense. A divided jury led to his acquittal—the first gay legal victory in modern history.

Hay would leave the organization over philosophical differences only three years after its founding, but because of his dream that every homosexual should achieve self-respect, today he can rightly be called the Father Of Us All.

Henry Hay may have conceived the modern gay movement, but **Franklin Kameny** instilled its soul. As an isolated young gay man growing up in Louisville, Kentucky, during the early 60s, I knew of only one other homosexual in the whole world—Franklin Kameny. Kameny wasn't just another gay man, he was an angry gay man; and through his toils he has delivered into the world millions of gay men and women.

Like so many other gay people caught up in the early years of the movement, Kameny would probably have preferred a life of comfortable anonymity. He received his Ph.D. in astronomy from Harvard in 1956 and assumed a position with the U.S. Army Map Service in Washington, D.C., in July 1957. But the federal government abruptly fired him five months later when investigators uncovered a previous gay-related arrest. Kameny sued, but after four years of poverty and hunger, lost his case before the Supreme Court.

Kameny was far from crushed, however. In late 1961, he founded the Washington Mattachine Society. Breaking away from the "debate society" atmosphere into which the national society had descended in the late 50s, he opted for a direct-action, confrontational style in step with Martin Luther King and the Black civil rights movement. "I take the stand," he declared early in his public career, "that homosexual acts engaged in by consenting adults are moral, in a positive and real sense, and are right, good, and desirable, both for the individual participants and for the society in which they live."

Kameny's victories were few and hard-fought, and as others began to assume upfront leadership roles he receded into the background. But as Barbara Gittings, another early leader, has said, Kameny "was the first one who articulated a complete, coherent philosophy for the gay movement." Had he not infused the early movement with such vigor and vision, it could not have achieved as many successes in years to come.

There are drags, there are drag queens, and then there are madames, but the only madame extraordinaire is **Jose Sarria**, a class of one. As a female entertainer at San Francisco's fabled Black Cat bar in the early 1950s, he became not just a master of high camp, but a brash commentator on the injustices directed against the city's small but growing gay population.

When at his urging the audience moved to the front door of the bar toward the end of his Sunday afternoon performances and sang "God Save Us Nellie Queens" to gay prisoners in a jail across the street, he demonstrated not just a boldness of spirit unusual for the times, but a strength of character that refused to accept the inferior status society forced upon him and his gay brethren.

Sarria was not destined to be common. Seeing hundreds of men getting arrested each month in San Francisco's parks on phony charges, he assumed the role of a one-man preacher and news service. When police began enforcing an archaic ordinance forbidding anyone from posing as a member of the opposite sex, Sarria simply got the city's drag queens to pin to their dresses slips of paper saying, "I am a boy." Case after case was dismissed. For those hundreds of gay men unfortunate enough to land in court on sex-related charges, Sarria urged them to demand as their right a trial by jury. The police, who seldom bothered to submit evidence in gay-related hearings (not having any), went away with quiche on their face.

Incensed by his tactics, the police and Alcoholic Beverage Commission tried repeatedly to shut down the Black Cat. Thanks in large part to Sarria, it took fifteen years.

Sarria's career eventually led him into the political arena briefly, where he became the first openly gay candidate for political office in American history, for San Francisco city supervisor in 1961.

Finally there is **Harvey Milk,** our most unlikely gay hero. Until he was 38, Milk opted for a series of establishment jobs as a statistician, information center supervisor and financial analyst. During the 1964 presidential campaign he even supported Barry Goldwater—vigorously. Five years before his death, he was still living an obscure life as proprietor of a small camera shop on San Francisco's dilapidated Castro Street.

Milk had often daydreamed about entering politics, but he never rose to his convictions until 1973, when his shop ran afoul of the California tax bureaucracy. Gays were just getting organized in San Francisco, and Milk felt he would have a natural constituency in any election. He ran for city supervisor as an openly gay candidate that fall, and almost made it.

Meanwhile, a boycott of six major beer distributors, including Coors, was gaining ground among local union drivers, and a representative of the Teamsters tentatively approached him to ask for his help in enlisting gay bars in the boycott. The gay bars proved to be the key, and all but Coors eventually signed an agreement with the union. Many establishment gays considered Milk an upstart rabble-rouser—they even threw their support to non-gay opponents in subsequent elections. But Milk's reputation as "The Mayor of Castro Street" was growing, and by 1977 he won a seat on the City Council as the first openly gay elected city official in the country.

Milk's subsequent assassination the following year, and the judicial travesties which resulted in his killer serving less than six years for the murders of Milk and Mayor Moscone, are well known. Had he lived, Milk might have gone on to achieve his ambition of becoming Mayor of San Francisco, and the country's most notable gay politician of the day. As it is, he has been immortalized in many plays and an Academy-Award-winning film. "If a bullet should enter my brain," he recorded shortly before his death, "let that bullet destroy every closet door." The irony of his life is that his death aroused gays much more than his brief public career. Milk remains a vision of hope for many gays and lesbians today.

There are others, of course. Ginny Apuzzo. The heroes of Stonewall. Gerry Studds, the first openly gay Congressman. Cultural heroes like Stein, Tschaikovsky, Tennessee Williams. Martin Luther King, whose life and ideals inspired gay Americans as well. Finally, Bobbi Campbell, a victim of AIDS, whose courage in the face of social ostracism helped others through the gay movement's darkest days.

Yet for every hero listed here, there are hundreds and thousands of unnamed souls struggling in their shadows. This list can therefore never be complete; as long as social forces continue to bear down upon the lives of innocent gay men and lesbians, the gay hero will continue to thrive.

Bibliography

Croft-Cooke, Rupert. *The Unrecorded Life of Oscar Wilde*. New York: David McKay, Inc., 1972.

D'Emilio, John. *Sexual Politics, Sexual Communities: The Making of a Homosexual Minority in the United States, 1940–1970*. Chicago: The University of Chicago Press, 1983.

Evans, Arthur. *Witchcraft and the Gay Counterculture*. Boston: Fag Rag Books, 1978.

Hyde, H. Montgomery. *The Love That Dared Not Speak Its Name*. Boston: Little, Brown and Company, 1970.

Karlen, Arno. *Sexuality and Homosexuality: A New View*. New York: W. W. Norton and Company, Inc., 1971.

Katz, Jonathan. *Gay American History*. New York: Thomas Y. Crowell Company, 1976.

Shilts, Randy. *The Mayor of Castro Street: The Life and Times of Harvey Milk*. New York: St. Martin's Press, 1982.

Teal, Donn. *The Gay Militants*. New York: Stein and Day, 1971.

Myths About Gay Men That Even Gay Men Believe

by Donald Vining

AS VISIBLE AS GAY MEN HAVE BECOME TO THE WORLD AT large in recent years, it's still not terribly surprising that many myths about homosexuals persist in the straight world. Some straight people perpetuate them out of ignorance, others to console themselves for dissatisfactions with their own lifestyle. There are those who belligerently insist the word "gay" is an inapropos label for homosexuals, since they're convinced we must be miserable. They point to the number of us in therapy as proof, as though heterosexuals never stretched anguished bodies on psychiatrists' couches, were a distinct minority in Alcoholics Anonymous, and had psyches as free of twists and bends as a highway across Kansas.

Since the onslaught of AIDS, some heterosexuals seem to have developed a convenient amnesia about syphilis and gonorrhea, which over the centuries have afflicted so many of their own sexual orientation. Some people depict us as living on a lascivious scale that would make Roman orgies look like a meeting of the Daughters of the American Revolution.

What is more surprising than the myths heterosexuals cherish about gays is the existence of several myths gays themselves continue to believe about their own world.

The harmless myth that the Stonewall Riots were the start of "Gay Liberation" is an example of myth employed as an effective symbol. The Boston Tea Party and the Fall of the Bastille didn't trigger the American and French Revolutions either, but these events have served for centuries in the popular mind as watersheds of history. Even though many quieter, more effective steps had been taken towards gay liberation before drag queens and street people fought police raiding the after-hours bar, and even though gay people were already benefiting from increased public tolerance brought about by the Sexual Revolution, clinging to the Stonewall myth can serve a useful purpose. Like Bastille Day, the weekend of the riots' anniversary falls in early summer, when the weather is most suitable for militant marches and rebellious rallies. Let the legend of Stonewall be blown out of proportion and endlessly embroidered. Let thousands, even hundreds of thousands of New York area gay men half-convince themselves and others that they were on the scene that weekend in 1969 when, in fact, they were partying or offering to slather suntan lotion on the back of a cute number occupying an adjacent blanket at the beach. No harm is done by giving the unruly incidents on Christopher Street more weight than a literal-minded historian might think they deserve.

There are other myths given credence in the gay world, however, which have less basis in fact and aren't similarly harmless. One of these is the belief that gay male relationships never last. Why this myth still persists in the face of so much evidence to the contrary is a mystery. One constantly hears sad and disillusioned young gay men mouthing this fallacy. It even finds its way into print in gay periodicals. In a recent interview with gay playwright Victor Bumbalo for one of the slick gay magazines, the presumably young journalist expressed surprise that Bumbalo and his lover had then been together for fifteen years. He wrote, apparently without contradiction from Bumbalo, that relationships of such duration were extremely rare. In fact, they are commonplace.

In the 70s and 80s, a number of books dealing with gay couples were published, each one of them attacking the myth: Charles Silverstein's *Man to Man: Gay Couples in America*; Mary Mendola's *The Mendola Report*; McWhirter and Mattison's *The Male Couple*; and *American Couples* by Pepper Schwartz and Philip Blumstein, which gives as much analysis to gay males and lesbians as it does to heterosexuals. The annual editions of Martin Greif's amusing *Gay Engagement Calendar* and his coffee-table volume *The Gay Book of Days*, refer to many long-lasting gay and lesbian couples in several countries and periods of history.

For the last two decades dozens of biographies of gay and lesbian achievers devote so much time to detailing the ups and downs of their subjects' homosexual "marriages" that they have few pages left to discuss the work that makes the celebrity worthy of a biography. No literate gay man should be unaware of the long male-male relationships of Edward Carpenter and George Merrill, W. H. Auden and Chester Kallman, Christopher Isherwood and Don Bachardy, Peter Pears and Benjamin Britten, or such lesbian pairings as Stein and Toklas, Bryher and the poet H. D., and the famous eighteenth-century Ladies of Llangollen, whose chief claim to fame, indeed, is the durability of their love.

The myth that older gay men are doomed to lives of lonely frustration and sexlessness haunts too many men as their birthdays roll around. A gray hair can cause hysteria, a wrinkle may produce trauma, and an encounter with a teenager who respectfully says "Sir" can send some off to a therapist wailing that life is as good as over.

Actually, the sexual and romantic life of gay men is every bit as long as that of their heterosexual counterparts. There are, fortunately, as many men in the gay world who think another man begins to be interesting at thirty-five as who feel he ceases to be. As for loneliness, gay men in their later years may well have a larger network of friends than straights, who've often invested so much of their time and energy in children they have neglected to open themselves to new friends or keep old ones. The phantoms about the horrors of gay old age haunt many younger gay men and drive them to grasp every sexual opportunity. It also may lead them to avoid commitment, fearing that if they confine themselves to one person, sexual opportunities will be missed which will never come again once they're 30.

Some of the young gay social workers and gerontologists who founded New York's Senior Action in a Gay Environment (SAGE) out of a very commendable desire to relieve the loneliness and isolation in which they imagined older gay males and lesbians lived, now confess they have a hard time locating such desolate older folks. They have discovered that most lesbians and gay men of advanced years lead happy and busy lives, which include a "significant other" and many friends. An intense outreach program is necessary to locate those who need such social services as "Friendly Visitors," telephone reassurance and escorts for visits to doctors, stores and social events.

Raymond M. Berger's *Gay and Gray* is a scholarly study of a sampling of over one hundred older gay men which finds them prevailingly happier than in their youth. These men feel freed of much of their former need for concealment, accepting of the unorthodox sexuality they perhaps once struggled against, and only in a minority of cases living alone. Most of the men surveyed reported that though they had fewer sexual partners than when young, and perhaps used a narrower range of sexual techniques, they had as much sex as ever and enjoyed it more.

Perhaps the most dangerous misconception circulating in much of the gay world is that the victories symbolized by Stonewall are irreversible. Because there has been a tremendous increase in societal acceptance of gay people, those without historical perspective imagine this acceptance to be permanent and likely to increase with time. Unfortunately, cultural tolerance is like an ocean tide. It can reach a high watermark and then recede out of sight.

Yet while the forces of repression and oppression muster, all too many gay people go smugly on their hedonistic way, leaving too few to fight the battles that secure and maintain our rights. It's unfortunate that most gay men give to the fight for gay rights neither the money they spend for one admission to a disco nor the time it takes to read a porno magazine. Meanwhile the underfinanced troops that do the fighting for all of us suffer fatigue and burn-out, and often aren't replaced since many believe the battle is won.

The myth that Stonewall was a decisive gay rights battle should be forever demolished. Stonewall was at best no more than the encounter of the Minutemen with the British troops at Concord and Lexington; the conclusive battle at Yorktown has yet to be fought. Now the gay revolution stands where the colonists did when Washington's weary, shoeless, poorly armed troops starved in the winter cold at Valley Forge, while nearby Philadelphians danced.

Some gay men worry too much about the wrong things and not enough about real problems. There's no need to despair about the possibility of lasting relationships and no need to dread the coming of age. There is, however, a very real need to put our money, time and energy on the line in the fight against those forces so eager to withhold those rights we have yet to win, and to snatch away those we have. What we need to fear isn't being alone due to breakups or old age, but of being all too together in a compound. Instead of shaking with fear at this prospect, we should shake with rage and ensure that it never happens.

The Gay Tao (The Way)

by Thomas J. Ho

The five colours blind the eye,
The five sounds deafen the ear,
The five tastes spoil the palate,
Excess of hunting and chasing makes minds go mad.
—Lao Tzu from *Tao Te Ching*

WHEN THE CHINESE PHILOSOPHER LAO TZU EXPRESSED these thoughts around 500 B.C., he couldn't have anticipated that his words would endure throughout history as the subject of so much inspiration and debate, comparable only to the teachings of Jesus Christ and the Bible. Societies have always produced philosophers and teachers—voices which extend hope of solving the personal conflicts and confusions of everyday life. Today, religious dogma still maintains its influence over our society's attitudes and behavior, when what is most needed are not gods and idols, but simple human understanding and peace of mind. In a disjointed world full of "inspired" politicians and popes, rabbis and gurus, sociologists and psychologists, we are virtually deafened by the noise, and homosexuals find themselves particularly vulnerable.

A Taoist understanding would put a stop to all of it. It would have us plug up our ears, cover our eyes, and mask over our mouths so that we might at last listen to our own voice.

As everyone must possess some opinion of himself in relationship to life, what becomes problematic is finding ourselves constantly struggling against the current. Our very nature in being homosexual is so challenged we become weak or confused in our own conviction. We become reduced to being like a rock in a stream when we should be like the water. In life there is nothing more difficult than to be a rock—hard, stubborn and immovable. Even when we believe we've attractively sculptured ourselves to be accepted in our environment, our hardened nature has not changed. As the rock we will always face conflict.

We encourage life to use its mallet and chisel against us, and we assume to live as others have shaped us.

On the other hand, if we are like water—flexible, flowing and expansive—we are offered limitless possibilities. To possess the nature of water we realize that we are powerful, but not aggressive; compassionate, but not weak; resourceful, but not ambitious. As water we're not hindered by the opinions and attitudes of those in our path; we flow over them and find we haven't been compromised. Those who would build dams to contain our flow will soon discover their walls will not withstand the nature of water. We will continue to flow freely over the top of the dam, or else they will see it burst and crumble.

So we may ask, "What do rocks and water have to do with being gay?" And the typical Taoist response would be, "What do birds' feathers have to do with their flight?" If we are to accept the value of our own lifestyle, we must be as free in our minds as the flowing of water. This freedom is absent of fear or aggression—fear, which is aggression turned inward; and aggression, which is fear turned outward. Both are the most wasteful and time-consuming emotions and activities of all.

Eastern thought is not so difficult to grasp as one might think. Yes, the Tao is filled with mystery. But all of life is mysterious and in constant change, so it's the purpose of Tao that we accept ourselves as part of the mystery.

Yin and yang are the "opposites" representing the active and passive forces of the universe. Yin is interpreted as the earth, female, passive, dark and receiving; yang as heaven, male, active, light and generative. As in a chemistry, both physical and metaphysical, all things exist through the interaction of yin and yang. One can't exist without the other—just as light can't exist without dark.

Gay men are in a unique position of being passive as well as aggressive; as strongly female as we are male. In our duality the possibility of discovering personal happiness is doubled. But also the effort in balancing our nature may find us pinned irretractably between yin and yang, so that we're unable to move because of our confusion. If we are pressed between two rocks, two strong "definitions," it is only because we've forgotten our most desirable quality—water.

Possibly one of our biggest cultural fallacies is that everyone must assume a "definition," an appearance or image of being one thing or another. So what are the "choices" for gay men? Are we resigned to cast ourselves as either "butch" or "nellie"? Topman or bottom? And are these roles forever ordered? What does it mean to be "a real man"?

Again, in the struggle for definition, we find ourselves trapped. When we have come to realize that as individuals our nature and needs can neither imitate nor be imitated, we'll have finally allowed our yin and yang to find its own balance.

I n balancing yin and yang, what we need most is moderation. If our need is for more, we should counter it with less. In the fulfillment of our excessive desires we can never be fulfilled, because in excessive self-fulfillment there always exists the constant need for more. Sensually, this perception pervades modern society. We are so consumed by what we see and hear and taste and feel, our threshold for sensuality is so elevated we can never be satisfied. The best is never good enough. Jaded like the precious Chinese stone, skillfully carved, we can neither be touched nor touch anyone.

Through moderation, we discover appreciation in simplicity; our lives become less complicated. We achieve a greater sensuality in our passions.

Throughout our lives gay men will always be regarded as "yin-yang guey chi," meaning strange or imbalanced. This opinion may never change, but we cannot be held by the opinions of others. Once we've accepted this opinion, we have ruled out the Tao in our lives. We deny that we're individuals capable of finding our own "Way," our own balance. The Chinese are a most superstitious people, and in using the term "yin yang guey chi" to describe the homosexual, we should understand the literal translation of the word "guey," meaning ghost. The word is often applied in reference to those groups of people whom the Chinese exclude from their realm of what is "normal" in appearance or behavior: e.g., "black ghosts" (black people) or "white ghosts" (caucasians). Homosexuals are ghosts because their nature can't generally be understood or defined as either yin or yang. Like ghosts our nature is elusive to the greater society, and also like ghosts our very existence frightens the imagination of most people. But on closer inspection we discover that our "Way" is perhaps closer to the universal Tao than most are willing to recognize.

Every culture has its fear of the "unknowable." The Tao itself is perhaps most feared by those who will not venture beyond their own doorstep. People always opt for protecting what little knowledge and understanding they have acquired, and then limit the possibility of further growth. They lose the courage to promote understanding. When this occurs they are closer to death than they realize—a frightened, unrevivable death.

When found in the company of other gay men, I wonder, "What fraternity have I joined?" and, "What is it that we can learn from one another to help make sense out of our lives?"

My own voice comes rushing back to me. I'm forced to realize that I must ultimately make sense for myself, discover my own "Way." Collective participation may resolve collective problems, but how am I to deal with myself once I am left alone? If I can learn to accept the following Taoist passage, I will have finally discovered the "Way" . . .

Those who know do not speak;
Those who speak do not know.
Block the passages,
Shut the doors,
Let all sharpness be blunted,
All glare tempered.
All dust smoothed.

Gay Men and Religion: Mixing Water and Oil?

by Craig Machado

IN THE SUMMER OF 1985 ONE OF SAN FRANCISCO'S LEADING gay papers, *The Bay Area Reporter*, published a series of highly critical editorials indicting Christianity, et al., for oppressing gay people. Not only was the church put on trial, but "Gay Religionists," those supportive of or involved in organized religion, were severely chastised for their collusion with "The Oppressor." Correspondence following the editorials was by no means unanimous. While some letters cheered the broadside against evil Christendom and their gay lackeys, many others defended the rights of gay people to their religious beliefs and practices, and cited the positive contributions of many churches and gay religious organizations to fighting anti-gay bigotry and injustice. Sure the church has been no angel in dealing with gay people, writers pointed out, but don't throw out the baby with the bath water.

To deny the suffering of gay men and women at the hands of religious persecutors and zealots would be to misread about two thousand years of Judeo-Christian history. Witch hunts, inquisitions, censures, and defrockings have known their place in the church, and to this day most major denominations in the United States won't knowingly ordain a "self-affirming" homosexual to the ministry. Despite the alleged biblical strictures ceaselessly trotted out against homosexuality (open to rampant speculation and interpretation), gay people continue to serve (albeit often closeted) in an array of religious vocations and careers.

Historically, lesbians and gay men have been just about everywhere in the church as priests, nuns, monks, bishops, lay workers and ministers, and more than one Catholic Pope is purported to have had sexual liaisons with members of the same sex. Gay historian John Boswell, author of the highly acclaimed *Christianity, Homosexuality, and Social Tolerance*, finds homosexuals playing a significant and visible role in the early Christian church. Other scholars are just beginning to unearth a wealth of gay medieval love poetry—much of it written between religious gays.

G ay men often have a lot of anger and mistrust for religious institutions, and rightly so. It's hard to garner respect for churches which have rather systematically vilified and condemned homosexuality on moral, biblical and ecclesiastical grounds—churches which offer heterosexual marriage/procreation or celibacy as the only viable sexual ethos. This isn't to say all churches take the same position on gay issues. Some churches have taken very strong stances on gay civil rights and a few will ordain openly gay candidates for the ministry. Churches which vest the power of ordination with the local congregation, such as the United Church of Christ, usually have an easier attitude about gay ministers than a church where such power must be approved by higher regional or national bodies—Presbyterians, Methodists, Lutherans and most other Protestant denominations.

The choice to (re)connect with a particular church/tradition/denomination involves a very self-conscious and sometimes prolonged search on the part of the gay person. Is the church known to be welcoming? Are there other gay people attending? Is the pastor accessible to the gay community? Is he or she open to dialogue? Does the denomination have a gay caucus or resources available to a prospective member? Is the church perceived as "socially activist" in the community, i.e., does it take stands on other critical issues of social justice—peacemaking, civil rights, women's rights, political persecution, refugees? Often an "activist" church may be more inclined to consider the concerns of gay and lesbian people. It's not uncommon for a gay man to try several churches before finding one where he feels totally comfortable and open about being gay.

G ay liberation has helped spawn a number of organizations bringing together gay people from established religious institutions as well as creating new, independent bodies, such as Dignity (Roman Catholic), Integrity (Episcopal), Affirmation (Methodist) and Affirmation (Mormon), Presbyterians for Lesbian/Gay Concerns, Lutherans Concerned, Unitarian Lesbian/Gay Caucus, Evangelicals Concerned (which is not tied to one denomination). These are some of the more prominent national caucuses.

There are also largely gay and lesbian Jewish organizations. Metropolitan Community Church, founded by Troy Perry, has established congregations throughout the United States and abroad. This church is a blending of several Christian traditions with a strong evangelical/baptist flavor. Dignity (not officially recognized by the Roman church, though some dioceses are more open and may permit use of facilities or priestly involvement in the mass) is one of the largest gay religious organizations nationwide and offers a range of social activities as well as weekly mass. Other groups like Presbyterians for Lesbian/Gay Concerns (PLGC) have an official relationship with the denomination (they must report each year to General Assembly, the national convocation of the church), don't consider themselves a "gay church," and work to make gay people feel affirmed and welcomed wherever they worship.

Some of the religious caucuses see their role as highly political: challenging the church to combat homophobia, recognizing the full dignity of gay men and women and the "gifts" (not the "sin") of sexuality, and ordaining qualified openly gay candidates. Others put less emphasis on confronting their denomination (this is due to some extent to the political structure of a church; Catholics are much more hierarchical, whereas Presbyterians have long had a constitutional/democratic form of governance) and more on personal needs, prayer, spiritual growth, common worship, and socializing.

The Metropolitan Community Church, since it exists independently, doesn't have to worry about changing a denomination's thinking (MCC did try unsuccessfully to gain official recognition from the National Council of Churches). The church has opened its arms to thousands of gay people and provided an invaluable ministry of presence and outreach to many urban gay communities. Some people though, at first drawn into a religious community through MCC, may find the mostly gay congregation somewhat limiting, and may want other supportive churches with a broader mix of people.

My own religious background was pure smalltown America; a "family-oriented" Presbyterian church complete with youth groups, Bible camp, choir, Saturday church clean-ups and Sunday school. Sex of any stripe in that best of prudish, Protestant traditions was never discussed. My Catholic peers at least were being exposed to the evils of masturbation. I knew by the time I was twelve that I took an unwavering fancy for other boys. The extent of my sex education/indoctrination, slipped to me one day by my mother, was *The Facts of Life and Love for The American Teenager*; one of those dreadful '50s question-and-answer paperbacks with heavily lipsticked girls and Beaver Cleaver dressed boys. Homosexuality, labeled "deviant sexual behavior," was summarized in two short, stinging sentences: It's wrong and don't do it. It was as if the author feared leprosy from any further elaboration on the topic. Like most other gay people during adolescence, I had to keep my sexuality to myself ("playing around with the boys" was occasionally okay, as long as you didn't get a crush on another guy), hoping for some vague future when "my secret" could be shared and maybe even appreciated.

By the time I was in college, religion, in the formal sense of church-going, seemed quaint, unsophisticated, dull, plain, anachronistic; certainly not something a college student with worldly pretensions wanted to do. Friends had discovered the East—Buddhism and Hinduism—so I dabbled with them, curious and excited about belief systems which seemed so different from the Christian ones I had experienced as a child. I was also maturing in my identity as a gay man. Gay liberation as a broadly-based civil rights movement began to flourish, as did some of its most vehement detractors: fundamentalist Christians and their Bible-thumping minions. Gay and Christian? How could you mix oil and water? I wanted nothing to do with a judgment-obsessed, damning religion that portrayed gay people as sick, sinful, immoral, even subhuman.

I moved to San Francisco in the late '70s along with thousands of other gay people. Initially I was overwhelmed by the numbers, the "candy store syndrome" as it was popularly referred to. If San Francisco wasn't the Promised Land it was dangerously close. After that first blush and intoxication of living among so many gay men—the bars, baths, parties, and discos—I started to wonder if something else didn't exist beyond this collective frenzy. But what was it?

And all this talk about the "gay community"—people threw the term around constantly—what did it mean? Weren't we more than our sexual bonds and habits? Like a lot of people in San Francisco, gay and straight, I had no immediate family present. Could I find a new family? People (and not just gay people) with whom I could develop deep friendships? People who could reinforce and challenge my own values and assumptions about life?

Wandering one night in San Francisco's Tenderloin, an area known for its poor and elderly residents, street people, wasted Vietnam vets, refugees, gays, transvestites and prostitutes, I walked into the Network Coffee House. There I met Glenda Hope, a Presbyterian minister, and her husband Scott, who ran the coffee house and directed an urban ministries program in the Tenderloin. A lot of rapping, '60s style, went on there: programs and discussion on work, ethics, sexuality, philosophy, religion, politics, creativity. Glenda and Scott considered the coffee house a key part of their ministry and they understood Christianity as a radical way of transforming a society which cared too little for its forgotten, its oppressed, and those who didn't fit the Middle American slot of "normality."

My friendship with the Hopes grew and I soon attended a small Presbyterian church (the first I had been in since my childhood) where Glenda regularly preached. The church was a good cross-section of the city: senior citizens, gay people, singles and single parents, students, gay and straight couples, divorced people. It was the first time I had ever heard a minister speak so articulately and compassionately about the dignity and worth of gay people, and about the message of Christ as liberation, hope and love. To hear religion rooted in the reality of this world and not in some lofty God talk, to hear the word gay used honestly and unflinchingly from the pulpit, to feel welcomed for who you were—this was indeed a revelation!

Glenda was a powerful preacher, a Georgia Baptist turned Presbyterian who had fought in the Civil Rights movement. She talked openly of her early reservations about gay people; then "the conversion" in which she saw us like anyone else, no better or worse. All were God's children and "all had a place in the choir." And Glenda practiced what she preached. She helped organize workshops on gay people in the church; she spoke out within the church for her gay brothers and sisters still suffering discrimination; she made sure gay folks were always welcome at Seventh Avenue church; and she started visiting and ministering to people with AIDS. For me and many other people, Glenda became a mentor and a hero, a model of what the contemporary church sees too infrequently.

Today, I am very much a part of Seventh Avenue Presbyterian Church, which unlike many urban churches in America is growing. Gay people are visible and active throughout Seventh Avenue, though it is by no means a "gay church." We are a rich, diverse family with lots of interests, talents, and concerns—one of them certainly the struggle of gay men and lesbians to live openly and proud.

Our own denomination, while taking some strong stands on civil rights for gay people, continues to practice discrimination within: no ordination of "self-affirming" or "practicing" homosexuals to the ministry or to positions of deacon and elder, the elected leadership of a local congregation. Our church and several other Presbyterian congregations have made public declarations at variance with official church policy: we affirm the right of all members to hold church office, including—and not least of all—gay people. As "More Light" congregations, we believe the denomination to be wrong in excluding a single category of people from leadership positions on the basis of sexual orientation. Methodists and Lutherans have made similar statements and call themselves "Reconciled Congregations."

Like other denominations with gay religious organizations, Presbyterians For Lesbian/Gay Concerns (PLGC) exists to support and affirm gay people in their sexuality and spirituality. PLGC hopes to persuade the denomination to drop all barriers to ordination. If fundamental change is to happen in peoples' hearts and minds, it has got to take place within religious institutions which *have* contributed their share of homophobia and heterosexism. Gay people, who have lived so long with fear, denial and scorn, have a lot to teach the churches about oppression, intolerance, hatred, as well as respect, acceptance, and unconditional love.

With the specter of AIDS, some gay men look to a church community for spiritual support, nurturance and care—especially when family and even other gay friends have deserted them.

If and when a gay person chooses to associate with a church, he may not find one as readily warm and welcoming as Seventh Avenue Presbyterian. Gay men not living in urban areas may have a harder time locating a sympathetic church. Most of the organizations mentioned in this article have monthly newsletters, and many list regional/local contacts. Checking a "gay yellow pages" services directory or local gay paper will usually yield announcements of gay religious/spiritual groups and their activities. Larger churches and organizations like MCC and Dignity meet in dozens of cities across the U.S.

Despite the well-founded "churchophobia" of some gay men, others are reevaluating religion as a positive and desired presence in their lives. In doing so they are taking back parts of their past, discovering new religious communities and most importantly, perhaps, their right to the freedom of worship. Metropolitan Community Church, the Unitarian and a few other Protestant churches are even willing and happy to perform "holy unions" or "ceremonies of commitment" between same-sex couples: a recognition that a gay relationship based on mutual respect, support, and love carries the same moral validity and meaning as heterosexual love. William Sloane Coffin, senior pastor of Riverside Church in New York City and uncompromising supporter of gay people, puts it this way: "I do not see how Christians can define then exclude people on the basis of sexual orientation alone—not if the law of love is more important than the laws of biology."[1]

[1] From *The Courage to Love*, by William Sloane Coffin, Harper & Row, 1982.

I Was a Double Alien: An Emigré Faces Gay Life in America

by Richard Plant

FOR MANY YEARS I HAVE LIVED IN AMERICA AS AN E.E.O.—an ethnic and erotic outsider. I have both suffered and profited from my status as a double alien.

When Hitler's hooligans began to roam the streets I fled from Germany to Switzerland. Living as a student in the border city of Basel, at the edge of the abyss, I watched what happened back home with mounting horror. The Nazis fired countless laws against the Jews, destroyed synagogues and drove out some of the best brains in science, medicine and the arts.

Under the leadership of Heinrich Himmler, the Nazis persecuted the gays. Himmler, a petty-minded bureaucrat, had claimed the top job of the SS police after Ernst Roehm, the only homosexual among the Nazi leaders, was murdered. With true religious fervor Himmler rejected everything that didn't fit into his narrow cosmic blueprint. Of course he loathed the Jews, but he also hated homosexuals with an intensity that would thrill homophobes everywhere. Soon I realized that not only had my liberal and Jewish friends disappeared into prisons, into camps, into nowhere, but that my gay friends also were vanishing.

In the late Thirties, when I first set foot on American soil, I felt lost and lonely. Holing up in a small furnished apartment near New York's Riverside Drive, I withdrew into myself. I knew almost nobody. Yes, there was an uncle who was well-off with two children, but he didn't hide his dislike of my life style. Fortunately I had saved a small nest egg: in Switzerland I'd illegally earned money, working for a newspaper under one fake name and writing thrillers under another. I spent these first solitary months studying English with an obstinacy I've lost over the years. Still, for quite some time my English was tainted and wobbly.

The worst part of this stage was my monastic lifestyle. Then one steamy evening as I slumped down on a bench in Riverside Park I noticed a pleasant-looking man who passed several times, pitching a stick for his German shepherd near my bench and throwing me an encouraging smile. The shepherd managed the introduction expertly, and soon Fred and I were talking. It was a slightly surreal conversation; I grasped about one third of his words and stumbled badly trying to respond, while Fred accepted my disjointed shards and mended them quietly. He was a music teacher who lived nearby with his mother, and I got to know him quite well. After a few weeks he even took me to meet his mother, a formidable keeper of the maternal flame. To my surprise, his mother was glad Fred had invited me—he used to pick up streetboys who occasionally would take more from him than he wanted to give. I slowly learned that what I felt to be my defect—being a language-crippled alien—made our friendship more challenging to him.

Perhaps Fred was especially kind. Even today I am not sure. But the various American men I met afterwards, including the two with whom a casual relationship grew into une *affaire de coeur*, displayed an innate generosity I hadn't expected. That I was foreign, that I possessed a sensibility different from new buddies-allies-comrades-friends, appealed to them and not only on a sensual level. The imagined liability turned out to be the real asset.

After I had learned to understand, speak and, most worrisome to me, write English, and after I started the hunt for a job, I discovered that no apologies for my accent or body language were needed. Of course, when one goes job hunting you count on failures; one becomes inured to rude rebuffs and insipid *don't-calluswe'llcallyou* litanies. And, when I finally landed a job as a third wheel on a semi-literary magazine, nobody—whether from Princeton or Dullsville Community College, whether male or female, whether straight, gay or in-between—ever attacked me as a "lousy foreigner."

My second longtime involvement in America didn't take place in New York, but in a small New England college town in the Forties. Cast of characters: Shawn, an Irish-American policeman, and I, by now a modest substitute lecturer, met under dramatic circumstances—two of my colleagues and I were stranded in a blizzard and a police car, driven by Shawn, had to rescue us. For me the rescue had a grade-B-movie flavor which I suspect I cherished more than Shawn or my straight colleagues. Shawn deposited the two others and then we were alone, with the snow spreading a protective blanket around us. To cover his nervousness, Shawn began talking. At nineteen he had been pressured into marriage with "the shrew next door" by his pious blue-collar parents. The war had transplanted him to Italy where his protective shell cracked and the closet door opened. Although Shawn was disappointed I wasn't Italian, I still was an alien to my last bone, and something deep within him responded.

Poor Shawn had to carry the major burden of our relationship. While I could slide in and out of the apartment I shared with a gay coworker, Shawn had to juggle his ever-changing job schedules and the demands of his home. I think he loved his children but, as he complained often, communications with his wife deteriorated. I should have felt guilty, but I did not.

Clearly, Shawn was a policeman and a husband against his will, caught in a trap I couldn't open. Like many gay American men I encountered, he could only "let go" when he was either away from home or connected with someone intrinsically foreign. I observed this pattern so often in later years that I'm amazed it's not mentioned in textbooks. The intelligent gay American male displays not only more interest in civilizations other than his own, but he usually develops a greater flair for working within their parameters than most straight men. This discovery, however, did not help me when after months of affectionate bonding Shawn began to develop "side effects."

Shawn, kept repeating that he was happy with me, but that our relationship was really a sin. The Bible said so. If "it" took place quickly somewhere in the dark with an anonymous stranger, he could ignore the fact. Now, however, he could no longer deny his actions. The next time at my place he knelt down, prayed for forgiveness and asked me to do the same. I was stunned. I could not do it.

He stayed away for weeks. After he came back, somewhat

grief-stricken, I told him the college had not renewed my contract; I would leave in two weeks. When he took my hand and asked for forgiveness, a powerful wave of compassion swept over me, a mixture of affection, pity and guilt for my inadequacy. I could barely stutter an answer. He promised to visit me in New York where I had gotten a new teaching job, as soon as he was "free." He never dropped a line. I truly hope Shawn has made an armistice with the warring factions within him and found peace.

For a long time nobody provided the energy with which Shawn had illuminated my drab existence. Perhaps I was personally too preoccupied with surviving in my new job at a huge college for the poor. Many colleagues kept their distance from me, but not because I was an alien. Half of them were also born outside the United States, and in the Department of Languages "native" speakers were as frequent as incompetent ones. However, almost all of the professors were married, in their fifties, and ensconced in nuclear families. I was the outsider. In addition, quite a few were religious fundamentalists. Whether Catholic, Jewish or Protestant, they seemed propelled by strong missionary urges. And here was I, the new guy, not married, and with a background of sophisticated atheism. I was additionally suspect because I had worked as a translator, a journalist and by then a novelist.

That I survived this initial decade of academic guerrilla warfare is due to the fact that I had nurtured one of the few talents granted to me: making friends easily and building a network of alliances. I found kindred spirits in the neighboring departments of English, music, the arts. Only a few shared my gay interests. The others were open-minded native-born Americans who were interested in my conjectures about the Nazi enigma. They even threw me a party when my first short story was published in a respected magazine. Of course I discovered gay men among the faculty, the students, the clerical help and the cleaners. But in those days the closets remained firmly shut with triple security locks.

B y that time, however, I was too involved to care much about college closets, because I had started on my third longtime relationship, that with Gino—a union to which I devoted all my strength and which promised to make me, finally, an integral part of the community into which I had drifted. Gino, a chemical engineer from California, of Sicilian and Mexican descent, was so much younger than I that I presumed he had stepped out of his closets without fear and trembling. Although it was now many years after Stonewall, although you could visit gay bookstores and browse among shelves of respectable gay books or hefty porno magazines, Gino dreaded the scorn of his family, "exposure" at the office, and his own subconscious.

What happened to us was devastating, and it confirmed what I had learned from Shawn. I reluctantly agreed to share an apartment with Gino. We were lucky because each of us could retreat to his own space. We shared an adequate bedroom and next to the living room, Providence had allowed a small storage space which I had ordained the guest room. Gino was forever studying and I was scribbling away as always. I felt a great tenderness for him—I was the older person—but when I listened to him talking about his family, I shivered. Such an unforgiving stance on all matters sexual and spiritual! Father had converted to new-born Evangelism, mother kept cleaning a clean house and went to mass at least once a day. His only brother had escaped early, while his younger sister appeared crushed by the parental double bill of religious fury.

When Mother announced her forthcoming visit to New York—officially to visit an old high school chum in the suburbs but actually, Gino was sure, to check up on him—Gino grew very nervous. Finally, he forced himself to ask my help: we must switch around the furniture so it would be clear I slept in the bedroom while he occupied the glorified storage space. Otherwise Mama might suspect and tell the family. Feeling sorry for Gino, I agreed, provided the visit would not extend over three weeks. With great ingenuity we created a new look and found hiding places for the few special magazines we kept. I played at being busy in the office and on coming home greeted Gino with a phony buddy-buddy heartiness. Mother watched and cleaned.

When alone with Mother, I begged her not to mop the kitchen floor daily and, please, leave the papers on my desk alone even if they were a bit dusty. I also avoided talking about Gino's prospects for marriage, a topic Mother would bring up without provocation. What distressed me was that even after Mother had left for the night to visit in the suburbs, Gino avoided me. His childhood engulfed him again and he started drinking on the sly. When he told me that Mother wanted to enjoy New York's cultural treasures for another month and suggested I move out for that time, I grew sad and angry. The apartment was leased in my name, I was responsible for it, and three motherly weeks was enough. I refused to move out, and as soon as Mother was alone with me I told her I expected relatives from Europe. Quite annoyed, she burst out with the question she had wanted to ask all along: did we really sleep in the same room? I said yes, and I saw nothing wrong with it. She remained silent and left soon afterwards for California. Within a week Gino packed his belongings. He accused me of being heartless and of needlessly shocking Mother.

I think I understand Gino's dilemmas. They still bedevil the hearts of our brothers and sisters. America's Puritanism is as deeply etched into the collective unconscious as the love of wine in the French. Ordinary sex is sin; gay sex is doubly sinful, especially if it brings pleasure, because pleasure leads to more sin. Without wanting to do so, the Shawns and Ginos of the world have accepted and internalized the homophobia of the authorities which ruled their childhood. We need information about homophobia, yet nobody has researched its many causes. In some countries it's as endemic as xenophobia and anti-Semitism.

What I dream of is the founding of a well-endowed Institute for Sex Research (ISR) run not only by psychiatrists and psychologists but by writers, artists, theologians, physicists, stockbrokers and, of course, musicians, policemen and engineers. My role would be modest. I just want to originate the programs and discreetly supervise them. Our motto will be Less Power to Guilt but, as always, I will be flexible.

Gay Switchboards

by Joseph Benjamin

HE SPOKE QUIETLY AND HALTINGLY. EVEN OVER THE phone, I knew he was in pain. He said his name was David and he wanted to talk about something. He then began a long, detailed account of his life as a self-described molester of small boys.

I was, at first, shocked by what he was telling me. One of the most dangerous stereotypes about gay men is that we like to run around accosting young boys. Many of the anti-gay crusades have masqueraded as movements to "save the children."

One of the cardinal rules for a volunteer on the hotline, however, is that one makes no value judgments. You are there to listen, and, if possible, to help. As David told his story, I quickly began to sympathize and to understand.

He said he had spent much time in prison where he was abused and often sexually attacked. He told me that the theme of the play "Short Eyes" was true. A child molester is considered the worst kind of human being, both by the guards and by his fellow prisoners. He becomes everyone's scapegoat and victim.

I had been a volunteer on the New York Gay Switchboard for less than a month when I received David's call. When I decided to join the staff of a hotline, my great worry had been about my ability to deal with potential suicides. I was happy to learn the switchboard receives few such calls. However, I was not prepared for a call like David's.

Here was a man who claimed that he seduced and sodomized young children but could not control himself. He said he had seen therapists, both in and out of prison, but they had been of no help. He was in his early thirties, but since the age of eighteen he had been in prison twice, the last time for about seven years. The next time would be a third offense and, he assured me, he would receive a much longer sentence. Much longer.

But now, he was out and among the boys again. He could not resist going after them. He rejected all of my suggestions for helping himself. He was resigned to his fate. Eventually, he would be caught in the act, as he had been before, and sent back to prison. There, he would be tortured. It was inevitable. There was nothing he could do.

I went home that evening, upset and shaken over the apparent hopelessness of David's situation. The next day, I discussed David's call with a switchboard veteran. He immediately laughed and told me not to worry.

David is a switchboard regular. He doesn't always tell the same story, and he never uses the same name twice. But in the story he tells most often, there are two key elements: his abuse of children and his being abused in prison. In another story he likes to tell, he is a slave in a disastrous S&M relationship. Whenever David is confronted and told we've heard his story before, he immediately hangs up.

This man apparently gets off on verbal self-abuse. He, undoubtedly, needs help of a kind which cannot be obtained by a call to a hotline.

This type of call is unusual. The great majority of calls to the switchboard are legitimate. One could even argue that David's call may be some kind of cri de coeur and is, in its own way, also legitimate. It was my perception of a collective gay cri de coeur that had brought me to the switchboard in the first place.

I joined the switchboard after Anita Bryant's campaign in Florida, in which she was able to rally Dade County voters against a civil rights statute for homosexuals. It was time, I thought, to get involved with my community—my gay community—and to offer whatever help I could. As it turns out, I probably have received more than I've given.

My involvement with the gay switchboard became a learning process. I discovered organizations and programs about which I was totally ignorant. Gay bankers and gay teachers, gay doctors and gay dentists, gay atheists and gay evangelicals were all new to me. I learned a great deal about my fellow gay men and I became much more comfortable with myself as a gay person. I attained a level of self-acceptance which, only ten years ago, I would have thought impossible. I was gay and that's what I wanted to be. Even if I could change, I would not.

Gay hotlines have been part of our lives for over a decade

now. To many of us life without them would be unthinkable. Whenever I arrive in a strange town, often the first thing I do is look in the phone book to see if there is a gay hotline.

In the United States and Canada there are over 100 such phone lines. In fact, only a few states do not have hotlines specifically for gay concerns. So whether you're in Honolulu (808–926–2910) or Houston (713–529–3211), there will be a friendly voice from whom you can obtain a wide range of information.

Various services are offered by the different hotlines. Some offer counselling and some don't. Some can tell you about the latest, cruisiest pub in town and some can't. The larger cities tend to have more complete services for their callers.

The hotlines have various names around the country (Gay Switchboard, Gayline, Gay Helpline, Gay Information and Referral, etc.) and are operated in a variety of ways. In some locations a religious group such as the Metropolitan Community Church runs the hotline, or it may be run in a gay community center. In a college town it may be a student group that will help get you through the day.

New York City's Gay Switchboard (212–777–1800) began operation in January, 1972, which makes it one of the oldest gay hotlines around. It operates from noon to midnight, 365 days a year. In San Francisco the gay hotline (415–841–6224) is actually located across the bay in Berkeley in the Pacific Center, a gay community center. Chicago's Gay Switchboard has one of those trendy mnemonic numbers (312–929–HELP). In Montreal you can call Gai-Ecoute (514–843–5652) if you wish to speak French and in Ottawa, you can be bi (lingual, that is) and call Gayline/Telegai (613–238–1717).

Smaller towns have hotlines also. For instance, if you ever find yourself in Iowa City, Iowa, you can dial the Gayline at 319–353–7162. And the Deep South? The Gay Switchboard's number in Jackson, Mississippi, is 601–353–7611. The point is, no matter where you are, in a big city or in the boondocks, there is a gay person not all that far away to whom you can talk.

David's call is classified at the switchboard as a "rap" call. (How those trendy words from the sixties and seventies stay with us!) The subject matter for these calls covers a wide spectrum. There are love affair problems ("My lover of five years is seeing other guys"), marital difficulties ("I've fallen in love with my wife's brother and we've been having really great sex for the last six months"), and even parental counseling ("I worry about my son's future—how can he be happy that way?"). Sometimes people are lonely or going through one of life's minor—or major—crises and merely need someone to talk to. And so we—if you'll pardon the expression—rap.

Often the first real contact a person has with another gay person is via a gay hotline. For someone who is just coming to terms with his sexuality, that first call can be scary. Some people approach the call as if it were part of an irreversible rite of passage. And of course, now and then, it is.

In the typical "coming out" call, the caller will usually start out by saying something such as, "I think I may be gay," or, "Lately, I've been sexually attracted to men." After discussing what may have brought them to this important juncture in their lives, many of the callers want you to tell them whether or not they really are gay. That, of course, is a question which only the caller himself can answer (besides, why should we let anyone into the club that easily?).

We give out a lot of information at the Gay Switchboard and we therefore must have a large and up-to-date set of files. There are of course listings for the dozens of gay bars and restaurants in the New York City area. We also maintain listings of sympathetic doctors, lawyers, therapists, and other professional types, and information about gay business, social, religious and sports organizations.

At New York City's Gay Switchboard about 25 percent of the calls are for information about the city's gay bars and restaurants. "I'm staying at the Plaza Hotel. Is there a good leather bar near here?" Or: "I'm in a leather bar in the Village. How do I get back to the Plaza Hotel?" In New York another large percentage of the questions is devoted to travel: "Tell me about the gay life in San Francisco." Or: "I'm going to Tierra del Fuego next month. Are there any gay discos there?"

Of course, we get our share of unusual calls: "I have a Coke bottle stuck up my ass. What should I do?" And obscene calls: "I want to suck on your balls and have you piss all over me." And intellectually curious calls: "How big is your cock?" Calls which are obviously obscene or masturbatory—known in the trade as "jerk-off calls"—are terminated immediately. We hate to be kill-joys but we really aren't there to provide that kind of service.

And what is the most frequently-asked question? What bothers our callers the most? That's easy: "How can I meet men?" Sometimes this poignant plea is prefaced with a statement such as, "I'm tired of the bar scene." What the caller is really asking is, How can I meet Mr. Right? I wish there were an easy answer but there isn't. I usually advise people to get involved in gay organizations (professional, sports, social or whatever)—at the very least they'll meet men with interests similar to theirs.

Almost ten percent of the calls in New York are related to health, and in recent years most of these calls have been about AIDS. Many callers merely want reassurance they do not have the disease. They'll ask about the symptoms of AIDS, and we patiently read them off. However, we always give these callers the same advice. If you have any doubts at all about your health, go see a doctor.

One result of the continuing AIDS crisis has been a proliferation of hotlines devoted exclusively to answering questions and providing counseling about the disease. The federal government and some state and local governments have established information lines to keep the public informed. The New York Gay Switchboard and other gay hotlines give their members special training to deal with AIDS questions. There are also gay organizations which have established phone lines to deal exclusively with AIDS-related inquiries.

The Gay Mens Health Crisis (GMHC) was founded in 1981 to help the gay community confront its own black plague. In addition to patient services, educational programs and support services for AIDS victims and their loved ones, the GMHC also staffs a 24-hour hotline in New York (212–807–6655).

The National Gay and Lesbian Task Force (NGLTF) has a crisis line with current information on AIDS and various support services related to AIDS. In New York State, you can reach the NGLTF crisis line by dialing 212–807–6016. In other states you can use a toll-free number, 800–221–7044.

Switchboards are an interesting phenomenon. They are a bit

like fire extinguishers. They aren't something you think much about until you need them.

And they are comforting. It's nice to know that even in some strange town, there will be a friendly person you can talk to. You may only want a bit of advice on where to go that evening. Or you may be looking for a sympathetic doctor or lawyer. Or an understanding priest, minister or rabbi. Or maybe you just want a nice book shop, but one that doesn't belong to B. Dalton.

You may have finally decided to get involved in a gay professional or business organization. Or with a gay softball team or outdoor group or bowling league. Maybe you like music and you want to get in touch with a gay choral group or a gay marching band.

Perhaps you just want to talk.

Well, don't be shy. Pick up the phone book and look for a gay hotline. Someone there wants to talk to you.

Get Your Mind Out of the Ghetto

by Alexander Wallace

I'VE KNOWN I WAS GAY SINCE AGE FIVE, BUT DOING SOMEthing about it took some time, and some maturity. As I was exploring the gay world I met David, who worked at New York University, knew all the best galleries, little theaters, gay bars and restaurants, and wore the latest "European" fashions. David lived in that gayest of gay ghettos, New York City's Greenwich Village. "The Village" could be very glamorous and exciting, with its legends of artistic greats, its tradition of tolerance and open-mindedness, its air of casual sex and the nonchalance of its denizens. That it could also be quite provincial did not enter my mind at the time. David, although younger than me, acted as my guide to discovering this daring gay world. I'd always known the Village was there—now was the right time to explore it— with David.

As I was born and raised in New York City, it was no mystery to me. I loved the city in all its diversity, allure, danger, beauty and charm. I never divided it into White or Black, uptown or downtown, gay or straight. It was all of a piece to me. I went everywhere, did everything. At first, spending all my time in an exclusively gay population was fun. We went to gay bars, gay restaurants, gay art galleries, gay shows and were entertained in gay homes. The park at Washington Square was gay, or so it seemed, and gay men were everywhere. They even walked arm in arm in the public streets. The atmosphere was relaxed, casual, natural; the rednecks who came to hoot and holler on weekends were worse than tourists—they were from another world. It was as if being gay were perfectly normal—and the other was not. Oh, there was artificiality to some attitudes, a feeling of, "Aren't we daring, Darlings?" But I did not recognize that, then, as a symptom of ghettoization. I went back uptown at night; and it never dawned on me that some people never left the Village. Spending time in an all-gay environment was like being turned loose in a Fanny Farmer's—fun, but there are limits.

I was raised what is now called "Born Again Christian," and very strictly, too. I believed as strongly as any Baptist minister, but I also knew I was gay.

It never dawned on me not to be. Being homosexual is natural to me, as natural as breathing. It's not what I do—it's what I am. I'm not naive—I know that some people don't like fags—and I knew it back then. I'd been called fag often enough to know the truth. But it didn't stop me from going out for plays instead of football. It didn't stop me from being the first to wear Bermuda shorts to school. It didn't stop me from going to museums instead of pep rallies—and it didn't stop me from drawing naked guys in social studies. I took some punches, realized that I was "different," and learned to cope. I learned to be proud of my individuality and my uniqueness. I was not like anyone else. Other people's problems with my being gay didn't stop me from getting what I wanted from life.

Once, while I was still seeing David, he declined to attend a party with me being given by a friend who lived at the Dakota (pre-John Lennon). My friend's first novel had just been published and he was celebrating. As one of the youngest tenants of the Dakota, he was the darling of the great and glorious of art and industry who inhabit that glamorous old pile—the essence of New York. I told David that they'd all be there—actors, writers, painters, producers, dress designers, moguls—names instantly recognizable, including a top ten quarterback and a candidate for the U.S. Senate. It would be a real New York party. There might even be a woman or two.

David said that the Dakota was "uptown" and that he did not go "uptown."

"David," I responded, "the Helen Hayes Theater, the Frick Collection, the Morgan Library, Saks Fifth Avenue, Tiffany's and my grandmother are uptown, as well as eighty-two of my favorite gay bars! What do you mean, you don't go uptown?"

"I have all that down here. I don't like your grandmother— she's a condescending old cunt just like you," he declared. "And besides, the Village is all gay."

He was wrong, of course. Nothing is all gay or all straight. One of the curious side effects of gay liberation has been that such divisions as straight and gay have become less clear. "Upwardly mobile," "yuppie," "gentrified," "world class," "liberated"— these new appellations know no color, race or sexual classification. More and more straights accept gay people as individuals, first—and then as gay somewhere down the line, after brother, father, doctor, artist, neighbor, friend and, "Oh yes, he's gay."

David could not know that then. I loved him and thought that, young as he was, he just was not comfortable in the company of people older, better educated or more accomplished than him. Perhaps he could not face an external examination of his worth and his persona, then.

People can be very demanding.

I tried. We tried. I'd get him to go uptown to the Metropolitan Museum on Sundays to the harpsichord concerts in the small auditorium. It was a great crowd, very mixed, very urbane. There was brunch in the Atrium Restaurant after. No way! As soon as the concert was over, he'd insist we go back to the Village. Same thing after a night at the theater, a film, ice hockey (which we both adored). Zammo! Back to the Village! Now I loved the Village gay bars, the company of those fast-mouthed old vipers who proved night after night that they were the funniest people alive. But not all the time! Give me a break! I thought, perhaps it's me. Perhaps I don't take being gay seriously enough. I wished, briefly, for stigmata. I even marched in a gay protest parade. I wondered how much thought straight people gave to being . . . HETEROSEXUAL! Were they HETEROSEXUAL when they did the dishes, went to work, found themselves in strange new situations, or were they simply people?

It never occurred to me to dwell on my homosexuality, and certainly not negatively. When I went to buy a theater ticket, I was a young man with twenty dollars to spend. When I went to a deb ball, I was someone great to dance with. When I went on a job interview, I was an applicant with a resume. I never saw myself as just gay, or gay first and the other things later, or oppressed; I'd never have gotten anywhere.

For me, being gay is being liberated. I am free of family and parental responsibility. I am free to travel, to change jobs, homes, cities. I don't have to worry about someone not taking the

Pill. Reading history, the Bible, the daily newspaper, I have a perspective no straight person can possibly have. I *could* live in two different worlds as many gay people do, and I sympathize with those who have to keep their gayness hidden. I have never liked to have to lie because someone else cannot handle the truth. But choosing to live in a ghetto seems to be a particularly gay phenomenon. It's rarely an economic necessity and no one forces us to live behind those walls.

I chose to live beyond the gay ghetto and my life is enriched because of that decision. I function as a member of society, not as a gay person or a straight person. Life is all of a piece. Not that I hide my gayness—I am probably more "out" than many of our community's so-called spokespersons. I see life as it is—not as gay or straight, us or them. I am also very active in civic and cultural affairs, again as a person, not as gay or straight, although most people I deal with know that I am a homosexual. My work and my commitment as a citizen comes first, and with pride, if asked, I can say, my uniqueness comes from being homosexual.

David finally moved from the Village to England, to evade . . . them. He felt he could be gayer there. Certainly, the English have always handled eccentricity better than us. But they do require a certain conviction, dedication, humor, panache and sass to their eccentricity—and there had better be great individuality to it.

People can be very demanding.

Do you think David made it over there?

Walls are funny things.

They are always designed to keep people out. Much too often they wind up keeping people in.

I've untied many bonds working to be openly gay—ties other people tried to wind around me. I've worked my way free of them—and free of the ropes gay people wind around themselves. There's only one way for me to live now.

Free—and outside the ghetto.

A Nation of Joiners:
A Brief History of Gay
Community Organizations

by Jay Weiser

THE OUTLAW COMMUNITY, 1850–1945

American cities grew explosively in the nineteenth century, and
with them grew the chance for homosexuals to meet. Homosexual men could find each other while remaining anonymous to
the outside world, but at any time a cop could entrap them and
haul them off to jail for sodomy, solicitation or indecency. In
Great Britain and Germany, where similar legal conditions pre-
vailed, small organizations for the advancement of homosexual
rights formed about 1900. There was nothing comparable in the
U.S., although informal networks existed: at the turn of the
century, black men held drag balls in Washington, D.C., and
there were interracial drag balls in St. Louis. A group of New
York drag queens calling themselves the *Cercle Hermaphroditos*
rented a room above a Bowery gay bar to change into their finery
and discuss the oppression they faced.

Henry Gerber learned of the German homosexual rights movement while serving in the U.S. army of occupation in Germany
after World War I. In 1924 he incorporated the Society for Human Rights in Chicago "to protect the interests of people who by
reason of mental and physical abnormalities are abused and
hindered in the legal pursuit of happiness . . . and to combat the
public prejudices against them . . ." Unlike the British and
German movements, which were upper-middle class, Gerber, a
postal worker, and his fellow founders came from the working
and lower middle classes.

Gerber hoped to create a mass movement, but soon after
founding the organization he was arrested, his room searched

without a warrant, and his diaries and typewriter confiscated. The headline in the *Chicago Examiner* read: "STRANGE SEX CULT EXPOSED." At his trial, a detective produced a powder puff, allegedly taken from Gerber's room, which was admitted into evidence as proof of effeminacy. Gerber and his fellow founders avoided jail since, this being Chicago, their lawyer fixed the case; but he lost his job. Years later he reflected:

> . . . The experience generally convinced me that we were up against a solid wall of ignorance, hypocrisy, meanness and corruption. The wall had won. The parting jibe of the detective had been, "What was the idea of the Society for Human Rights anyway? Was it to give you birds the legal right to rape every boy on the street?" . . .[1]

THE CLOSET OPENS A CRACK:
HOMOPHILES AND THEIR FOES, 1945–1969

World War II drew millions of men away from their families and into same-sex environments, and accelerated the pace of urbanization. American leaders denounced the Nazi persecution of minorities and black people launched a militant civil rights movement. In 1947 Kinsey's *Sexual Behavior in the Human Male* revealed that 37 percent of American men had had gay sex. A few gay men began thinking of themselves as part of an oppressed minority group. When the Cold War set in, in the latter 1940s, many gay people lost their jobs as alleged security risks and threats to the moral fiber of the nation. Henry Hay, a long-time Communist Party lecturer, wanted to fight back. While the communists had little use for homosexuals, their radical commitment to black civil rights in the 1930s and 1940s influenced him. So did Hay's 4'8", freethinking Great-Aunt Kate, who took him to trade union meetings as a kid.

In 1950, Hay and a few others (including Rudi Gernreich, later the creator of the topless bathing suit) formed an organization that viewed homosexuals as a distinct minority group, like blacks. Although its early literature referred to "our physiological and psychological handicaps," the group anticipated the agenda of gay liberation by advocating "progressive sexual legislation," "reform of judicial, police and penal practices," and the establishment of "a collective outlet for political, cultural and social expression to some 10 percent of the world's population."[2]

By spring 1951, the organization was incorporated as the Mattachine Society, named for medieval societies of masked unmarried townsmen who performed to protest oppression. In order to protect against police infiltration, the Mattachine Society was divided into cells, like the Communist Party.

Mattachine was not the first post-war gay organization. In New York, the Veterans Benevolent Association, founded in 1945, operated as a social club, drawing 400 or 500 men to its dances. In the late 1940s the Knights of the Clock, an interracial Los Angeles social group with some political aims, was formed. Mattachine, though, fought entrapment, questioned political candidates and leafletted in gay areas. By 1953, 2000 people regularly attended more than 100 Mattachine discussion groups, which tried to forge gay men and lesbians into a cohesive and self-respecting minority.

Mattachine's militance didn't last. The communist backgrounds of Hay and other founders were hazardous in the McCarthy era, and the rapid expansion of membership brought in closeted types who were frightened by the organization's radical goals. "Respectables" took over and rejected the concept of a gay minority and gay identity, insisting that homosexuals differed from heterosexuals only in what they did in bed. Out of fear of alienating the heterosexual majority, they called themselves "homophiles" instead of "homosexuals" and stopped fighting the sodomy laws. Instead, they sought out leaders in medicine, law, religion and mental health to lecture on whether homosexuals were sick. They hoped that without any visible action by gay people, straight elites would educate the public that homosexuals were really human beings.

Mattachine virtually collapsed. The 1953 convention—before the takeover—had drawn 500 people. The 1954 convention drew 42. By the late 1950s, according to pioneering lesbian activist Barbara Gittings, "everyone in the movement literally knew every other person active in the movement."[3]

Gay groups found visibility hazardous in the 1950s, especially outside New York, San Francisco and Los Angeles. Mattachine chapters were founded around the country, but they were tiny. A month after the 1959 Mattachine convention was held in Denver, the police raided the home of the local chapter's librarian, confiscated the organization's mailing lists and arrested him for violating Colorado's anti-pornography law. He lost his job. In 1960, Mattachine membership nationwide was only 230.

By the early 1960s, spurred by the civil rights revolution, people with more affirmative visions were entering the ranks. Frank Kameny was fired from the U.S. Army Map Service for being gay, fought in the courts and lost, then founded Washington Mattachine to fight against discrimination. The rising militance helped New York Mattachine raise its membership from under 100 in 1963 to almost 200 in 1964 and to 445 in 1965.

Although Mattachine expanded from 15 chapters in 1966 to 50 in the spring of 1969, its emphasis on respectability and education turned off many gay men whose lives centered on the bar scene. Broader based organizations grew up in San Francisco. Police attacks on gay men, including repeated mass arrests of bar patrons and revocations of bar licenses, triggered the formation of the San Francisco Tavern Guild in 1962. The Tavern Guild was a business association, but it held social events, distributed a legal guide and registered voters in bars in an effort to mobilize the community.

Two years later, also in San Francisco, the Society for Individual Rights (SIR), was founded to create a mass movement and a sense of community. While Mattachine had shunned social events (at first out of fear of arrest for encouraging illegal sexual behavior and later because they might drain energy from civil rights), SIR organized bridge clubs, art classes and dances, and opened the first gay community center in the country. By the end of 1967, SIR had 1000 members. But while SIR stood for a community that could do more together than drink in bars, only a few members were political activists.

By 1969, there were hints of what was to come. The amorphous radicalism known as "The Movement" was in the air: black power agitators, the New Left, hippies and women's liberationists rejected conventional morality and the nuclear family, championed oppressed groups and demanded revolutionary change. Within the gay community, there was spreading activism. Columbia University's Student Homophile League was founded in 1967 and, radicalized by the 1968 student strike, began preaching a revolutionary gospel to gay people at other universities around the country. Most major cities had small homophile organizations and the "respectables" were losing their dominance.

AN ORGANIZATIONAL EFFLORESCENCE, 1969–PRESENT

The Stonewall riots ignited gay liberation. In New York, as in San Francisco before, police provocation led to gay reaction. This time, drawing on The Movement's radicalism, gay people saw the rioters as fighters against the oppressor and decided to fight back too. About two weeks after the riots, the Gay Liberation Front (GLF), named after the Vietcong's National Liberation Front, was born in New York, followed by other GLFs in major cities and on college campuses. Using the apocalyptic and vague rhetoric of the New Left, GLF demanded the abolition of existing institutions and complete sexual liberation. Gay libbers demonstrated across the country and disrupted hostile groups like the American Psychiatric Association.

The Gay Activists Alliance (GAA) was formed in New York at the end of 1969 by a group fleeing from GLF's utopian visions. GAA fought for gay rights, "zapped" offending politicians and institutions, and made the media's coverage of the gay community a political issue. GAA rented a former firehouse in SoHo (in lower Manhattan) and fostered a gay culture with lectures, dances and discussions on literature, art and film. GAA had 300 members by 1971, when it rented the firehouse, and the dances often drew a thousand.

GAA dwindled away, but its gay pride ideology flourished. Tens of thousands of gay men across the country became affiliated with gay social, political, cultural and religious organizations. In 1973 there were already 1100 organizations around the country. By 1985, a dozen years later, there were 9 national political and advocacy organizations, 31 national religious organizations, 15 professional organizations and 10 archives. There is a Gay Veterans Association, a National Association for Gay and Lesbian Gerontology, and a national Gay Harvard Alumni group. The 20 local organizations of the International Gay and Lesbian Outdoor Organization have about 5000 members. The organizations within the Gay Fathers Coalition International have over 2000 members. The chapters of the National Association of Black and White Men Together have 1400 members.

Most of the national organizations are weak coordinating bodies, with the bulk of activity taking place locally. In 1985, 80 groups used New York's Lesbian and Gay Community Services Center. You can join Girth and Mirth in Dallas, trill with Omaha's Midcity Chorus, hang-glide with the Chiltern Mountain Club in Boston, and butch out with the Dukes Levi-Leather club in Chapel Hill, North Carolina. You can join the Gay Activists Alliance in Anchorage, Alaska, and Hackensack, New Jersey, and even still join the Mattachine Society in Washington, D.C., and Buffalo. Hundreds of thousands have turned out each year for festive marches on Gay Pride Day, but except for the 1979 March on Washington for Lesbian and Gay Rights, only a few thousand have marched for civil rights or AIDS funding. The following table gives an idea of the changes in organizational life since 1972.

Gay organizations are mainly a big-city phenomenon. Almost every city with more than 200,000 people has at least one gay group. They are also found at most major colleges, because college students are often willing to be openly gay, and because colleges were at the cutting edge of the movement in the early 1970s. Organizations are blossoming in many suburbs, too: Suburban Gay and Lesbian Youth of Oak Brook, Illinois, and the Association of Suburban People of Plymouth, Michigan, are two.

The table shows the steady growth of gay organizations around the country. In 1972, cities with less than 300,000 people (other than college towns) often had no formal gay presence, as was the case in Akron. Smaller cities in the South, such as Birmingham and Shreveport, usually had no gay organizations, while larger ones like Houston were underrepresented compared to northern cities like Seattle and Minneapolis/St. Paul. By 1977, the number of organizations more than doubled in many of the cities surveyed. By 1985, even a small city like Billings had its Yellowstone Lambda Alliance. The explosive growth in Houston and Birmingham, along with the establishment of a Metropolitan Community Church (MCC) in Shreveport, indicates that gay organizations have established themselves in the South. Growth rates of over 400 percent between 1972 and 1985 are not uncommon, and even more established gay communities such as San Francisco and Los Angeles have roughly doubled their number of organizations.

Community Organizations[1,2]

City	Population (1980)	Community Center?			Movement/ Social			Religious		
		1972	'77	'85	1972	'77	'85	1972	'77	'85
Los Angeles, CA (and vicinity)	2,967,000	Y	Y	Y	22	18	25	4	7	18
Houston, TX	1,595,000	N	N	N	3	7	12	1	2	9
Baltimore, MD	787,000	N	N	Y	1	4	6	1	3	4
San Francisco, CA	679,000	Y	Y	N	17	28	31	6	10	11
Minneapolis/ St. Paul, MN	641,000	Y	N	Y	4	3	22	1	5	8
Seattle, WA	494,000	Y	Y	N	5	5	6	1	4	4
Birmingham, AL	284,000	N	N	Y	0	0	3	0	0	1
Akron, OH	237,000	N	N	N	0	1	2	0	2	2
Shreveport, LA	206,000	N	N	N	0	0	0	0	0	1
Hartford, CT	136,000	N	N	N	2	1	7	1	2	4
Billings, MT	66,798	N	N	N	0	0	1	0	0	0
TOTAL		4	3	4	54	67	115	15	35	62

City	Social Service[3]			Business/ Professional			Total			Change
	1972	'77	'85	1972	'77	'85	1972	'77	'85	'72–'85
Los Angeles, CA (and vicinity)	3	6	4	1	2	10	31	34	58	87%
Houston, TX	0	0	2	0	0	2	4	9	25	525%
Baltimore, MD	0	0	2	0	0	1	3	8	14	367%
San Francisco, CA	3	6	14	1	4	3	28	49	59	111%
Minneapolis/ St. Paul, MN	1	7	6	0	1	3	7	16	40	471%
Seattle, WA	4	2	2	0	1	1	11	13	13	18%
Birmingham, AL	0	0	1	0	0	0	0	0	6	NA
Akron, OH	0	0	0	0	0	0	0	3	4	NA
Shreveport, LA	0	0	0	0	0	0	0	0	1	NA
Hartford, CT	0	1	7	0	0	0	3	4	18	500%
Billings, MT	0	0	0	0	0	0	0	0	1	NA
TOTAL	11	22	38	2	8	20	87	135	239	175%

[1]Source: *Gayellow Pages* (New York: Renaissance House), March '73 fall '77, 1986.
[2]Includes gay and mixed gay-lesbian organizations, but excludes exclusively women's or lesbian organizations.
[3]Includes Alcoholics Anonymous-type organizations as well as other nonprofit social service organizations.

Most joiners seem to be middle and upper-middle class. New York's Sundance Outdoor Adventure Society, Inc., includes many computer-programmers, word-processor operators, graphic designers, lawyers and teachers among its members. There are about 1000 members of lawyers' groups across the country. The table shows that business and professional organizations have grown impressively in the larger cities. Many of those who cut their gay activist teeth in college organizations in the 1970s probably began founding professional organizations after graduation.

The working class and poor seem less likely to join gay groups. Blue-collar Akron has always been less well-organized than smaller, white-collar Hartford. Working-class Gary, Indiana (1980 pop. 152,000), and Bridgeport, Connecticut (1980 pop. 143,000), have no gay organizations at all. There are signs of change in New York, where police have formed the Gay Officers Action League and black and Hispanic MCC churches have started.

The AIDS crisis has accounted for most of the recent institution building, and has also produced modest government funding for gay organizations. New York City, after inexcusable neglect, allocated $1,000,000 in contracts to Gay Men's Health Crisis (GMHC) in 1985–86, half of its budget. With a paid staff of 18 and 1100 volunteers, GMHC tries to cope. AIDS Project/Los Angeles had a 1984–85 budget of $738,600. Philadelphia Community Health Alternatives (PCHA) had a 1985–86 budget of $91,710 and, courtesy of a Philadelphia City Council grant, one paid staffer for the affiliated Philadelphia AIDS Task Force. In 1985 the United States Conference of Mayors and the federal Centers for Disease Control granted $185,664 for public education to AIDS service organizations in 11 cities, but the size of the grants was tiny compared to the size of the problem.

When Troy Perry founded the Metropolitan Community Church in 1968, he created a gay religious community. Generations of gay people had imbibed religious poison declaring that homosexuality was evil. Perry stepped outside the bigots' box and founded a denomination that affirmed gayness, an achievement comparable to the founding of the first independent black church in 1787. MCC had 32,000 members worldwide by 1985. It remains the only national gay denomination, but members of existing denominations, inspired by Perry, have chosen to worship together on their own terms. Integrity, the Episcopalian organization, has 2000 members nationwide in 35 chapters. Dignity, the Roman Catholic organization, has 4500 members in 110 chapters in the U.S. and Canada. There are 25 American Jewish organizations with 3000 members. Gay Baptists, Mennonites, Methodists, Mormons and Seventh Day Adventists, among others, also have organizations.

Political activism increased after Stonewall and swelled again with Anita Bryant's anti-gay crusade in the mid-1970s. Gay organizations have become a permanent and important part of the political scene in San Francisco and a few other places, but they are often ineffective. Houston's gay rights organizations have been more successful than most, helping to elect Mayor Kathy Whitmire and persuading the Houston City Council to pass an ordinance banning discrimination in city employment. Even Houston's community was shocked in 1985 when a referendum repealed the law and few gay people seemed to bother to come out and vote.

National gay rights organizations with professional staffs formed throughout the 1970s and early 1980s. Lambda Legal Defense and Education Fund, Inc., in New York City, was founded in 1972 to fight for gay rights in the courts. Along with National Gay Rights Advocates (San Francisco) and Gay and Lesbian Advocates and Defenders (Boston), it has won some important battles over freedom of speech, sodomy laws and custody rights, and lost some too.

In 1973, a group of political activists, disgusted with GAA's impractical politics, organized the National Gay Task Force (NGTF) with grand hopes. Despite an early success in persuading the American Psychiatric Association to remove homosexuality from its list of mental disorders, and some flickers of activity when it was headed by Virginia Apuzzo, the organization has not been a very visible advocate. NGTF spun off the Gay Rights National Lobby (GRNL) in 1976 to lobby Congress, and the two organizations promptly began fighting. GRNL, in turn, begat the Human Rights Campaign Fund political action committee in 1981, which has cut the first professional figure in the national gay political community.

Like the social service organizations, the gay rights organizations are under-funded. Too many gays, in the tradition of the homophiles of the 1950s, are waiting for some fairy godmother to bestow rights on them, and don't contribute. GRNL collapsed and was absorbed by The Human Rights Campaign Fund, while NGTF (now rechristened The National Gay and Lesbian Task Force) teeters along financially in appropriately campy Perils-of-Pauline style. Lambda Legal Defense remains small but fiercely solvent. None operate on the scale of black civil rights organizations. In 1984, NGTF had about 8,000 members and a $450,000 budget. In 1983, the NAACP increased its membership by 60,000 and had a $4,114,581 budget. In 1983, Lambda had one staff lawyer and a $135,092 budget, while in 1983–84, the NAACP Legal Defense and Education Fund, Inc., had 24 lawyers and a $6,732,050 budget.

Leaders of gay organizations are respected enough to testify before Congressional committees, and gay organizations have been admitted to the National Conference on Civil Rights. Despite this, and recognizing that progressive politics in a reactionary era is not easy, the community has had more of a gift for spawning national gay rights organizations than for doing anything with them.

Henry Hay is 74. He has lived long enough to become a movie star of sorts in the documentaries *Word Is Out* and *Before Stonewall*, and to see the development of a national community with a rich organizational life. Gay people now have their own institutions to turn to. In a world filled with homophobes, they have places where they are valued and where they can make a future for themselves. The community that Hay worked to build faces a massive public health challenge in AIDS, and it lacks a tradition of giving and organization of social services. If gay people remain politically quiescent in the age of AIDS and public hysteria demands a quarantine, a civil liberties crisis could occur. As Japanese-Americans who were interned during World War II found out, bigotry can devastate the lives of politically unorganized minorities. The achievement of the last thirty-five years is amazing. It is also not enough.

Notes

[1]Reprinted from Jonathan Katz, ed., *Gay American History* (New York: Avon Books, 1976), p. 591.

[2]Reprinted from Jonathan Katz, ed., *Gay American History*, p. 616.

[3]Quoted in Jonathan Katz, ed., *Gay American History*, p. 651.

Design for Living: Strengthening the Body Politic Seven Ways

by Armistead Maupin

SEVERAL MONTHS AGO MY FRIEND TIMOTHY LEARY GAVE me some advice about my upcoming national book tour.

"Before you go," he suggested, "figure out exactly what you want to say, and don't be embarrassed to say it over and over again. It may be the hundredth time you've said it, but it's the first time they've heard it, so make sure you sound like you mean it. The hundredth time is just as important as the first."

He was so right.

Three weeks and 15 cities later, I had summoned up the same answers so often that I felt like a cross between Dr. Ruth Westheimer and the audio-animatronics Abe Lincoln at Disneyland. Most of the questions were about my books ("When will Mouse find a lover?" and "Didn't you kill Connie twice?" were two of the biggies), but a surprising number of them cast me in the role of Coming-Out Consultant, a keeper of the mysteries of Happy Homohood.

Remembering Tim's suggestion, I surveyed my most frequent responses and discovered the following blueprint for a more fulfilling life. Read it once, and I promise I won't bring it up again.

1. STOP BEGGING FOR ACCEPTANCE.

Homosexuality is still an anathema to most people in this country—even to many homosexuals. If you camp out on the doorstep of society waiting for "the climate" to change, you'll be there until Joan Rivers registers Democrat.

Your job is to accept yourself—joyfully and with no apologies—and get on with the adventure of your life.

2. DON'T RUN AWAY FROM STRAIGHT PEOPLE.

They need variety in their lives just as much as you do, and you'll forfeit the heady experience of feeling exotic if you limit yourself to the company of your own kind.

Furthermore, you have plenty to teach your straight friends about tolerance and humor and the comfortable enjoyment of their own sexuality. (Judging from *Donahue*, many of them have only now begun to learn about foreplay; we, on the other hand, have entire resorts built around the practice.)

Besides, it's time you stopped thinking of heterosexuals as the enemy. It's both convenient and comforting to bemoan the cardboard villainy of Jerry Falwell and friends, but the real culprits in this melodrama are just as queer as you are.

They sleep with you by night and conspire to keep you invisible by day. They are studio chiefs and bank presidents and talk-show hosts, and they don't give a damn about your oppression because they've got their piece of the pie, and they got it by living a lie.

3. REFUSE TO COOPERATE IN THE LIE.

It's not your responsibility to "be discreet" for the sake of people who are still ashamed of their own natures. And don't tell me about "job security." Nobody's job will ever be safe until the general public is permitted to recognize the full scope of our homosexual population.

Does that include the teachers?

You bet it does. Have you forgotten already how much it hurt to be 14 and gay and scared to death of it? Doesn't it gall you just a little that your "discreet" lesbian social-studies teacher went home every day to her lover and her cats and her Ann Bannon novels without once giving you even a clue that there was hope for your own future?

What earthly good is your discretion, when teenagers are still being murdered for the crime of effeminacy?

I know, I know—you have a right to keep your private life private. Well, you do that, my friend—but don't expect the world not to notice what you're really saying about yourself. And about the rest of us.

Lighten up, Lucille. There's help on the way.

4. STIR UP SOME SHIT NOW AND THEN.

Last spring I wrote a commentary for the Los Angeles Times on the subject of television's shoddy treatment of homosexuality. The piece originally contained a sentence to the effect that "it's high time the public found out there are just as many homosexuals who resemble Richard Chamberlain as there are who resemble Richard Simmons."

The editor cut it. When I asked him why, he said: "Because it's libelous, that's why."

To which I replied: "In the first place, I'm not saying that Richard Chamberlain is gay; I'm simply saying there are plenty of gay men who resemble him. In the second place, even if I were saying that Richard Chamberlain is gay, it wouldn't be a libelous remark, because I'm gay myself and I don't say those things with malice. I don't *accuse* anyone of being gay; I state it as a matter of fact or opinion."

Three years earlier, I confronted a similar problem with an editor at the New York Times who forbade me to make reference in an essay to "gay film writer Vito Russo" without some written proof from Vito—an affidavit, no less—that he was, in fact, one of *those*.

I asked the editor if the Times took similar precautions when mention was made of black or Jewish people. Surely there are plenty of Americans who would hate to be mistaken for black or Jewish, so why isn't their bigotry protected by the strong arm of the newspaper libel law?

"Because," said the editor, "it's just not the same thing."

And they're doing their damnedest to keep it that way. When the new city of West Hollywood assembled its council last month, the Associated Press identified the three openly gay members as "admitted homosexuals." Admitted, get it? Fifteen years after the Stonewall Rebellion, the wire service wants to make it perfectly clear that homosexuality is still a dirty little secret that requires full confession before it can be mentioned at all. If you don't raise some hell, that isn't going to change.

5. DON'T SELL YOUR SOUL TO THE GAY COMMERCIAL CULTURE.

Well go ahead, if you insist, but you'd better be prepared to accept the Butt Plug as the cornerstone of Western civilization.

I am dumbfounded by the number of bright and beautiful men out there who submerge themselves completely in the quagmire of gay ghetto life, then wonder why their lives seem loveless and predictable.

What the hell did they expect?

If you have no more imagination than to swap one schlock-heavy "lifestyle" for another, you haven't learned a god-damned thing from the gay experience.

I'm not talking about sex here; I'm talking about old-fashioned bad taste.

No, Virginia, we *don't* all have good taste. We are just as susceptible to the pitfalls of tackiness as everyone else in the world. Your pissing and moaning about the shallowness of *other* faggots falls on unsympathetic ears when you're wearing a T-shirt that says THIS FACE SEATS FIVE.

Not long ago I sat transfixed before my TV screen while an earnest young man told a gay cable announcer about his dream of becoming Mr. Leather Something-or-Other. He was seeking the title, he said, "in order to serve the community and help humanity." He wore tit rings and a codpiece and a rather fetching little cross-your-heart harness, but he sounded for all the world like a Junior Miss contestant from Modesto.

If our fledgling culture fails us, it will be because we forget how to question it, forget how to laugh at it in the very same way we laugh at Tupperware and Velveeta and the Veterans of Foreign Wars.

6. STOP INSULTING THE PEOPLE WHO LOVE YOU BY ASSUMING THEY DON'T KNOW YOU'RE GAY.

When I began my book tour, a publicist in New York implored me to leave his name out of it, because "my family doesn't know about my . . . uh, lifestyle."

Maybe not, but they must be the dumbest bunch this side of Westchester County; I could tell he was gay *over the telephone.*

When my own father learned of my homosexuality (he read about it in *Newsweek*), he told me he'd suspected as much since I'd been a teenager. I could've made life a lot easier for both of us if I'd had the guts to say what was on my mind.

7. LEARN TO FEEL MORTAL.

If AIDS hasn't reminded you that your days are numbered—and always have been—then stop for a moment and remind yourself. *Your days are numbered, Babycakes.* Are you living them for yourself and the people you love, or are you living them for the people you fear?

I can't help thinking of a neighbor of mine, a dutiful government employee who kept up appearances for years and years, kept them up until the day he died, in fact—of a heart attack, in the back row of an all-male fuck film.

Appearances don't count for squat when they stick you in the ground (all right, or scatter you to the winds), so why should you waste a single moment of your life seeming to be something you don't want to be?

Lord, that's so simple. If you hate your job, quit it. If your friends are tedious, go out and find new ones. You are queer, you lucky fool, and that makes you one of life's buccaneers, free from the clutter of 2,000 years of Judeo-Christian sermonizing. Stop feeling sorry for yourself and start hoisting your sails. You haven't a moment to lose.

Reprinted by permission of *The Advocate* (Issue 411, January 8, 1985). Copyright © 1985, Liberation Publications.

About the Contributors

Joseph Benjamin (New York, NY) is a playwright and one of his plays is set at a gay hotline. He is involved in community affairs and for several years was a volunteer at the New York Gay Switchboard. He has recently written a filmscript, a comedy which has nothing to do with crisis phone calls.

Michael Bronski (Cambridge, MA) has been active in gay politics for more than sixteen years and has been watching movies for more than thirty. In the past eleven years he has covered popular culture, politics and sex for Gay Community News. His articles have appeared in The Advocate, Radical America, Fag Rag and the Boston Globe. He has also published Culture Clash: The Making of Gay Sensibility (South End Press).

Arch Brown (New York, NY) is a produced and published playwright (News Boy, Sex Symbols, Brut Farce, Backtrack (with Joseph Hansen), a filmmaker (The Night Before, Dynamite, Musclebound, Pier Groups), a video director (English as a Second Language, Longjohns, Rough Idea), and a critic (New York Native, The Advocate, Manhattan Gaze, The Villager).

Joseph R. De Marco (Philadelphia, PA) is a writer and activist whose work has appeared in the Philadelphia Gay News, The Advocate, the Philadelphia Inquirer, Gaysweek and In Touch. He has been the editor-in-chief of New Gay Life and The Weekly Gayzette. In 1983 he was awarded the prize for excellence in feature writing by the Gay Press Association for his article "Gay Racism," later anthologized in Black Men/White Men (Gay Sunshine Press). Among his other publishing credits he lists fiction, drama and poetry.

Charles Henry Fuller (Cambridge, MA) is a freelance writer who, after pursuing a career as a classical singer for nine years, has returned recently to his first passion—writing. Many of his essays and articles have appeared in Gay Community News. Currently he is at work on an extended piece of fiction.

Craig G. Harris (Washington, D.C.) has written for *New York Native, The Connection, Blackheart Ltd., High Times* and *In The Life.* He has worked in various editorial capacities at McGraw-Hill, Scholastic, Avon and Bantam Books. Harris has also produced off-Broadway theater and a radio show entitled "Gay New York."

Dick Harrison (*Caribou, Maine*) is a rural gay activist and graphic artist living at the edge of the time zone. He edits a regional gay newsletter, has written for *Our Paper: A Voice for Lesbians and Gaymen* in Maine, and would like to have a gay guesthouse in the country.

Terry Helbing (*New York, NY*) has been active in gay theater for the last thirteen years as producer, publisher, critic and actor. Currently he is artistic director of Meridian Gay Theatre, cofounder and copublisher of Gay Presses of New York, founder and publisher of JH Press, and theater editor of *New York Native.*

Ronald E. Hellman, M.D. (*New York, NY*), is a psychiatrist, general practitioner, and researcher. His articles have appeared in *Science, The Archives of General Psychiatry,* and other publications. He was the first openly gay medical student to be accepted into a psychiatric residency. He organized the first gay medical professional organization in the United States in 1972—the Gay Medical Student Alliance. He has appeared on the "Regis Philbin Program," Cable Network News, and other television and radio programs.

Michael Helquist (*San Francisco, CA*) is a freelance journalist who since 1982 has written about the AIDS epidemic. His articles have appeared in several publications, including *MS.* magazine, *American Medical News, The Advocate, Coming Up!* (San Francisco), and the *Philadelphia Gay News.* The Gay/Lesbian Press Association recognized Helquist in 1985 with two "outstanding achievement" awards for his coverage of AIDS research and the San Francisco gay bathhouse controversy.

Mike Hippler (*San Francisco, CA*) is a columnist for the Bay Area Reporter who has contributed to *Christopher Street, New York Native,* the San Francisco *Chronicle,* the *Bay Guardian, Los*

Angeles Update and others. He earns his living, however, not as a writer, but as a waiter, presently on San Francisco's Pier 39.

Thomas J. Ho (*Westchester County, NY*) has been published in *New York Native*, *High Times*, *Pacific Bridge* and *The New Press*. He is a writer of essays, short fiction and journalism, with interests in philosophy, sociology, agrarian culture and pacifism.

Gregg Howe (*San Francisco, CA*) is a writer who has written for *Gay Community News* and *The Alternate*. He is currently writing mystery novels and living with his lover and three eccentric stuffed bears.

Greg Jackson (*Boston, MA*) is a teacher and freelance writer and a ten-year veteran of life in Boston's gay ghetto.

John E. Jones Jr. (*Columbus, OH*) has written extensively for Catholic, black and gay publications, including *The Advocate*, *In Touch*, *In Style* and *New York Native*. He is a former organizer in the Catholic youth movement, a civil rights activist, lay missionary and anti-poverty warrior, and has been published in various magazines and newspapers in his hometown.

Stan Leventhal (*New York, NY*) is a former composer/performer who writes regularly for the gay press on the subjects of music and literature. He was Music Editor of *New York Native* from inception to May, 1985, is currently Book Editor of *Torso*, and freelances for *The Advocate*. His fiction has been published in *The James White Review*, *No Apologies* and *Blueboy*; he is preparing a collection of short stories tentatively titled *The Buddy System and Other Short Fictions*.

Craig Machado (*San Francisco, CA*) a ruling elder at Seventh Avenue Presbyterian Church, is newsletter editor for Presbyterians For Lesbian/Gay Concerns (PLGC), San Francisco. He collaborated on a ground-breaking work, *Homosexuality and Social Justice*, through the Social Justice Commission, Archdiocese of San Francisco. He has contributed to *The Advocate* and writes regularly for *Coming Up!* magazine. He teaches English as a Second Language for the San Francisco Community College.

Ivan Martinson (New York, NY), opera nut and frequent standee, has written about books, music, theater and various combinations of these for the New York Times Book Review, American Theatre, The New Leader, New Times, Christopher Street and New York Native, for whom he is opera critic. He is writing a novel, The War With The Fags.

Armisted Maupin (San Francisco, CA) is the author of the Tales of the City series (Harper & Row). His most recent novel in the series is Sunset Scavenger.

Eric McMahan (Louisville, KY) has had a successful professional career in modeling in California and nationwide. He is currently pursuing a second career in the secretarial field.

Brian R. McNaught (Gloucester, MA) is a certified sex counselor, lecturer and author. His syndicated column, "A Disturbed Peace," has appeared in gay periodicals since 1975. A collection of his writings was published in 1981 under the same title. Mr. McNaught served as Mayor's Liaison to the Gay and Lesbian Community in Boston (1982–1984) and has spoken at over forty universities on the topic of homosexuality.

Rondo Mieczkowski (Provincetown, MA) is a writer and poet who writes about Provincetown for Boston's Bay Windows. His poetry chapbook Vivisection is out of print. He has worked as a literary editor and in theater. His poetry has won awards (he was a finalist for a Massachusetts Fellowship in Poetry, 1986) and been published in small press journals across the country.

Gregory E. Miracle (East Lansing, MI) is a philosopher, theoretical linguist and founder of the Society for the Benefit of Young Men. His books in progress include The Doctrine of Nonverbalism, Colloquial English and Formal Written Standard and The Gay Tarot.

Bryan R. Monte (Pawtucket, RI) received his Masters degree in creative writing from Brown University. He is the editor of No Apologies, a gay literary magazine. In December, 1985, Mr. Monte presented a paper at the Modern Language Association's annual convention entitled "The Blockages and Erasures of the Gay Discourse, in R. W. Fassbinder's *Berlin Alexanderplatz.*" Mr. Monte's work has appeared most recently in *Bay Windows* and *The James White Review.*

Jesse G. Monteagudo (*Fort Lauderdale, FLA*) is a regular contributor to *The Weekly News* (Miami) and *The Front Page* (Raleigh, NC) where he specializes in book reviews, and an occasional contributor to other publications. He currently serves as president of the Stonewall Library Committee (Fort Lauderdale) as well as member of several other community organizations in South Florida.

Hugh Murray (*New York, NY*) has written for *Gay Community News, Christopher Street, Phylon, Journal of Ethnic Studies, The Nation* and *Science & Society.*

Phil Nash (*Denver, CO*) has spent the last decade in Denver, preparing for the very special kind of mid-life crisis that happens to outspoken gay writers and activists. When it happens, he'll write about it.

Philip Pannell (*Washington, DC*) is a former D.C. Human Rights Commissioner and president of the D.C. Democrats. By being black and gay, he has felt the double edge of discrimination.

Mark A. Perigard (*Boston, MA*) has written for *Bay Windows, Gay Community News,* the Boston *Phoenix* and the Boston *Globe,* and has had heterosexuals in his life for as long as he can remember. He is working on a book about gay parenting.

Richard Plant (*New York, NY*), a Ph.D. from Basel, Switzerland, has written on many subjects in both English and German. His first novel, *The Dragon in the Forest* (Doubleday, 1950), dealt with pre-Hitler Germany, a period he also treated in several stories published by *The New Yorker.* He has written essays and reviews for *The Nation,* the New York *Times Book Review, The Advocate* and *New York Native,* among others. At present he is finishing a major study of the Nazi extermination of gay people, to be published in spring 1986, by Holt, Rinehart & Winston. A preview was published in *Christopher Street* in 1977.

John Preston (*Portland, ME*) is a novelist whose works include *Franny: The Queen of Provincetown, I Once Had a Master and Other Tales of Erotic Love*, and the continuing Alex Kane adventure novels (all published by Alyson Publications). His erotic novel *Mr. Benson* was published by Alternate Publishing. He contributes regularly to the gay press, including two syndicated columns: "Letter from Maine" and "Books of the Month."

Paul Reed (*San Francisco, CA*) is the author of *Facing It: A Novel of A.I.D.S.* (Gay Sunshine Press). He has written for the *Bay Area Reporter* and the San Francisco *Chronicle.*

Darrell Yates Rist (*New York, NY*) has written for such varied publications as *New York Native, Christopher Street, The Advocate*, the New York *Post*, the *Village Voice, Harper's* and *Film Comment*. He is the author of *Going to Paris to Live* (Irvington Publishers), the story of American men who exiled themselves in Paris in 1985 in search of a cure for AIDS at the Pasteur Institute.

H. W. Seng (*San Francisco, CA*) is a former features editor and managing editor of Boston's *Gay Community News*, for which he still writes book reviews.

Samuel M. Steward (*Berkeley, CA*) has had three careers: university professor, tattoo artist and writer of erotica under the pen name of Phil Andros. He has published sixteen volumes, some of which document his long friendship with Gertrude Stein and Alice Toklas, and others which recount his association with Dr. Kinsey and his Institute.

Edmond C. Sutton (*New York, NY & San Diego, CA*) is a finalist of the California Spelling Bee and Optimist Club Speech contests. He has written about film, music, video, style, and fashion for various publications including *New York Native*.

Donald Vining (*New York, NY*) is the author of *A Gay Diary* (four volumes, covering 1933 to 1975), editor of *American Diaries of World War II* (all The Pepys Press). A collection of his pieces from the major gay periodicals was published in 1986 by The

Crossing Press under the title *How Can You Come Out If You've Never Been In?*

Alexander Wallace *(Atlanta, GA)*, a native New Yorker, is a gay atheist, writing and trying to survive deep in the Bible Belt. As a publicist his efforts appeared in all the New York media. Since moving to Atlanta, he has written for *Atlanta Magazine, Cruise, Etc., Atlanta After Dark, Metropolitan Gazette, Torso* and *New York Native.* He is currently Fashion Editor of *Creative Loafing.* Raised in a New York ghetto, he knows it's no place to stay.

Jay Weiser *(Brooklyn, NY)* is a member of thirteen gay community organizations and the jazz critic for the *New York Native.* He is also the author of articles in *Dissent* on Sid Caesar, and in the *Native* on the World War II internment of Japanese Americans.

David Williams *(Louisville, KY)* has served as a correspondent for *The Advocate* since 1979. In addition, he has been active in several local gay organizations in Louisville, including a stint as editor of *Lamba Louisville News.* He is currently working on a book of short stories.

T. R. Witomski *(Toms River, NJ)* has written for *Penthouse, The Connection, Drummer, Philadelphia Gay News* and numerous other publications. He contributed to *Hot Living: Erotic Stories about Safer Sex* (Alyson), *Wads* (Gay Sunshine), and the forthcoming *In Defense of the Erotic Imagination* (Arbor House). When not writing, he may be found in opera houses or gay bars.

Roy P. Wood (Athens, GA) was born in New York City but spent most of his life in the south, in Georgia. He served eight years in the USAF, then attended the University of Georgia, where he earned BA and MA degrees in history. He is the author of *Restless Rednecks, The Long Exile* and numerous short stories. He was active in gay rights movements at the University of Georgia in the seventies. (Mr. Wood developed AIDS and died before publication of this book.)